World Poverty For Dummies

Millennium Development Goals: The Eight-Point Plan

- **Goal 1: Eradicate extreme poverty and hunger.** Halve the proportion of people who live on less than one dollar a day; achieve full and productive employment and decent work for all, including women and young people; and halve the proportion of people who suffer from hunger.

- **Goal 2: Achieve universal primary education.** Ensure that children everywhere, both boys and girls, complete a full course of primary schooling.

- **Goal 3: Promote gender equality and empower women.** Eliminate gender disparity in all levels of education; and increase the participation of women in the paid workforce and national parliaments.

- **Goal 4: Reduce child mortality.** Reduce by two-thirds the number of children who die before the age of 5.

- **Goal 5: Improve maternal health.** Reduce by three-quarters the number of women who die during pregnancy and childbirth; and achieve universal access to reproductive health services.

- **Goal 6: Combat HIV/AIDS, malaria and other diseases.** Halt and begin to reverse the spread of HIV/AIDS; ensure universal access to treatment for HIV/AIDS for all those who need it; and halt and begin to reverse the incidence of malaria and other major diseases.

- **Goal 7: Ensure environmental sustainability.** Integrate the principles of sustainability into development; reverse the loss of environmental resources; reduce the loss of biodiversity; halve the proportion of people without sustainable access to safe drinking water and basic sanitation; and achieve a significant improvement in the lives of at least 100 million slum dwellers.

- **Goal 8: Develop a global partnership for development.** Develop fairer trading systems with a commitment to good governance, development and poverty reduction; address the special needs of the least developed countries, landlocked developing countries and small island states; provide debt relief; improve access to affordable essential medicines; and make available the benefits of new technologies, especially information and communications.

Take Action

- **Write to politicians.** Ask your elected representatives what they're doing about world poverty. Is your government committed to achieving the Millennium Development Goals?

- **Engage in the debate.** Write to your newspaper, phone talkback radio and let other people know that there's something they can do to end world poverty.

- **Organise an event.** Raise awareness and money to help end poverty.

- **Donate time and money.** Volunteer at a not-for-profit, or donate cash if you don't have time.

- **Join a campaign for change.** Campaign for a better world. Take action that's timely and effective.

For Dummies®: Bestselling Book Series for Beginners

World Poverty For Dummies®

Cheat Sheet

Personal Choices

- **Consume less and buy fair trade.** Try to buy fewer things, and support fairly traded goods.
- **Leave the car at home.** Reduce your carbon footprint and walk, ride a bicycle or catch public transport whenever you can.
- **Invest ethically.** Put your money where your heart is and invest in sustainable companies.

Find Out More

Become part of the Make Poverty History campaign to achieve the Millennium Development Goals.

- **Australia:**
  www.makepovertyhistory.com.au
- **United States:**
  www.one.org
- **United Kingdom:**
  www.makepovertyhistory.org
- **United Nations:**
  www.endpoverty2015.org

Best Online Resources

- **Worldmapper:**
  www.worldmapper.org
- **Gapminder:**
  www.gapminder.org
- **The Millennium Development Goals:**
  www.un.org/millenniumgoals
- **Human Development Report:**
  hdr.undp.org/en/

How the World's Money Flow Gets Divided

When you add all the numbers up, there is about US$5 trillion legally traded in the international arena each year. Most of that is involved in trading between the developed nations. Some of the other amounts of money that change hands are listed below.

- US$25 billion is spent by tourists in the developing world
- US$100 billion is given in aid by rich countries
- US$130 billion is paid in interest by developing countries
- US$200 billion is sent home by migrant workers
- US$500 billion is estimated to be spent in the international drugs trade
- US$700 billion is spent by tourists worldwide
- US$1,000 billion is officially spent on military hardware
- At least US$1,000 billion changes hands in the form of bribes
- Up to US$3,000 billion changes hands in money-laundering schemes.

For Dummies®: Bestselling Book Series for Beginners

World Poverty

FOR

DUMMIES®

by Sarah Marland, Ashley Clements,
Lindsay Rae and Adam Valvasori

Foreword by Tim Costello,
Chief Executive, World Vision Australia

WILEY

Wiley Publishing Australia Pty Ltd

World Poverty For Dummies®

published by
Wiley Publishing Australia Pty Ltd
42 McDougall Street
Milton, Qld 4064
www.dummies.com

Copyright © 2008 Wiley Publishing Australia Pty Ltd

The moral rights of the authors have been asserted.

National Library of Australia
Cataloguing-in-Publication data

Title:	World Poverty For Dummies / authors Sarah Marland [et al.].
ISBN:	978 0 731 40699 9 (paperback).
Notes:	Includes index.
Subjects:	Poverty. Poverty — Research. Poverty — Social aspects.
Dewey Number:	362.5

Cover image: Getty Images/Peter Macdiarmid

Printed in Australia by
McPherson's Printing Group

10 9 8 7 6 5 4 3 2 1

About the Authors

Sarah Marland joined World Vision in 2002 and was involved in running the Make Poverty History campaign before moving to Amnesty International, where she now manages a campaign on human rights and poverty.

In 1985, on a balmy night in tropical North Queensland, 11-year-old Sarah watched Live Aid on TV and resolved to devote her life to the glamorous pursuit of saving the world. From there she became a teenage environmentalist, and a professional good-gal — getting a degree in social work and building creative and engaged communities in Brisbane and Melbourne. In 2002, she got a relatively normal job in an international non-government organisation. She's still waiting for the glamour to kick in.

Ashley Clements has worked and lived with Burmese refugees on the Thai–Burma border, and now spends much of his time working with Iraqi refugees in Jordan. If you count the slightly unusual dialect of English he has developed over the years, Ashley speaks three languages and is working on his fourth: Arabic. He is also living in his seventh country, and thinking very hard about where his eighth will be.

He hasn't been able to shake a passion for global politics acquired at the heart of the international community in Geneva, Switzerland. He studied Politics, Philosophy and Economics in the United Kingdom and, being a glutton for punishment, went on to do a Master's in International Politics in Australia.

Lindsay Rae manages research and education at World Vision Australia, and is also doing research on social capital and global civil society. He worked as a secondary teacher and spent several years working with newly arrived young refugees in Melbourne's suburbs. He studied Politics, Asian languages and Education and later taught politics at La Trobe University, Melbourne. Since 2000 he has worked as an education consultant in Australia and Indonesia.

Adam Valvasori is currently loving being the Values Manager at The Body Shop Australia, helping to turn consumers into activists. He has been a social marketer for World Vision, where he proudly created Stir (Google it!) and worked on Make Poverty History campaigns.

Unlike Sarah, Adam watched cartoon superheroes and TV ads. He studied public relations and marketing at uni and thought he'd be making spectacular ads by now. The determination of his heroes to do good and not sell out must have rubbed off, though. Their influence has led him to campaign for a better world rather than the ultimate sports deodorant. He has worked on Australia's Youth Parliaments and youth initiatives like the National Youth Roundtable, National Youth Week and the youth Web site *the source*.

Dedication

To everyone who does their bit to help end global poverty.

Authors' Acknowledgements

Thanks to Charlotte Duff who believed in the project right from the get-go, and kept believing despite everything. To Maryanne Phillips who helped us get off to a great start and enormous thanks to Giovanni Ebono, without whom this would never have been finished and whose steady hand and enthusiasm made it all come together in the end.

Sarah writes: Thanks to Jennifer Campbell Case and Amnesty International Australia for cutting me a lot of slack to get this project done. And to my husband Andrew Macrae, who put up with the nights and weekends when I was working — or worse, avoiding it.

Ashley writes: Thanks to my high-school English teachers for making me believe I could change the world. Thanks to my family for getting me here, my friends for keeping me here and to my fellow Dummies for seeing this through, despite becoming scattered from the hive in Burwood.

Lindsay writes: Thanks in so many uncountable ways to Viktor Fischer, Russell Hocking, Melanie Gow, Linda Ng-Tatam, Lindy Stirling, Joelle Stoelwinder, Victoria Wells, Derek Streulens and Nicole Wiseman.

Adam writes: I'd like to thank all the aid workers — real live action heroes on minimum wage. Thanks also to the funky campaigners, volunteers and ordinary people who aren't 'aid workers' but seeing a drum in front of them and feeling outraged at an injustice said 'Damn it I'm going to make some noise'. For the people who realise they have a skill, a gift, and think, 'I can give something back', not 'I'm going to make a lot of money'.

All we can ever ask: no matter who you are or what you do — be passionate about a justice issue outside your own bubble and just give the making of change a good, pirate-like, rum-go.

Publisher's Acknowledgements

We're proud of this book; please send us your comments through our For Dummies online registration form located at www.dummies.com/register/.

Some of the people who helped bring this book to market include the following:

Acquisitions, Editorial and Media Development

Project Editors: Giovanni Ebono, Maryanne Phillips

Acquisitions Editor: Charlotte Duff

Editorial Manager: Gabrielle Packman

Production

Layout and Graphics: Wiley Composition Services and Wiley Art Studio

Cartoons: Glenn Lumsden

Indexer: Don Jordan, Antipodes Indexing

The authors and publisher would like to thank the following copyright holders, organisations and individuals for their permission to reproduce copyright material in this book.

Fairtrade Australia: page 66 (figure 4-1)

United Nations: page 29 (figure 2-1) from *The Millennium Development Goals Report*, © United Nations 2007. Reprinted with the permission of the United Nations.

Every effort has been made to trace the ownership of copyright material. Information that will enable the publisher to rectify any error or omission in subsequent editions will be welcome. In such cases, please contact the Permissions Section of John Wiley & Sons Australia, Ltd who will arrange for the payment of the usual fee.

Contents at a Glance

Table of Contents

Foreword

• •

*I*f you've picked up this book, you may well share my feeling that poverty is one of the great moral and political issues of our time. Thinking about poverty it's easy to get depressed, and easy to get angry — but I believe we now have good reasons to be optimistic.

As never before, we now have the resources to tackle what Bono calls 'stupid poverty'. This is the stupid poverty where children die for lack of a 20 cent immunisation. The poverty that allows famine and malnutrition while European taxpayers subsidise every cow by over $2 a day. The same poverty that denies people basic needs like clean water and a safe place to call home, and the same poverty that leaves people vulnerable to trafficking and slavery.

For too long we have tolerated human suffering on a massive scale — suffering that is wrong and avoidable.

But now we have entered a new time and a new generation is finding its voice. Today's generation can be remembered for much more than iPods and Facebook. This can be what Nelson Mandela termed 'the great generation' — one that leaves the world better than it found it.

Eradicating extreme poverty needs a real partnership involving both developed and developing nations. But it needs to be a partnership between people, as well as between governments. We need ordinary citizens in their millions to add their energy, their skills and their voices to this great global movement for justice. We have the resources — we just need the will to act.

I hope this book will help you to understand better the many and complex issues surrounding world poverty. But most of all I hope it will move you to action — to join the millions who are seizing this moment to make poverty history.

Tim Costello
Chief Executive, World Vision Australia

Introduction

. . . .

For nearly all our professional lives, the four authors of this book have worked in organisations dedicated to helping other people. The sense of satisfaction we feel at the little we have achieved is almost overwhelmed by humility. The little bit we have done is insignificant compared to the enormity of the challenge presented by world poverty.

It is exhilarating to work on a project that makes a difference and it is close to the ultimate reward to see people who once struggled living a much better life. Exciting as those experiences are, it is breathtakingly disappointing to realise that there are billions more people in the same boat.

That's the point of this book. The four of us can do so much, but with you on our side we can do a whole lot more. We need you to know, in detail, what the problems are, what can be done about them, and how you can help make those things happen.

That's why we wrote this book and, we hope, that's why you've picked it up.

About This Book

World Poverty For Dummies is an overview of the situation that faces billions of people in the world that you share. Because it describes the condition of whole populations, it summarises those conditions using statistics, facts and figures that regularly reach into the millions. This is a very impersonal way to talk about human lives. To counter the impersonal nature of those abstract numbers we have peppered the book with stories. Stories from our own experience, stories from other people who have worked in the field and stories from the people the book is about — the poorest people in the world.

Sometimes the statistics and the stories are overwhelming. Reading about people who are starving to death — or writing about it, for that matter — can leave you feeling flat and emotionally drained. This book is the tip of an iceberg though. For every number in every table, and every person in every tale, there are more people, more stories, and more aid workers getting on with life.

The great thing about the *For Dummies* style is that it encourages you to view those numbers and stories as pieces in a puzzle. It puts together the almost overwhelming amount of information in a logical and easy-to-digest manner. You can use this book as a reference, and get an overview of how extreme world poverty is; or you can treat the stories and statistics as a call to action, and head off to do something about this global tragedy.

Conventions Used in This Book

To help you navigate through this book, we use the following conventions:

- *Italic* is used for emphasis and to highlight new words or terms that are defined.
- **Boldfaced** text is used to indicate keywords in bulleted lists or the action part of numbered steps.
- `Monofont` is used for Web addresses.

Foolish Assumptions

Every author must make some assumptions about her audience, and we've made a few assumptions about you:

- You care. We say it often enough in this book to become a cliché, but it's important. You wouldn't pick it up unless you do, and because you do, we know that you will act on some of the suggestions we make.
- You are probably one of the world's wealthier citizens. You read English, that's a pretty good head start, and you have access to this book. That means you are probably not working in sweatshop conditions, or eking out a living with your bare hands in a drought-stricken landscape.
- You are educated. Most of the world's wealthier citizens are. You can read. That means that you have skills that could be useful to an organisation trying to help the world's poor.
- You can get access to the Internet if you want it. This will help you find out more about some of the organisations we mention in these pages and the programs they undertake. You can even participate in some of those programs online. So, get onto your Web browser and start helping.

If you fit any of these descriptions, then you've picked up the right book. We hope that our work in getting it into your hands helps you do your bit to help the world's poor.

How to Use This Book

World Poverty For Dummies covers each topic in its own separate chapter. That means you can start anywhere. You can flick to any part of the book and start reading at random, or you can scan the table of contents and turn to a topic that catches your eye.

You probably know more about some topics than others and feel the urge to fill in some of the gaps. That's the great thing about this format. You don't have to follow our lead. Go where the urge takes you.

If you are a complete newbie to the issues driving world poverty, you're probably best off to start at Chapter 1 and follow your nose. There are plenty of cross-references to lead you astray, but the disciplined among you will, no doubt, read it from one cover to the other. We'd like to think so anyway.

How This Book Is Organised

We've organised *World Poverty For Dummies* into six parts. The first three parts provide the background on poverty. They look at how it came to be the way it is, what impact that has and how it affects the individuals in the world's poorest countries. Parts IV and V focus more on the bigger picture: What's driving the global economy and how we can use those tools to relieve the agony of the world's poor.

That leaves Part VI, the famous *For Dummies* Part of Tens. Each chapter in this part is a succinct list of top tips on a particular topic.

Part I: For Richer or Poorer

One in three people in the world has a real struggle surviving and the vast majority of them live in Africa, parts of Asia and South America. Part I of the book provides an overview of world poverty. It outlines who's poor and who's not, what impact this has on their lives, the characteristics of poverty around the world and what you can do about it.

Part II: Poverty's Building Blocks

This part focuses on the factors that make nations poor. It starts with an historical overview, reviewing the history of colonialism, the impact of two world wars and the legacy of the cold war. It looks at the influence of the weather, climate and other natural features on the economies of the world's poorest nations. Finally it examines the cultural influences of corruption and other attitudes that prevent nations from climbing out of crippling poverty.

Part III: Poverty Under the Microscope

Poverty not only threatens the lives of individuals in the poorest countries, it makes it almost impossible for them to put programs in place that will help them get ahead. The impact of poverty on women flows on to the health of whole communities and the education of their children, extending the damage into future generations.

Poverty prevents people from getting enough to eat, or drink. That damages their health, their physical and mental development, their education and their ability to produce goods to trade with. Their society is poorer as a result. The effects of poverty add to each other to create a compound result. Part III examines each of these effects, their long-term consequences and the strategies required to overcome them.

Part IV: Poverty's Outlook

Major challenges face the world's poor. With large numbers of poor people, human life is devalued and those further up the food chain are all too willing to take advantage of it. As a result, exploitation, slavery and sacrifice are horrifically common. The development of enormous cities with more than 20 million people, many of them living in unofficial settlements, adds organisational challenges to the mix. The influence of global warming threatens to reduce food and water supplies that are already stretched to the limit.

This part examines the depth of these challenges and the scenarios for surviving them.

Part V: Economics and the Levers of Change

The world economy and the institutions that drive it are the most influential forces on the future of rich and poor nations alike. A clear understanding of these forces and their impact on poverty is an essential prerequisite for eradicating the most extreme poverty. The chapters in this part follow the trail of the money. It looks at where the resources are, where the money flows in international finance, aid and trade. It looks at the impact these flows of cash and resources have on the lives of the global poor. It also examines the tools used by these global institutions to shape the future. Most importantly, it looks at how the systems that govern global trade keep countries poor.

Part VI: The Part of Tens

Four snapshots of global poverty, with ten frames in each. This part of the book lists the ten most exciting changes that have recently taken place and more than ten of the greatest challenges facing the world's poor. Then it's over to you. First up, the easy option of ten scintillating movies about world poverty, and the more difficult task of choosing among ten actions that you can take.

Icons Used in This Book

When you see this icon, you don't want to forget the accompanying info — pretty subtle, huh?

This piece of art clues you in on hands-on advice that you can put into practice. In most cases, this icon tells you how to get involved in some activity that is already taking place on the other side of the world.

Ignore this information at your own peril. We use it to warn you about mistakes, missteps and traps that can cause despair in even the most enthusiastic worker on behalf of the world's poor.

When we send you off to the Web for more information, we let you know by plonking this icon in the margin. Just tap in the address provided and let your mouse lead you to the resources you need.

This icon flags places where we get really technical about poverty. It might be the definition of an economic term or the economic analysis of a particular aspect of world trade. Although it's great info, you can skip it and not miss out on the subject at hand.

The stories that illuminate the facts have been highlighted with this little fella. They might be personal stories from one of the authors, but more often they are tragedies or stories of hope from somewhere in the world.

Where to Go from Here

For Dummies books are designed so that you can jump in anywhere and get the information you need. Don't feel like you have to read every chapter — or even the entire chapter. Take advantage of the Table of Contents and Index to find what you're looking for, and check it out. But, if you need an introduction to world poverty, take a close look at Parts I and II for the scoop on the field.

Part I
For Richer or Poorer

Glenn Lumsden

'All this poverty and suffering is making
me feel so guilty, I'm compelled to do
something. Let's holiday in a richer country.'

In this part . . .

One in three people across the globe struggles to survive every day. In a world of extremes, there's nothing more extreme than the difference between the way that the rich and the poor live. In this part, you find out how everyone in the world is connected. We provide an overview of what it means to be poor and how being born into poverty affects all aspects of a person's life. You also discover how the continent a person is born in determines how they experience poverty.

Want to know what you can do about the plight of millions living a desperate hand-to-mouth existence? This part also shows you the kinds of jobs that you can take on to help end world poverty.

Chapter 1

Rich World, Poor World

. . . .

. . . .

Almost one million people die because of poverty every year. This is not because they are marooned on desert islands, or are lost in the desert. Neither is it because there's not enough food in the world to feed the six billion people you share it with. Those people die because the political systems that govern how food and money move around the world are designed to protect the economy that makes you rich, even if it costs those people their lives.

The starving people in the world are only one part of the problem of poverty. Poverty damages the billions of the world's poor every year. These folks are affected by water shortages, diseases caused by filthy water, overcrowding and mass violence. They experience the helplessness that comes from owning nothing, learning little and having no opportunity to get ahead.

Most of the world's poor are poor because violence has taken away the land that should support them, they are denied health care and education by a dysfunctional government, or their resources are being taken by international companies to make cheap products for rich countries. If you understand how these problems conspire to keep the world's poor at the bottom of the barrel, you can do something to help them.

The organisations formed to help the world's poor operate at multiple levels. They work with governments to address these structural imbalances, they work with a wide range of people to collect the money and resources needed to do the job and they work on the ground with the world's poor, trying to make a difference. Chapter 4 explains how they do their job — so that if you want to, you can help them to the best of your ability.

Taking Off the Rose-Coloured Glasses

As well as the shocking truth that about one million people die every year because of poverty, there's the even more shocking reality that one billion people live in misery. The chapters in Part III deal with the effects of poverty on these people. These extremely poor people don't get enough food to eat, or water to drink and wash with, and they have no hope of earning enough money to improve their lives. It is these people whom this book is about.

Many people assume that the world's poor starve because:

✔ A drought affected their country for years so their crops failed

✔ They have no natural resources and so have nothing to trade

✔ A natural disaster destroyed their homes and national infrastructure

✔ A plague of locusts or mice came and ate all their crops

The shocking truth is that natural disasters and disadvantages are not the cause of extreme poverty. Those disasters do cause problems and do cause some people to be poorer than others. In general, though, extreme poverty kills millions of people because:

✔ Their governments sell the national resources for next to nothing

✔ Their government is in disarray owing to internal fighting

✔ They have been herded off their land and into refugee camps

✔ They work for foreign companies who pay them slave wages

In other words, the extreme poor of the world are extremely poor because someone is ripping them off. And, more often than not, the villain of the piece is rich. The extreme poor are condemned to a life of misery because someone else is making money out of their poverty. That someone else is often a company, a government or an individual from the rich half of the world.

In February 2008, the Special Court investigating crimes against humanity heard that 75,000 people in Sierra Leone had been killed and many times that number had their hands amputated in an attempt to control the diamond trade. Millions of landmines and cluster bombs were spread around the country to prevent ordinary people from mining for diamonds. The dictator of neighbouring Liberia, Charles Taylor, is on trial for this genocide. The developed countries that sold the landmines and cluster bombs, the neighbouring countries that trained the militia, and the diamond traders who purchased the diamonds and are alleged to have paid private militia to distribute the landmines for over forty years, apparently, broke no laws. The humanitarian disaster evolved over ten years and was reported in the global media as a civil war, exacerbated by a drought.

The North–South divide

As well as the billion people living in misery, the world currently has about a billion people living in luxury. If you have enough food to eat and a house to live in, are warm in winter and comfortable in summer, and have an education that allows you to make some choice about the work you do, then you are one of the luckiest people in the world. Many people in rich countries can also afford:

- ✔ Eating out from time to time

- ✔ Entertainment — such as movies, concerts or sporting events

- ✔ Driving for pleasure on the weekend

- ✔ Holidays from work, and the opportunity to travel

- ✔ Personal computers, televisions, stereo systems

- ✔ Their own cars, holiday homes, investments

These luxuries are unimaginable to more than half of the people in the world.

Most of these billion wealthy people in the world live in North America and Europe. These rich countries are known as the *North*, or the *first world*, or the *developed world*. Until Japan became one of the richest countries in the world, the term *the West* was reasonably accurate, and it is still widely used. The map in Figure 1-1 shows at a glance why many diplomats divide the world into North and South, even though Australia and New Zealand are among the richest countries in the world and are in the Southern Hemisphere.

The most significant fact is that about 85 per cent of the world's wealth is owned by 15 per cent of the world's people. If you earn more than two hundred and fifty dollars a week, you are among the world's wealthiest people. Part V lists some of the problems that make this imbalance of wealth an entrenched problem.

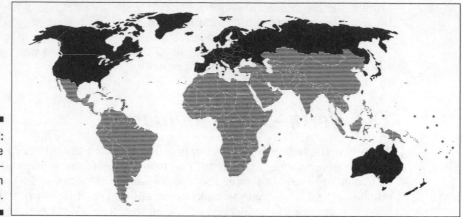

Figure 1-1:
Map of the
North–
South
divide.

You may have heard that one billion people who live in extreme poverty live on less than US$1 a day. It doesn't mean that they literally have one United States dollar to live off. That figure is based on what's known as *purchasing power parity*, or PPP for short. PPP is a measure of equivalent spending power. So when you say that someone lives on less than US$1 a day, it means each day, they can purchase in their own country the equivalent of what a person living in the United States could buy for $1 — say, a bag of rice and a newspaper. To put it another way, imagine your wage was $365 a year. With that minuscule amount of money, you have to feed, clothe, shelter and educate your family. Another billion people live on less than US$2 a day!

The wealth of wealthy nations

This number of extremely poor people has not changed much over the last sixty years. At the end of World War II there were around two and a half billion people and around one billion of them (40 per cent) were extremely poor. Sixty years later, there are six and a half billion people and around one billion of them are still extremely poor.

There are more people in the world who are better off, but there are still a billion people suffering. Poverty has been almost eliminated in Western Europe and North America, and a greater percentage of the population in South America and Asia are better off. The challenges faced by each continent are discussed in Chapter 3.

Might, right and liberal humanism

The authors of this book recognise that poverty has existed as long as humanity. We accept that it is human nature for some people to accrue wealth and power. Every community has winners and losers. If you assemble a group of people (or animals) who have never met each other and put them onto a deserted island, they will quickly establish a pecking order. The people higher up the pecking order will get more than others, will be better fed and stronger, and will live longer. This occurs quite naturally.

There are plenty of people in the world who feel that poverty is natural. Because all creatures compete and some are more successful than others, many people feel that attempts to help the poor and the dispossessed are a waste of time. They think that those attempts simply oppose the natural order of things.

It is true that some people naturally do better than others. It is also true that the organisation of human society allowed its members to survive better than they did as hunters and gatherers. The development of agriculture allowed societies to stockpile food so they had enough to eat in lean years, and so they could support specialists — such as potters, builders and metalworkers — who did not contribute directly to the production of food.

That organisation, and the specialisation it allows, institutionalises inequity. The value that society places on particular skills determines who eats better than others. The rules that society puts in place to govern access to those skills determines whether people can improve their circumstances. In traditional Hindu society, for example, your caste determines the work you do and the income you can earn.

The authors of this book do not promote one particular sort of social organisation over another. We understand that rules tend to be written in favour of the wealthy. We acknowledge that history is written by the victors. It's important to remember, though, that this book is written because we do not accept that one-fifth of humanity should starve. We actively work in our day jobs to ensure that the rules that govern our world should not condemn a child to a life of misery.

When we write about the 'lie of the level playing field' in Chapter 19, it is not because we believe in a particular economic model, or because we are advocates on behalf of a particular group of countries. We devote that chapter to the impact of unfair trade laws because we see people dying as a result of them. We see the developing countries of the world walking out of global trade talks and threatening to organise opposing trade blocs.

The alternative to negotiated settlements is generally conflict. If you feel that it's sensible to determine how to share the world's resources by shooting it out, then you'll probably be frustrated by this book. We have written in the belief that it's possible to govern in the interests of all people on the planet, just as it has been proved possible to govern in the interests of all people in a particular country.

As well as the billion extremely poor people with purchasing power equivalent to less than $1 a day there are two and a half billion more people in countries that are struggling economically. That means three and a half billion people are likely to have children who won't be much better off than they are. Another two billion people, mostly in China, India and Brazil, are getting richer. There's a detailed account of how this growth rate will impact on the world economies in Chapter 16. Individual Indians and Chinese are still extremely poor — on average they have less than one-thirtieth of the income of people in the United States. The middle class people (increasing in number) in those countries, however, have enough money to own houses and cars and to travel to other places in the world. On current growth rates, it will take them 40 years to catch up to the developed world.

If you prefer to see things visually, you might appreciate the tools provided by WorldMapper. On the Web site at www.worldmapper.org you can visually represent this disparity on a map. If you want to compare income, for example, the area of the country is adjusted by the ratio of income to population. The United States and Europe are very large, and Africa is so skinny it resembles a daddy-long-legs spider. You can choose to display a wide range of criteria.

Just how rich are you?

The Global Rich List at www.globalrichlist.com has an income calculator to help people work out where they personally fit in terms of world income. If you don't live in the United States, you'll have to convert your income into US dollars using a currency calculator.

Here are some figures from the richest English-speaking countries of the world.

The Annual Survey of Hours and Earnings in the United Kingdom in 2007 estimated that the average adult income across Britain is £457. The equivalent of about US$900 each week, or US$46,800 each year, this salary puts the average Brit well inside the top 1 per cent of people in the world.

In March 2007, the Australian Bureau of Statistics estimated that average weekly earnings (salaries and wages) of full-time Australian workers was A$1,070.40. Australian wages, like their cricket scores, are a little higher than the British at about US$950. Multiply by 52 to get an annual income of US$49,400. Enter this into the rich list calculator and, again, the average Aussie is well inside the richest 1 per cent of people in the world.

Canada, with an average weekly income of CAN$747 comes in at US$38,500 per annum, which puts them in the top 3.5 per cent of global incomes.

Residents of the United States join their colleagues in Australia and the United Kingdom with an average salary just short of US$50,000.

This is a very rough estimator — it compares data from different years and ignores government policies that complement personal income — but it indicates just how wealthy the average person in a developed country is when compared with the rest of the world.

The World Institute for Development Economics Research did a study of the world distribution of household wealth. Using information from 2000, they estimated that:

✔ The richest 1 per cent of adults in the world own 40 per cent of total global household wealth

✔ The richest 10 per cent of adults in the world own 85 per cent of global household wealth

✔ The poorest 50 per cent of adults in the world own barely 1 per cent of global household wealth

The countries in the North, shown in black in Figure 1-1, control more than 80 per cent of the world's wealth. You will be reminded again and again throughout this book that the governments of these rich countries make laws and regulations, and support military activity, to maintain this inequity. Chapter 19, for example, is devoted to the imbalance of trade and how this unfairly affects the poorest people on the planet.

Consuming like there's no tomorrow

You probably don't feel particularly wealthy. Especially when your kids demand the latest gadget, or your friends pour you a glass of expensive wine or boast about their latest holiday. It's more than likely, though, that you have nearly everything you really need. You feel poor because there's still lots of stuff you want. Mohandas (Mahatma) Gandhi observed that there are sufficient resources to satisfy all humanity's needs, but not enough to satisfy everyone's greed. Realistically, there's no limit to what you want. That's human nature.

Every year the United Nations releases a Human Development Report that compares various indicators of wealth around the world. The 1998 Report compared the spending priorities of the world's wealthiest nations with the funds needed to provide basic services to everyone on the planet. What the UN found was:

✔ Cosmetics purchases in the United States $8 billion

✔ Basic education for all $6 billion

✔ Ice-cream purchases in Europe $11 billion

✔ Basic water and sanitation for all $9 billion

✔ Cigarette purchases in Europe $50 billion

✔ Basic health and nutrition for the planet $13 billion

The point is not to whip yourself every time you buy moisturiser or an ice-cream, but to put aside some of your energy and money for the world's poor. You'll still have a great lifestyle and, hopefully, they can have a better one too.

Acting to End the Agony

Knowing how bad life is for one billion of the world's poorest people can make you feel a bit miserable . . . unless you do something about it. Chapters 4 and 24 describe actions you can take that will make a real difference to someone who's struggling to stay alive. The most important actions, though, are taken by governments who determine the regulations that control the flow of money around the world. The whole of Part V is dedicated to the impact that government policy has on the global sharing of wealth. If you understand how that works, you can do your bit to influence the decisions that your government makes.

Goals for a new millennium

The Millennium Declaration was signed in 2000 along with a set of goals, called the Millennium Development Goals (MDGs). These goals form an eight-point plan to end poverty.

You can read up on the goals, together with the 18 targets that define those goals and the 48 indicators for measuring progress towards them, at www.un.org/millenniumgoals. The detail of these goals, the targets and the indicators are listed in detail in Chapter 18.

- Goal 1: Eradicate extreme poverty and hunger
- Goal 2: Achieve universal primary education
- Goal 3: Promote gender equality and empower women
- Goal 4: Reduce child mortality
- Goal 5: Improve maternal health
- Goal 6: Combat HIV/AIDS, malaria and other diseases
- Goal 7: Ensure environmental sustainability
- Goal 8: Develop a global partnership for development

Suffering from affluenza?

Endlessly trying to keep up with the Joneses? Is the pleasure of purchasing beginning to fade? Got lots of stuff but still feeling empty? You may have contracted affluenza.

The *Macquarie Dictionary* defines affluenza as 'the dissatisfaction that accompanies consumerism as a path to happiness'. You have needs and, once they're met, you start thinking of wants. Then you move on to luxury items, but they just don't seem to make a lasting impression — you keep feeling you need more, because you just aren't fulfilled. Many people also waste a lot of wealth and resources on things that don't get used, stay hidden away in cupboards and, eventually, are thrown out. One path to a cure is to start thinking about what things you actually *need*. Could you live a simpler life and, in doing so, maybe free up some resources, redistribute the wealth, and have a positive impact on the environment?

The Public Broadcasting Service (PBS) in the United States has run a few programs on affluenza. Why not check out their Web site www.pbs.org/kcts/affluenza and take the Affluenza Test.

Other campaigns

Ending world poverty takes a commitment. It's everyone's responsibility to help halve extreme poverty by 2015.

The Global Call to Action Against Poverty is a global campaign to call on world leaders to achieve the Millennium Development Goals. This campaign has different guises in different countries. In Australia, the United Kingdom and Canada it's called Make Poverty History. In the United States, it's the ONE campaign. Its aim is to mobilise ordinary people to call on their leaders to do their bit to end poverty.

Nelson Mandela launched the campaign in Trafalgar Square in 2005, comparing it to the movements to abolish slavery and apartheid. He said, 'In this new century, millions of people in the world's poorest countries remain imprisoned, enslaved, and in chains. They are trapped in the prison of poverty. It is time to set them free. While poverty persists, there is no true freedom.'

These campaigns encourage governments to meet the Millennium Development Goals, and in particular to do this by:

- ✔ Giving more and better aid
- ✔ Dropping poor country debt
- ✔ Making trade fair
- ✔ Helping poor communities keep their governments accountable
- ✔ Tackling climate change

There's lots of ways you can get involved in the campaigns to end poverty. See what's happening in your country:

- ✔ **Australia:** www.makepovertyhistory.com.au
- ✔ **United States:** www.one.org
- ✔ **United Kingdom:** www.makepovertyhistory.org
- ✔ **United Nations:** www.endpoverty2015.org

Actions you can take in your life

Citizens of rich countries can do a lot to help people living in poverty by donating, lobbying and volunteering. One of the most effective tools is to use your voice and your vote to encourage your government to do everything possible to act as a responsible global citizen. Go to the campaign Web sites listed in the preceding section for tips and ideas. Here are some other ways to help end poverty:

- ✔ Ask yourself, are *you* a responsible global citizen? What impact does your consumption and waste have?
- ✔ Keep yourself informed about the issues of poverty.
- ✔ Donate your money or time to an organisation working for positive change.
- ✔ Look into ethical investment portfolios.
- ✔ Investigate when making purchases — does this company use child labour? What's their environmental record? How do they act in poor countries?
- ✔ Let someone else do the investigating for you — purchase Fairtrade goods.

The rights way to go

There is a century of experience gained by organisations working to eradicate extreme poverty. At the beginning of the twentieth century, the effort was almost entirely an extension of the religious missions of the century before. It was based on giving food and encouragement to poor people. After World War II, the focus shifted to ensuring economic independence. Now, the focus is moving more to human rights.

The Millennium Declaration starts with values; in particular, freedom, equality, solidarity, tolerance, respect for nature and shared responsibility. It also makes reference to the Universal Declaration of Human Rights. That declaration was adopted by the United Nations in 1948. It has 30 Articles covering various rights. Several of the points in the Millennium Declaration link directly to these rights, including:

✔ A standard of living that gives every-one adequate access to food, clothing, housing, medical care and social services

✔ Access to education

✔ Special care for mothers and children

✔ Other economic, social and cultural rights

You can read the full text of the United Nations Declaration of Human Rights at www.un.org/Overview/rights.html.

Does Aid Actually Work?

Many people ask, 'Does aid work?' Given the scale of the problem and the myriad factors working against the poor, does it actually make a difference to the Asia–Pacific, or the Caribbean, what aid rich countries deliver? The short answer is, 'Yes'. The longer answer takes all of Chapter 17 to spell out. It all has as much to do with the type of assistance that's provided as the amount.

Foreign aid, combined with local efforts, has contributed to some amazing achievements:

✔ Smallpox across the globe has been eradicated, and significant decreases have been achieved in the infection rates of polio, river blindness and tuberculosis.

✔ Primary school enrolment has increased by 8 per cent in developing countries since 1991, with the most improvement being in the new millennium.

✔ The percentage of the population with access to proper sanitation has increased by 21 per cent across Eastern Asia, 12 per cent across Northern Africa and 9 per cent across Latin America and the Caribbean.

This is not to say that aid does not face challenges when not enough is provided to really get the job done, or when it's too narrow in focus. Chapter 18 examines those challenges more closely. Health, for example, is proving to be a big problem in the Asia–Pacific region. World Vision Australia estimates that to provide even a basic service, aid of about US$16 per person is needed in the region annually. The aid contributed falls well short of these targets. In 2003–04 Papua New Guinea had only about US$5.20 per person for health services, and the Philippines had as little as US$0.40.

As well as receiving more aid, poor countries need that aid to be properly focused and well delivered and, most importantly, they need it to deliver services that allow them to get on with their lives, not become dependent on handouts from rich countries.

Introducing the Grameen Bank

Bangladeshis don't always have the easiest of lives. Fate hasn't been too kind to the South Asian country. Bangladesh is essentially a massive delta that floods every year when the monsoon hits. With most of Bangladesh being within 10 metres of sea level, it's in a rather precarious position!

When it's not flooding, Bangladesh commonly experiences famine instead. As if that's not enough, almost every year typhoons and tornadoes pay the country a visit. And it's not made any easier by the 150 million people who cram into the country at an average of over 1,000 per square kilometre.

In 1974 famine struck Bangladesh. Spurred on by a particularly severe array of natural disasters and political factors, up to one million Bangladeshis died (although the government estimates were closer to 25,000).

In the wake of the famine, a US-educated Bangladeshi economist, Muhammad Yunus, was inspired to do something about the poverty in his own country. He saw a need for the poor in Bangladesh to be given loans with reasonable terms to help them recover from the devastation. Before the arrival of microfinance, the only way to get a loan was through money-lenders who offered extortionate interest rates. They insisted on strict repayment conditions with severe consequences for those who didn't keep them up.

So Yunus made some small loans to artisans and farmers, and soon began a research project that trialled the system on a larger scale. This experiment grew into what came to be known as the Grameen Bank. The name means 'bank of the villages' in Bangla.

The Grameen Bank doesn't require collateral for loans, and claims the poorest of the poor are therefore able to make use of the institution. At the end of 2006 the bank had just shy of seven million borrowers — virtually all of these are women.

The unprecedented success of the project led to Muhammad Yunus and the Grameen Bank being jointly awarded the 2006 Nobel Peace Prize.

Chapter 2

What's Wrong With Being Poor?

The poverty confronting one in five people on this planet is not the sort of poverty depicted by Chaplin's tramp or in Kerouac's *On the Road*, or experienced by the 'rubber tramps' (living voluntarily in mobile homes) exploring the underbelly of the developed world. The world's poorest people are starving to death, they are dying of thirst and disease, they are herded into refugee camps and exploited. A modern slavery has emerged where the victims are free to earn money to pay their employer for rent and food, as long as they don't get sick or injured.

This chapter explores the reality of life on earth for that one-fifth of humanity and the terrible impact this grinding poverty has on their bodies and societies. It describes plans for lifting them out of poverty and the help they need to make those plans reality. Finally, it looks at the shocking truth that the biggest challenge they face is the world's rich. People in rich countries, like you, enjoy a luxurious lifestyle partly built on the suffering of the world's poor. This chapter outlines the impact of that imbalance.

Living Hand to Mouth

There are some aspects of modern life you probably consider luxuries: Air-conditioning, a choice of gourmet food and drink, designer clothes and fast cars. You may enjoy these things, but you don't count them among life's necessities. A roof over your head, enough food on the table and the security of your loving family, those are the things that really matter, right?

Well, those necessities are exactly the things missing from the lives of the world's poorest two billion people. They don't have a roof over their head or enough food to eat, and they can't guarantee their family will be with them from one day to the next.

Gimme shelter

Did you know safe housing is a basic human right defined in the United Nations Declaration of Human Rights? It ranks up there with food and clothing as a basic component of an adequate standard of living. Despite this, millions of people don't have a home.

In the developed world, the problem of homelessness is less dramatic and less visible. The homeless people in your city or town are probably restricted to a relatively small area. They live on the streets of a small number of suburbs and drift from shelter to shelter. Many people feel pity, disgust, annoyance or discomfort when confronted by these drifters, hoboes, tramps — if they see them at all.

Across the rest of the world, poverty is more visible. Whole communities live on rubbish dumps, construction sites, the median strips of freeways and the land around airports and railways. One billion people on earth live in slums. It's a staggering statistic. It threatens to multiply threefold by 2050, if left unchecked. Many of these slum dwellers live in cardboard boxes, or simply pull a sheet of plastic over their heads at night. Chapter 14 goes into more detail about the challenges facing the homeless in the world's largest cities.

Homelessness can come about as a result of low income; lack of affordable housing, education or health care; a disaster; violence; substance abuse or addiction; or mental or physical illnesses. The vast majority of the world's homeless have simply been left on the street because they have no other option.

In 2001, about one million Argentines found themselves thrown out of the middle class overnight. The Argentine government along with the International Monetary Fund restructured the financial system. Part of that restructuring converted people's home loans into US dollars, instead of the pesos that they were paid at work. The exchange rate for the peso collapsed, and millions of people found their mortgage repayments increasing by ten times or more. They simply had to walk away from their homes. The economy collapsed in 2002 and over 25 per cent of Argentines were unemployed and 57.5 per cent lived below the poverty line. The position has improved slightly in the last five years, but 22.5 per cent of Argentines remained unemployed in 2004.

The trickle-down theory stops here

The *trickle-down theory* was made famous by Ronald Reagan. Simply put, the theory is that when you look after the rich, everybody will be better off. This idea has usually been promoted by lobbyists for big companies and the wealthy, as a means of lifting the incomes of the working poor without taxing the rich or big business.

However, the UN-Habitat Report notes that there is little evidence to support this idea. The consensus among those working to end global poverty is that any trickle-down is confined to a relatively small part of society. Most aid agencies now seek to address global poverty through a variety of programs that involve direct intervention.

This is a stark reminder that the economic system supporting you is actually very fragile. The parents of kids born and bred in the rubbish dumps of a megacity in the developing world may have been comfortably well off before an international financial crisis ruined their lives.

You can get actively involved in protecting the housing rights of vulnerable groups (the poor, the elderly, children, people with disabilities, displaced persons, people living with HIV/AIDS and indigenous people). In Australia, you can get involved with homeless people and even talk to them through Internet forums like the one at forums.homeless.org.au. It offers them a community to connect with, peer support and a method of speaking out. If you're more globally focused, have a look at the Amnesty International Web site www.amnesty.org.au and take action against housing violations around the world.

Feed me!

Famine is one of humanity's oldest foes and still stalks the world's poor. Famine, one of the four horsemen of the apocalypse, condemns more people to the embrace of Death than the other two — War and Pestilence — put together. Even today, famine kills more people than AIDS, malaria and tuberculosis combined.

From 1970 to 1997 the number of hungry people dropped from 959 million to 791 million — mainly due to development in India and China. The global effort to defeat famine was making ground, but 791 million people is a lot of victims! Sadly, famine is on the rise again. In 2003 the number suffering from hunger rose again to 854 million.

There's enough food in the world to feed everyone, yet one child still dies every four seconds. Today, one in nearly seven people doesn't get enough food to be healthy and lead an active life, making hunger and malnutrition the number one risk to health worldwide.

Rich nations have the voracious appetite of a teenager. A hungry teenage boy can demolish a dinner prepared for a whole family without a second thought. The statistics on the consumption of food around the world underline the adolescent appetite of rich nations. Despite having less than 20 per cent of the world's population, the developed world consumes about one-third of the world's cereals and one-half of the animal products.

More than one-eighth of the world's population doesn't have a secure supply of food. Eight hundred million people don't get enough to eat, and the vast majority of them live in Africa, South Asia or South America.

In the United States, about 4 per cent of people experience hunger at least once a year and, on any given day, about half a per cent of people will be hungry. The figure is 13 per cent in Asia and 33 per cent in Africa. In raw numbers, this means that one and a half million citizens of the world's richest country do not have food security, nor do half a billion Asians and 200 million Africans.

Because of this global disparity, the Food and Agriculture Organization (FAO) of the United Nations expects at least six million children under five years old to die of hunger this year.

Right now, as you read this book, one in four of the world's children under five is underweight. Their immune system is weaker, they're more prone to infection and disease, and more likely to grow up physically and mentally underdeveloped. Chapters 9 and 12 examine the causes and solutions of this grim toll in human life.

Quenching the thirst of billions

Humans depend on water for agriculture, transport and industry. Our very survival depends on clean fresh water. It is our most valuable commodity. Yet clean water remains out of reach for billions of people around the world.

Human health suffers from the lack of good water. Over 80 per cent of all diseases are caused by unsafe and unclean water. Five million people, mostly children, die each year from waterborne diseases.

A poor tax

Access to water goes hand in hand with wealth. Those with cash have clean water. Take the slum dwellers of Nairobi, Manila, Lima or Jakarta. Low-income households in the slums of these cities pay up to ten times more for their water than high-income residents of the same city.

Wasted potential

In many parts of the world, poor people — usually women or children — are forced to walk long distances for their day's water. In South Africa alone, women walk the equivalent of 16 return trips to the moon each day just to fetch water, according to the Web site www.waterpolicy.com. That's more than 300 times round the world! Think of what these women could achieve if they didn't need to waste their days fetching and carrying water.

Education and vulnerability

In many countries, children fetch water for their families. As a consequence, they have less or no time for the education they need and deserve. Women and children walking long distances are also highly vulnerable. Both are at risk from sexual abuse or abduction.

Agriculture

The lack of available water also limits agriculture. Agriculture uses 70 per cent of the world's water. The chairman of Nestlé, Peter Braebeck, predicted in 2007 that food prices will rise radically in the near future because of competing demands for water. This prediction came true in April 2008.

Scratching for a living

Many of the world's poor are reduced to eking out a living at the margins of society. People in the slums of Mumbai, Manila and Rio de Janeiro live on the scraps of the city that tourists see. Chapter 14 describes the cities of more than 20 million people. These places have no hope of feeding or housing the poor that flock there hoping to escape rural poverty.

These urban poor are vulnerable to every form of exploitation. They'll work for minimal amounts of cash under the most horrendous conditions imaginable. Because there are so many of them, and the governments do not have sufficient resources to protect them, there are not enough regulations and not enough officials to enforce whatever regulations may be in place.

The rural areas that the poor leave behind are not much better off. The conversion of small-scale family farms to industrial agriculture produces higher yielding crops, but the beneficiaries of this increased productivity are sitting in offices in Amsterdam, Shanghai and New York. The traditional farmers of that land are begging for a coin in the gutters of the nearest capital city.

Caught between a traditional way of life that simply can't compete with the demands of the global economy and the vortex of global poverty, those people that remain on the land are vulnerable to violence and exploitation. Famine, violence and mass population displacement across Central Africa are a typical result of the collision of these two worlds. The victims of that collision enter the twenty-first century by being thrown on the bottom of a very large pile. Six billion humans are better off than they are, and everyone is fighting to get a step ahead of the next guy.

The working conditions of the world's poor are generally viewed as secondary to housing, feeding and giving them water. Chapter 11 gives an overview of the challenges facing the working poor. The eight Millennium Development Goals set by 190 countries in September 2000 only peripherally address the problem of working conditions. The reality is that their survival comes first and their education comes second. Once those basic building blocks can be assured, then there's some hope they'll be able to make a decent living in decent conditions. Chapter 13 outlines just how dire the situation is, with millions of people in slavery around the world today.

Struggling to Get Ahead

Poverty creates conditions that make survival difficult, and when you're focused on surviving it's hard to put the energy into the projects that can help you climb out of poverty.

The solutions are well understood. The key components include:

- Creating a hygienic environment that keeps people healthy
- Protecting and supporting mothers
- Providing education for boys and girls

The challenge, of course, is that each component requires a long-term effort and education, and has to be put in place at the same time as dealing with the problems that caused people to be poor in the first place. The elimination of rubbish and raw sewage from European cities, for example, took almost a century and involved building sewers, rebuilding whole sections of major cities and educating the population not to throw their waste out the window. Taking on projects of this size requires considerable financial resources and political will.

Plagues affecting nations

There are three great pestilences of our times — Acquired Immune Deficiency Syndrome (AIDS), malaria and tuberculosis. These three diseases, between them, kill almost as many people as starvation, or unclean water. All three diseases affect the world's poor in much greater numbers than they affect the rich.

Although these diseases are difficult to cure, prevention is relatively simple and treatment is very effective in developed countries. Malaria, for example, can be prevented by a treated mosquito net; AIDS by using condoms and practising safe sex. Tuberculosis is prevented by identifying, isolating and curing its victims as early and quickly as possible. Education is required so people know what the solutions are. Sufficient income to afford the solutions and the power to choose to practise safe sex are necessary for the solutions to work. All those components are missing in many of the world's poorest countries.

Have a look at Chapter 12 to get the lowdown on how these diseases can be brought under control. Even a complex and relatively new disease like AIDS is effectively treated in the developed world these days. Very few people in rich countries who contract the human immunodeficiency virus (HIV) that causes AIDS actually develop AIDS. Even fewer die from it. In southern Africa, the opposite is true. Thirty per cent of all adults are infected with HIV and 14 million children have been orphaned by AIDS. Globally, just under half of all people living with HIV are female, but in sub-Saharan Africa it's a startling 60 per cent. These terrible statistics are the result of a combination of:

✔ The stigma of being HIV positive

✔ The unequal status of women

✔ A lack of political will by international governments

✔ Denial on the part of local governments and authorities

The good news is that global attention to these relatively simple problems is beginning to have some impact. Nevertheless, it will be decades before the problems can be brought under control.

Nurturing mothers

Women perform two-thirds of the world's work, but earn only one-tenth of the income and own less than 1 per cent of the world's property. Across the world, they do most of the feeding, health care and domestic duties. Women also grow the bulk of the food in agricultural societies. Yet they are usually the last to be fed and cared for, and are often prevented by law, tradition, or both, from receiving an education, owning land or having any money of their own. As Tammy Wynette said, 'It's hard to be a woman.'

Any number of studies indicate that the most effective way to have a positive impact on the world's poor is to educate and empower women. Because women hold the family and community together, educate children and pass on culture and knowledge, any benefits they receive are generally amplified and passed on to the whole society. That is why equal opportunities in education for girls and an end to discrimination against women are prominent among the Millennium Development Goals listed in Chapter 1. The role of women in eradicating extreme poverty is discussed in Chapter 8.

Of course, mothers are the very source of life itself. You are only here because your mother gave birth to and nurtured you. For that reason, improving maternal health is a separate Millennium Development Goal, in addition to the goal of reducing infant mortality. The statistics on mortality among infants and mothers are provided in Chapter 12.

The overwhelming trend in these statistics is the strong relationship between mortality rates and access to medical care during birth. Nutrition and hygiene also play a critical role, but are secondary compared with access to skilled attendants at the birth and are complicated by a range of regional factors. Figure 2-1 shows the increase in the availability of midwives, nurses and doctors for developing regions over the 15 years from 1990 to 2005.

School's out . . . of the question

Education is critical to national development. Educated people are more resilient in the face of disasters and grasp opportunities more readily. The United Nations (UN) Human Development Index (HDI) puts a large emphasis on education in rating the countries around the world. The HDI awards points based on the adult literacy rate, as well as enrolments in primary, secondary and tertiary education.

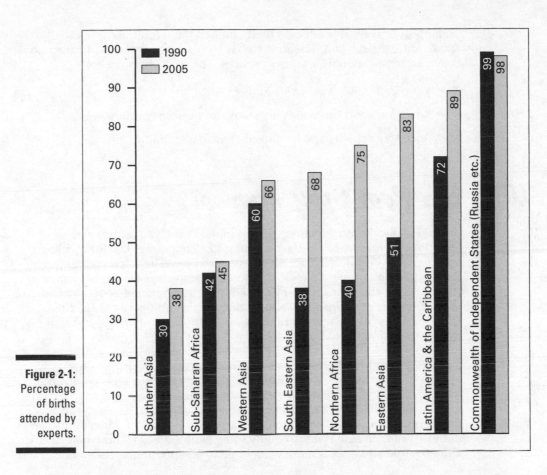

Figure 2-1:
Percentage
of births
attended by
experts.

Education helps cure poverty so effectively because it has a compound effect. A high income means you're not poor today, but it may leave you exposed to disaster if that income dries up. Education, by comparison, enables you to do well even if your oil well, speculative investments or guano deposits stop producing money. Most countries with low school enrolments are poor now, and are highly likely to remain poor in the future. Lack of education locks in disadvantage because it guarantees that the adults of the future will be uneducated. They will:

✔ Struggle with literacy and numeracy

✔ Earn less because they have fewer skills

✔ Experience more health problems

✔ Be less active in government and decision making

To help poor countries educate their children and stop the cycle of disadvantage is difficult. The first step is to support parents and carers so they can send children to primary school. The next steps are to:

- ✔ Keep children in school for longer
- ✔ Ensure schools have the curriculum and resources they need
- ✔ Encourage children to be citizens and leaders in the future.

Why the Poor Stay Poor

The same disadvantaged countries are in the news, year after year. Sometimes a reasonably well-off country, like Zimbabwe, fails dramatically and the list is reshuffled. Success stories like China, India and Brazil prove that the world's poorest people can scrape themselves off the bottom of the list. Have a look at Chapter 16 to see how a diversified economy and strategic trade relationships helped China, India and Brazil escape the traps that keep most of the world's population poor. These are the handful of exceptions, though, that prove the rule.

The general pattern is that once you're down and out, luck tends to run against you. It's not that poor countries just have the bad luck to be in the wrong place, or deserve divine retribution, it's that once a country has taken a serious body blow to its economic or cultural strength, it's vulnerable to the next problem that comes along. Disasters strike harder when homes are not well built, disease is more deadly when people are malnourished, and industry that struggles is more vulnerable to competition.

The picture is complicated by the fact that competitive forces fan the flames of poverty, to keep prices down. Rich nations want to buy resources at the cheapest price. It's not in the interests of the customer to help a supplier get economic independence and more bargaining power, so governments of rich countries discourage activities that help poor countries develop economically. The following sections introduce the factors that compound the problems of poverty.

Living on the edge

Many people who live in poverty live on the edge of things: The sides of mountains, floodplains, marginal land in drought-prone regions. Living on the edge makes the poor vulnerable to disasters. If it doesn't rain, crops fail — if it does rain, the crops are washed away. With climate change, these disasters may happen more often and may be worse. For the two billion people who live on less than US$2 a day, that's bad news.

Bangladesh sits on the mouth of the Ganges, Brahmaputra and Meghna rivers in the Bay of Bengal. This enormous river delta has been built from the sediment that is picked up by those rivers as they flow from the Himalayan mountains and deposited when that water hits the Bay of Bengal. The vast majority of the nation is less than 10 metres above sea level; about 20 per cent of the land area is less than one metre above sea level. It is estimated that 100 million people will be displaced if the sea level rises by one metre. Those people are overwhelmingly the poorest people in one of the world's poorer countries.

The water supplies of some megacities of South America depend on melted snow and glaciers of the Andes. Those glaciers have shrunk as global temperatures rise. The impact of global warming worsens the already dire circumstances in which those poor people live.

The shift in climatic conditions creates another threat to the world's poor: When the climate changes so does the appropriate use for their land. Aborigines in Northern Australia, for example, have ownership of vast tropical swamps in perpetuity. Now that global warming threatens the agriculture in the more temperate south of the continent, the government has commissioned scientific reports on converting the tropical north into the food bowl for the continent. The people of Patagonia in Argentina live near some of the nation's best fresh water sources. As water becomes scarce, they're fighting for the right to manage their own resources.

Across the world, the poor face increasing competition for scarce resources from the world's rich. There are no prizes for guessing who's more likely to win those competitions.

In the path of disaster

Chapter 15 details the sad irony that although the world's poorest people contribute least to global warming, they suffer most. The World Bank's Global Risk Analysis estimates that more than half the world's population, that's 3.4 billion people, live in areas where at least one hazard could have a significant impact on them.

One disaster can wipe out decades of development in a matter of hours, in a manner that rarely happens in richer countries. Table 2-1 lists the ten deadliest natural disasters of all time. The fact that they have all taken place in economically poor countries is not an indication of where the weather and geology is most threatening, but where they have the worst impact.

Table 2-1		The Ten Deadliest Natural Disasters Ever	
Rank	**Event**	**Location**	**Death Toll (Estimate)**
1.	1931 Yellow River flood	Yellow River, China	4,000,000
2.	1887 Yellow River flood	Yellow River, China	2,000,000
3.	1970 Bhola cyclone	Ganges Delta, East Pakistan	1,000,000
4.	1938 Yellow River flood*	Yellow River, China	up to 900,000
5.	1556 Shaanxi earthquake	Shaanxi Province, China	830,000
6.	1839 India cyclone	Coringa, India	300,000
7.	1642 Kaifeng flood	Kaifeng, Henan Province, China	300,000
8.	2004 Indian Ocean tsunami	Indian Ocean	250,000
9.	1976 Tangshan earthquake	Tangshan, China	240,000
10.	1138 Aleppo earthquake	Syria	230,000

* Triggered by military events.

Debt sucks!

Say it again, Sam. Debt sucks. It sucks money away from essential services like health care and education — things that could make a real difference to the lives of the poor. Cash from abroad can fund much-needed health care and education projects, or build essential infrastructure like roads, rail lines and sewerage. But borrowing foreign cash means debt, and debt can grow so large it destroys nations. The following subsections look at some ways that national debt hits the poor.

Sucking the health budget dry

The debt payments made by African nations are enough to save the lives of 19,000 children each day. African countries spend an average of $14 a year per person on debt repayments. Only $5 goes towards health.

For decades health care and life expectancy improved in countries like Zimbabwe, Zambia, Nicaragua, Chile and Jamaica. The debt crisis of the 1980s reversed these gains. Now, more children die before the age of 5 than 25 years ago. Diseases such as tuberculosis and yellow fever — previously thought to have been eradicated — have made a comeback.

Robbing the public purse

Another debilitating impact of debt is that governments cut spending to meet the repayments. Public services and infrastructure decline; businesses suffer, levels of unemployment rise, and the unemployed stay unemployed. With a shrinking workforce, the number of tax-payers goes down too, tax revenue falls, government revenues are down, and so once again public spending needs to be cut. It's a vicious cycle.

Fuelling instability and violence

If you think the effects of debt are limited to the wallet, think again. The burden of debt is met, across the world, with strikes, political unrest and violence. In response to large debts that doubled food prices and quadrupled the price of medicines, riots in the Dominican Republic in 1984 turned bloody. After days of violence at least 60 people were left dead and 500 injured across the country.

Loan after loan to bail out an ailing Argentine economy ended in tears. The country had been on shaky ground since the early 1980s, but patches of growth had seen it through. But by 2001, Argentina's debts caught up with the country and it descended into turmoil.

Debt-driven destruction

Unless you've been hiding under a rock, you've probably heard that our rainforests are disappearing faster than a cheetah on steroids. In fact, they're being mowed down at a rate of one football field each and every second. Over the course of a year that's an area the size of 30 million football fields that are lost. Greed and the push for economic development are usually blamed for this destruction. And that's right, but debt is one of the tools used by the greedy to drive economic development.

Brazil chops down more trees than any other country. Maybe it's no coincidence that the country is also the world's largest debtor.

Aid: A helping hand or a twist of the knife?

Flip to Chapter 18 for tales of some of the amazing things that have been accomplished through aid. But today's international debts dwarf the current spending on aid. For every $1 given by rich countries, up to $13 is returned in interest repayments. A good deal of the money claimed to be aid by Western governments is actually just loans that must one day be repaid with interest.

Playing with loaded dice

You'd have to be pretty stupid to play at a casino where you know the games are rigged. Your odds of winning a hand of poker aren't so hot if the dealer knows what cards you're holding. But this is exactly the kind of game that poor countries play when they open up to free trade and liberalise their economies. The problem is, no-one's letting them stay out of the game. The sidebar 'The Cancun round: A revolution in the sun' describes what happened at the Cancun trade talks when poor countries simply refused to play any more.

Empires expand by dragging resources from the edge of the empire to the centre. When someone at the edge resists, they get to meet the imperial army. The general Cassius sent the Roman army to Syria and Asia Minor (Turkey) in 42 BC to force them to pay ten years' taxes in advance as punishment for resisting Rome's terms. During the Opium Wars (1839–1842), the British navy shelled the ports of China when it refused to trade tea and silk for opium grown in British India. Every war undertaken to protect the commercial interests of a major power has the, often unintentional, impact of expanding the reach of the empire.

The game is played these days with bullion instead of bullets. Aid dollars and investments are offered in exchange for trade agreements. The following subsections describe some of the rules, tricks and tools of the trade that the rich countries of the world use to make sure the odds work in their favour. Chapter 19 examines the impact this trade imbalance has on the poor.

Subsidies: Rich cows, poor people

Subsidies are payments to producers to supplement the price they get for goods at market. They can be a direct payment, but are more often given in the form of tax breaks or grants. Poor countries can't compete with these subsidies even when they produce goods very efficiently.

The average European cow is subsidised by about US$2.50 a day, according to the World Bank. But more than three-quarters of all people living in sub-Saharan Africa live on less than US$2 a day. Rich countries spend 16 times more on aid to their own farmers than they do on aid to Africa!

The United States offered to cut cotton subsidies by 80 per cent at the 2007 Doha round of trade talks. At the time, the world price for cotton was about 60 per cent what it cost to grow and it was being sold for less than the farmer in the United States was paid. Tens of thousands of Indian cotton farmers had gone bankrupt, 20,000 cotton farmers committed suicide and thousands sold their kidneys to pay their fertiliser bills to US companies.

The Cancun round: A revolution in the sun

Cancun's a pretty decent place to relax. The warm sun and golden beaches are enough to lull most people into complacency. Sit back, sip a margarita, and let your troubles drift away. But not for the trade delegates of the world's poor. For them Cancun in September 2003 was a place to make a stand against unfair trade.

Delegates from poor countries were sick of getting a bad deal. At Cancun, they banded together and walked out when it became clear that the United States and the European Union were not taking their claims seriously. The bad news is that years later the talks have reached a stalemate. The United States and the European Union aren't budging and trade continues to be unfair for the world's poorest countries.

Tariffs: When subsidies aren't enough

Tariffs are the other side of the coin to subsidies. Subsidies mean you can sell your goods more cheaply. Tariffs are a tax added to the cost of goods coming into a country. They mean that everyone else's goods are more expensive.

The average tariff on agricultural goods coming into rich countries from poor countries is more than 15 per cent. For manufactured goods such as clothing and textiles it's nearly 10 per cent. Footwear regularly attracts tariffs of 15 per cent or higher. By contrast, African nations apply tariffs to about 5 per cent of imported goods and those tariffs average much less than 10 per cent. How can poor countries compete with penalties like this?

Downright dirty dumping

Dumping is sending goods to foreign markets at prices lower than the cost of production. This undercuts local producers who can't compete with heavily subsidised goods from abroad. Dumping seriously damages the economies of poor countries. Dumping is considered unfair and is 'discouraged' by the World Trade Organization but it still goes on.

European farmers produce more food than Europe needs. Because they're paid by government subsidies, it doesn't matter to them if anyone's buying their goods or not. So they just keep on producing. This unwanted produce is regularly 'dumped' in Africa.

Tomatoes are one of the most controversial products that regularly make the news for being dumped. Farmers in Canada and the United States regularly lobby their respective governments to act on dumping of tomatoes from the other side. In 2001 anti-dumping penalties applied by the US government to Canadian greenhouse tomatoes exceeded 34 per cent. Thousands of African tomato growers marched in Ghana, Africa, in September 2007 against the dumping of European tomatoes onto the African market.

Back-door protection

Protection — as opposed to protection rackets — is the term used for the rules designed to make sure that products are safe and fit for use. A global compliance regime can enforce sanitation, labelling, packaging and contents standards. On the surface, this sounds fair and just.

Sometimes, though, these standards are used as a way of avoiding competition from abroad. The European Union's regulations on *aflatoxins* (poisons produced by mould on poorly stored cereals) far exceed the recommendations of the United Nations. The World Bank estimates that these rigged regulations cost Africa tens of billions of dollars but saved only a handful of European lives.

Chapter 3

The Geography of Poverty

Human beings enjoy a far higher quality of life and can expect to live longer than ever before. Today, people in the most impoverished region of the world — Africa — have longer life expectancies at birth than people in the most privileged region — Europe — did two centuries ago. On average people may be better off across the board, but 'average' doesn't offer much comfort if you're at the bottom of the barrel.

In 1960, one-fifth of the world's people in rich countries had 30 times the income of the poorest fifth. But four decades later this figure had grown enormously. The richest fifth now earn nearly 75 times what the poor do. The top 10 per cent receive one-third of the world's total income, 165 times more than the bottom 10 per cent (UN Human Development Report 2006).

Western Europe, North America and Oceania are all richer today than they were in the past. Sub-Saharan Africa and Eastern Europe are becoming poorer. On average, people in these regions are worse off today than they were two decades ago. Latin America and Arab countries are improving a little, but not nearly as fast as the West. So their relative position in the world has been in decline over the past quarter of a century.

This chapter gives you a feel for the connections between where people live and how poverty affects them. You get an understanding about what drives poverty in each region. Gender, age, rural/urban location, region, ethnicity and religion can all affect how individuals experience poverty, and these interact in different ways in every region. For example, death from war and starvation is common in Africa but unusual in the rest of the world.

Beyond Borders

While the world's various geographic regions face unique poverty challenges, common themes do exist. These issues include:

- ✔ **The wealth is not spread equally.** Some continents, like Europe, are wealthier than others; some countries, like Japan, are wealthier than others on the same continent; and some people in each country are wealthier than others. When there is an extreme disparity between rich and poor then the poor are probably in trouble. The profile of poverty changes considerably around the world.

- ✔ **Conflict adds to poverty.** Chapter 6 discusses in detail the destructive effects of conflict. Needless to say, when lots of people are killed and lots of infrastructure blown up, the economy suffers and the poor are further marginalised.

- ✔ **The rural poor suffer most.** The nature of poverty is radically different in rural and urban areas. The escalating problems of rapidly growing cities are highlighted in Chapter 14. The rural poor are usually the last to get access to services, and are often the hardest hit by natural disasters and conflict.

- ✔ **Women and children face greater hurdles.** For a variety of reasons, women and children struggle to get a fair go in many countries. They are worse off in some parts of the world than others. One thing that's common is that where women suffer most, society suffers as well. Head on over to Chapter 8 for an account of the fascinating and disturbing relationship between gender discrimination and poverty.

Africa: The Bankrupt Continent

Africa is home to some of the worst poverty in the world. It has the largest proportion of people living below US$1 a day and, in many instances, the number of poor people is growing. Conflict and disease make Africa's poverty worse.

No country in Africa is rich enough to be considered a developed country, but at the same time, there's lots of variation in wealth between countries. Africa, the continent, has lots of natural resources — including oil, gold and diamonds — but few Africans have benefited from this natural wealth. Even so, there are some remarkable examples of change that inspire hope for the continent and prove that there is a way forward.

Democracy and economic growth

One of the biggest triumphs of the twentieth century happened in Africa when South Africa peacefully shifted from apartheid to democracy. The number of countries that regularly hold democratic elections has increased significantly in the past two decades. That list includes Benin, Cape Verde, The Gambia, Ghana, Malawi, Nigeria, Senegal, Tanzania, Uganda and Zambia. These countries exhibit Africa's aspiration for democracy and upholding human rights.

Not all countries are going backwards economically. Cape Verde, Mauritius, Mozambique and Uganda have sustained annual growth rates of close to 7 or 8 per cent. Other countries are firmly on the path to long-term poverty reduction. Levels of education have increased in Guinea, Malawi and Tanzania, and rates of child mortality have decreased in The Gambia. There's even been success in containing the spread of HIV, particularly in Senegal and Uganda.

Deserts and jungles

Africa is a vast and ancient continent, with deserts, jungles and plains that have shaped its development over thousands of years.

Historically, Africa's deserts and jungles acted as barriers to trade — the key to growth and development. Thick jungles in the west and centre of the continent made the transport of goods and people difficult. The Sahara Desert to the north blocked trade with the wealth in Europe, and the Kalahari Desert inhibited trade with the wealthier south. To a lesser extent, these physical impediments still inhibit trade today. In modern Africa few roads are paved, and during the wet season unpaved tracks become impassable mud.

Northern Africa has always operated as part of the Mediterranean trading network. Egypt was the granary of the Roman, Greek and Persian empires. The relationships between the 'Moors' and Mediterranean Europe are old and deep. Sub-Saharan Africa is what Europeans called the Dark Continent and has generally done very poorly from its international relations.

Tropical Africa has a high proportion of mountainous, landlocked countries and rivers that are not easily navigable. Despite their isolation, these countries are densely populated because they happen to be blessed with rich volcanic soils, providing lots of land that can be used for agriculture.

Hoarded treasure, blighted children

Africa is one continent where the disparity of wealth within nations is a major cause of extreme poverty. In Zambia, for example, the richest 10 per cent of the population earns a total income that is 42 times larger than that of the poorest 10 per cent.

In Guinea the poorest 20 per cent of people have such limited access to medical services that they make up only 4 per cent of the hospital population. Across sub-Saharan Africa, 37 per cent of children do not go to school.

Africa also displays the tragedy of extreme poverty in rural areas. People living outside cities are likely to be significantly poorer than those living in urban centres. In the dry rural savannah regions in the north of Ghana, poverty runs at 70 per cent, much higher than in the capital, Accra. Africa is also a continent where women suffer discrimination. School-age girls, for example, are often too busy collecting water and firewood to get to school.

Death by design and disease

The Democratic Republic of Congo (DR Congo), in the heart of Africa, has abundant reserves of diamonds, copper and crude oil. At the same time it's one of the poorest countries in the world. Millions of people have died of starvation and disease in the last five years. Life expectancy is 44 years for men and 42 for women. DR Congo is so poor partly because it's only just emerging from 40 years of brutal conflict. All of the poorest states in Africa are engaged in, or just emerging from, civil wars. Sierra Leone, Burundi, Central African Republic, Rwanda, Somalia and Angola are examples.

The malaria curse

If you were a lonely malarial mosquito looking for love, you'd move to sub-Saharan Africa. The climate's just right. There's the ideal amount of rainfall, the right temperature and plenty of mates to make it *the* hot spot to breed and wreak havoc. More than one million people die of malaria every year, mostly infants, young children and pregnant women — most of them in Africa. Malaria doesn't just kill people; it costs approximately $12 billion a year in lost productivity. It puts a huge strain on the health system and accounts for up to half of all hospital admissions and outpatient visits in Africa each year. When people are sick, they can't work. It also takes kids out of school and leads to a lifetime of ill health. The tragedy is that malaria is easily preventable and treatable.

HIV and AIDS pandemic

HIV and AIDS are killing Africa's doctors, teachers, mothers, fathers, business owners and farmers. Twelve million children have become orphans. By 2010, one in five children in southern Africa will be an orphan. Life expectancy has dropped by decades. In Swaziland, a country with high rates of HIV infection, people can expect to live to the age of 33.

The more HIV spreads, the poorer Africa gets. Households lose their main income earners, health systems lose doctors and nurses and become overwhelmed with sick people, and workplaces lose workers. Economies grind to a halt and that makes it even more difficult for countries to deal with the pandemic. HIV and AIDS is an emergency on a huge scale.

The Crucible of the Middle East

The complex relationships between conflict and poverty, resources and global politics are on graphic display in the Middle East. Extremely wealthy royal families and some of the world's poorest people inhabit this troubled region, suffering from conflicts fanned by the military exploits of the world's richest nations. *The Middle East For Dummies* (Wiley Publishing Inc., 2003) details the many factors that underlie these problems.

The economies in countries like Iraq, Egypt, Sudan, Somalia and elsewhere are erratic. The reasons are manifold, varied and complex. It's worth noting that most of the region's nations have little or none of the oil for which the region is famous. So countries with huge populations, such as Pakistan and Egypt, lack sufficient natural resources to offset extreme poverty.

Among other barriers to economic development are the following:

- **Bureaucracy and corruption:** Huge, sluggish bureaucracies racked by corruption serve as effective barriers to development.
- **Failed strategies:** Oil-producing nations, like Saudi Arabia, have attempted to invest petrodollars to improve social services. Because oil-rich countries have failed to diversify, their economies are hopelessly linked to oil exports. When the global oil market suffers, so do their economies.
- **Failure to modernise:** Most Middle Eastern countries have failed to modernise. Without modern secular education, modern technology, economic strategies, industries, tax structures and infrastructure, nations can't compete.

- **Population:** Unfettered population growth may be the most alarming deterrent to economic development.

- **Unequal distribution of wealth and resources:** Among oil-producing nations, governments or a handful of the elite generally control the petrodollars, and therefore the money doesn't trickle down. The wealthy landholding elite in many nations, at times bordering on feudal lords, stand in the way of development.

Asia: More Than Its Fair Share of Woes

Asia is the world's largest and most diverse continent. The climatic extremes of the continent result in wild variations in vegetation and animal life. The world's two most populous countries, China and India, are in Asia.

Although Asia is home to two-thirds of the world's poor, between 1965 and 1990 East Asia grew faster than any other region in the world. Asia represents one of the most important parts of the world economy, with 56 per cent of the world population, 26 per cent of the world gross domestic product (GDP) and a quarter of the world's trade. These nations provide the proof that it's possible for poor countries to create wealth and achieve a good standard of living.

- Recognising the link between education and wealth, many Asian countries have set themselves the task of providing universal access to basic education, especially for girls. It's likely that the region as a whole will achieve universal primary education in the next few years.

- Employment rates, opportunities for work and trade are also improving, and many individuals and companies in Asia are flourishing.

- The emergence of India and China as economic powerhouses offers the entire region the promise of an even greater future, despite the challenges this growth represents for the global economy and climate.

Monsoons and high, cold deserts

Asian countries are affected by almost every conceivable natural hazard: Earthquakes, landslides, volcanoes, cyclones or typhoons, droughts, epidemics, insect infestations and forest fires. Human activity adds further instability. The destruction of tropical forests, intensive agricultural activities and exploitative mineral extraction pose a significant threat to future growth and prosperity in the region.

In some ways, the richness of Asia's flora and fauna is a curse. On one hand, those diverse natural assets provide the resources for development, but the harvesting of those natural resources is becoming an environmental catastrophe.

Raging tigers, bleeding sparrows

A key feature of growth across the Asian region has been inequality. Figure 3-1 shows clearly that some Asian nations approach the wealth of the United States, whereas others are poorer than the war-torn African state of Rwanda. Over the last ten years or so, the majority of countries in the region have recorded increases in income inequality. In some cases, the income gap has widened by 35 per cent.

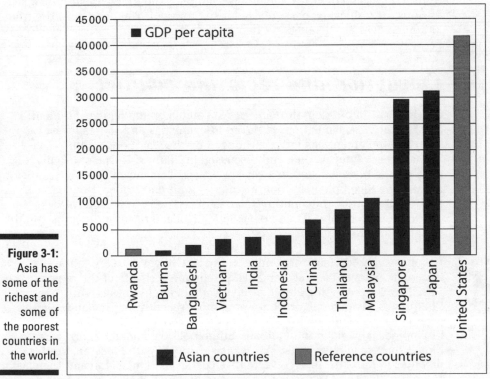

Figure 3-1: Asia has some of the richest and some of the poorest countries in the world.

Source: United Nations Human Development Report 2007.

The main difference in income is within countries — between rich and poor states, rural and urban centres and coastal and regional areas. For example, the gap between rich and poor states in India has widened. Relatively rich states have, on average, grown two to three times faster than poorer ones over the last three decades. This kind of disparity entrenches poverty — it's harder for people to get ahead, move up and create wealth. Although the rural–urban divide is common throughout the world, Asia also suffers polarisation between coastal and inland regions. If current trends continue, the coastal-inland gap will eventually surpass the traditional rural–urban divide.

Child labour, trafficking and slavery

Asia has the largest number of working children under 14 — about 127 million — more than double the total number of children in the United States. Children work mainly because they have no choice. There's a range of jobs that children do to boost their families' incomes. Some work in factories, on farms or as domestic help in homes. The unlucky ones are trafficked. Asian countries, including Cambodia and Thailand, are recognised as hubs for trafficking, particularly for sex tourism. The horrors of the traffic in human lives are detailed in Chapter 13.

Corruption and recurring conflict

Corruption is a problem throughout Asia and is cramping development. Most of the 22 Asian nations received low rankings and scores in the 'Corruption Perceptions Index' produced by the watchdog group Transparency International and discussed in Chapter 7. One of the biggest problems is that civil servants get low wages. This means that they look for other ways to supplement their income — graft and bribes. How bad can it be? In Indonesia, the monthly salaries of civil servants usually cover the cost of living for only 10 to 12 days. In Mongolia, a third of the judges in the countryside are homeless.

Asia has suffered plenty of conflict in the last 40 years to erode the economic potential and sustainable development efforts of the region. There are long-standing ethnic or civil conflicts in Indonesia, the Philippines, Myanmar, East Timor and, most recently, in Thailand. There's poor governance in countries such as Cambodia, Laos, East Timor, the Philippines, Myanmar and Vietnam. Ethno-political conflict in Sri Lanka, India's inter-religious conflicts as well as disputes with Pakistan, border disputes in Kazakhstan, Kyrgyzstan, Tajikistan, Turkmenistan and Uzbekistan since the demise of the Soviet Union, and ongoing conflict in Afghanistan continue to cast a pall over the region.

One hundred million missing girls

Can't find a good man? Maybe you need to search in Asia. Because girls and women are seen as inferior, there's a strong preference for baby boys over girls, particularly in China, Bangladesh, India, Nepal and Pakistan. This has led to the phenomenon known as 'missing girls' — the females who were conceived but aborted and are simply absent from the population. It is estimated that 100 million females are 'missing' across Asia, 50 million of them in China. As a result, the biological norm for women to marginally outnumber men is reversed in some regions in Asia. In China there are now whole villages of men coming of age who can't find a partner.

Being female in Asia also means that you're worse off. Girls are more likely than boys to be malnourished, suffer poverty, face violence and be refused an education.

Latin America: Countries in Contrast

South and Central American nations are not as poor as Africa or poor Asian countries, but the wealth in those nations is less equally shared than anywhere else in the world. This inequality has persisted for centuries but has fallen strikingly in recent years, along with increased political stability. Between 2002 and 2006, the number of Latin Americans in extreme poverty fell from 97 million to 81 million.

Latin America is well placed to take advantage of new markets emerging as a result of concern about climate change. Countries like Brazil already have robust alternative fuel industries, such as ethanol and bio-diesel. The demand for carbon credits from the developed world can potentially bring significant economic benefits to those nations with significant areas of wilderness.

Conflict between poor and rich continues to play a big part in Latin America. Indigenous communities, which represent more than half the population of countries like Bolivia and Guatemala, are particularly marginalised and often involved in that conflict. Check the section 'Indigenous People: The Poor on Your Doorstep' to see the problems indigenous people face everywhere in the world.

South America projects a notoriously macho culture that, as in other poor regions, oppresses women and disadvantages future generations.

The Andes and the Amazon

There's a wide variety of climatic regions and landscapes across Latin America. Dominating South America is the Amazon rainforest, known as the earth's lungs because it produces about 20 per cent of the world's oxygen and has the highest diversity of plant species on earth. Deforestation of the Amazon is a serious concern, not just for South American citizens, but globally. The Amazon basin is fed by the Andes mountains, stretching down the west coast of the entire continent and dominating the weather of the continent and the landscape of Colombia, Ecuador, Peru and Chile.

This dramatic climate and geology has a tendency to be unstable. Central America and the Caribbean face the constant prospect of natural disasters including earthquakes, volcanoes and hurricanes. Extreme weather events are getting worse as the impact of global warming takes hold. For example, climatic phenomena such as *El Niño* (a weather system that begins in Peru and influences drought across the South Pacific) are recurring more frequently and at greater magnitude.

Landowners lording it over locals

Guatemala, Brazil, Colombia and Chile suffer from the most unequal distribution of wealth in the world. Some of this inequality has its roots in Latin America's colonial past. The colonial land tenure systems put ownership of land in the hands of a few who also controlled the indigenous labour that worked the land. These colonial masters controlled the natural resources and revenue from all activity on the land under their management.

Since colonial times there have been major political changes, which have included land reforms, under a wide range of democratic and military regimes. But those changes have not resulted in the widespread redistribution of property. Land and power are still concentrated in the hands of the elite.

Alongside the indigenous poverty prevalent in South America, race and ethnicity also keep people poor. Across South America non-Hispanics — defined as having a maternal language other than Spanish (or Portuguese in Brazil) — are horrendously poor. Latin America's African descendants have lower education, lower nutrition levels and worse access to health care and other social institutions than any other group.

Slipping values in banana republics

Latin America generally has high rates of crime, violence and political instability that coexist with the high degree of inequality. In almost all Latin American countries, violence is now among the five main causes of death, and is the principal cause of death in Brazil, Colombia, Venezuela, El Salvador and Mexico. Overall, Latin America is home to more murders than anywhere else in the world apart from sub-Saharan Africa.

Alongside high crime and violence generally, gender-based violence is relatively common. Between 30 and 50 per cent of women in Latin America suffer from psychological violence, and between 10 and 35 per cent are affected by physical violence in their own homes.

Crime and violence damage the economy and social infrastructure as well as people's lives. Money that could be spent on alleviating poverty has to be spent undoing years of conflict. Infrastructure such as roads, telecommunications, bridges, electricity generators is targeted in wars, and it takes vast resources to rebuild post-conflict.

Wars between guerrillas and governments in South and Central America set back economies by billions of dollars and many years. As an example, repairs to a destroyed oil pipeline in Colombia cost approximately US$4 million, and El Salvador suffered approximately US$1.6 billion worth of damage to infrastructure between 1992 and 1996. This devastation was often part of a wider pattern involving the destruction of homes, churches, marketplaces, schools and health centres.

Indigenous People: The Poor on Your Doorstep

No matter what region of the world you go to, one thing remains the same — and we're not talking about a McDonald's hamburger. The fate of indigenous people appears universally tragic. There are about 370 million indigenous people living in more than 70 countries worldwide and, in most places, they're worse off than everyone else. Whether in rich countries (Australia, the United States or Canada) or in poor countries (the Philippines or Peru) poverty is pervasive among the indigenous populations.

Indigenous poverty has its roots in the history of colonisation and dispossession. Many indigenous populations don't have the legal right to live on the lands that once were exclusively theirs. Nor do they have access to the resources they managed sustainably for thousands of years. For many indigenous communities, outsiders exploit these resources, with few benefits flowing back to them and little regard for the natural environment. For most ancient cultures, the land is inextricably linked to the people's identity. When they're kicked off the land, they suffer not only economic loss, but also the loss of identity and culture.

Denied their right to land, many indigenous communities were driven into extreme poverty and ill-health. Many chronic conditions are endemic in indigenous communities because there's little or no access to quality health care and because of poor nutrition. Indigenous people in most countries have much higher mortality rates than the national average. For example, in Peru, indigenous children die at nearly twice the rate of the non-Indigenous population. Indigenous Australians die nearly 20 years younger and their children are three times more likely to die than non-indigenous Australians.

The figures are alarming worldwide, even in those countries where the indigenous communities actively participate in the national economy. In Bolivia and Guatemala, for example, more than half of the total population is poor, but almost three-quarters of the indigenous population are poor. Poverty among indigenous people in Ecuador is about 87 per cent and reaches 96 per cent in the rural highlands.

Colonial shame: Australia's Aborigines

The Indigenous people of Australia have been living in the region for at least 40,000 years. At the time of colonisation in the late eighteenth century, there were between 350 and 750 distinct cultural groups across the country, each speaking its own language or dialect. These societies were mostly hunter-gatherers. European colonisation led to the decimation of many communities in waves of disease and violence, and many indigenous Australians were driven off their traditional lands. It wasn't until 1967 that Indigenous Australians were even counted in the census.

Indigenous Australians are still worse off than other Australians. Discrimination persists and many Indigenous Australians live in the kind of poverty that is comparable with developing countries. In remote communities there is often no clean water and sewerage.

Smoking, obesity and alcohol abuse are also more prevalent in Indigenous communities than in the rest of Australia. As a result, Indigenous Australians are affected by diabetes, circulatory system and respiratory disorders, ear disease, eye disorders, cancer, urinary tract problems and physical injuries at much higher rates than the rest of the Australian population and at a much younger age. Untreated middle ear infections and bad nutrition are common in Aboriginal children and affect their performance at school.

Inadequate housing also contributes to ill-health. Indigenous Australians live in crowded conditions, and in accommodation where there's poor maintenance and inadequate basic utilities. As explained in Chapter 12, these living conditions cause higher rates of infectious diseases such as skin, eye and ear infections, and respiratory infections. If left untreated, they can cause long-term medical problems.

The first item of business for the new Australian government elected in November 2007 was to officially say 'Sorry' to thousands of Aborigines, known as the *stolen generations*, who were removed from their parents and institutionalised or fostered out. The statement of the government said, 'We take this first step by acknowledging the past and laying claim to a future . . . where we harness the determination of all Australians, indigenous and non-indigenous, to close the gap that lies between us in life expectancy, educational achievement and economic opportunity.'

Chapter 4

So You Want to Make a Difference?

So, you want to help fellow human beings out of the desperate poverty trap, but you don't know Bono or Bob Geldof? Well, you could become an aid worker!

The idea of going out to address world poverty conjures up images of heroic acts like these:

✔ Pushing food-aid packages out of a B-52 flying over a conflict zone

✔ Clearing a field of landmines to be replaced with a field of rice

✔ Helping create an entire micro-climate by reforesting a dustbowl

✔ Establishing child safe areas in regions susceptible to nefarious human traffickers

✔ Lobbying governments to reduce tariffs for imports from developing countries

These activities certainly sound more adventurous than being assigned to a beige cubicle, crunching numbers on a spreadsheet or knocking up another report for the board of directors. The unfortunate reality is that unless you're Angelina Jolie, all jobs require a stretch of time in the cubicle.

The good news is that aid and development organisations need all kinds of support staff, as much as they need on-the-ground development experts. It takes a diverse set of skills for an organisation to be effective. To be an aid worker you don't have to fit the movie star stereotype of the heroic food distributor in the middle of nowhere. Of course, you might want to make a contribution in your spare time, without giving up your whole life. Whatever you can do will be gratefully accepted.

This chapter outlines the variety of jobs that need doing to help the world's poor, the skills and talents you need to do them and some of the ways you can help. It gives you some ideas about where to start and how to use the skills you have to be part of the solution to world poverty.

Commitment Comes First

Perhaps your empathy for people struggling to survive poverty began at a very young age — ever since you can remember, you've wanted to do something to make the world a better place. Or maybe your social conscience developed over time as you sought more meaning in your life.

Sometimes it takes a disaster — natural, man-made or on a personal level — to inspire someone to change course and dedicate their working life to helping others to escape poverty. No matter how you arrive at your decision, there are a few steps you have to take to make that decision a reality. The first step is to make the commitment:

✔ Write down the things that drive you. What are your motivations? What are your ultimate goals? Take it from us, with the relatively low pay you get in the sector, you're going to need all the passion and commitment you can muster.

✔ What are the goals of agencies that interest you? Aid and development organisations generally have mission statements that outline their priorities — eliminating poverty, improving lives and upholding human rights, for example.

✔ How do your goals match up with the goals of the agencies? If you want to be employed by an aid agency, no matter what the role, you need to be committed to the organisation's goals and you will need to behave according to the code of conduct of that organisation.

✔ What relevant things have you done? Make a note of any letters or articles you may have submitted to a newspaper or to politicians. Make a list of community-oriented groups and activities you have been engaged in. If you can't think of anything at all, maybe you need to volunteer for a while before you apply for a position within an aid organisation.

You don't have to work in Kenya or Papua New Guinea to help the poor. If you're serious about making the world a better place, hundreds of great local, national and international organisations champion very noble causes. They all need your help. If there's a cause you believe in, there's likely to be an organisation that supports it. Think about throwing the weight of your career behind these groups, too.

The road less travelled

Tamara, a close friend of co-author Sarah, started her career as an aid worker very differently from most people. She trained as a commercial lawyer and then launched a corporate career in risk management for a major bank. She enjoyed a strong career path, salary and opportunities to expand her skills and experience.

She reflects on that now: 'I have always been committed to social justice movements, but at the time I worked in the bank, that commitment was secondary and definitely limited to after office hours. I was searching for something that would allow me to get more personally involved. So, a small group of colleagues and I decided that we would start a not-for-profit organisation and send computers to a school in a small village in Northern India. Our aim was to provide a resource for students who had no access to technology, or ability to access the Internet and engage in the wider world.'

This incredibly challenging project was ultimately successful. She raised the funds with her colleagues to provide the computers. It was a life-changing experience; it opened her eyes to the complexity of international development and the extent of the injustice experienced by the majority of people in the world. 'When I finished that project, I knew I wanted to get more involved in the issue of poverty, but other than a short stint in India, I felt I had little to offer an international aid agency.'

Here is how she assessed her skills at the time. 'I could develop and implement strategy, design operations for a large-scale and international business, and I could manage and influence different interest groups. With my offering firmly in mind, I met with and closely questioned everyone I knew in the aid industry. I volunteered, I applied for roles and eventually World Vision gave me an opportunity to be part of their International Program.'

Looking back now, she notes the profound effect the work has had on her. 'Over the past two years I have used my corporate skills to develop a key program strategy, redesign business operations and take part in program design. I actively advise on carbon trading and poverty reduction, implement strategies to address mother and child nutrition, and develop business efficiencies to ensure that more resources can be provided to people living in poverty. I work with incredibly passionate and talented people, and personally feel that I play a part in addressing poverty.'

She also notes the wildly different backgrounds of the aid workers she has met. 'There have been former teachers, mechanical engineers, occupational therapists, agricultural scientists, documentary makers, social workers and even musicians. No one person's path into aid work is the same. However, they do have two things in common — a skill that is valuable to a not-for-profit agency and a passion for social justice.'

Types of Aid Workers

Not everyone who works in aid and development is an *aid worker*. Within the sector, not many people use that title to refer to themselves. But that's how the rest of the world knows us so, for ease, we use the term aid worker throughout this chapter. In fact, the term refers to a wide range of jobs, such as:

- Advocate
- Aid and development worker
- All-round good guy/gal
- Community development worker
- Humanitarian worker
- International development worker
- Lobbyist
- Relief worker, development worker
- Researcher

People who work for modern aid agencies are typically divided into these groups:

- Advocates
- Development workers
- Emergency relief workers
- Support staff

An aid and development organisation, often called a non-government organisation, might specialise in one or more of these types of activities, and some of the big agencies — like Oxfam or World Vision — do all four. Of course, no matter how many aid and development activities these organisations pursue, they also need support staff for their marketing, fundraising, finance, legal activities, human resources and the myriad other activities required to keep an organisation in the field.

Chapters 4 and 18 discuss the impact aid workers have in the real world. The following sections provide a breakdown of the tasks carried out by each of the major types of aid workers.

Emergency relief workers

You've probably heard the saying, 'Give a man a fish and you feed him for a day, but teach him how to fish and you feed him for a lifetime.' That's all well and good, but sometimes the poor guy just needs a fish right now! That's when humanitarian aid, or emergency relief, is needed. Emergency relief is about saving lives, alleviating suffering, today.

The high-profile end of emergency relief is food aid. From time to time emergency relief gets a bad reputation because the media profile is out of sync with more long-term programs. Nevertheless, emergency relief is a critical component of emergency aid, encompassing a wide range of food-aid activities that can be rolled out when the going gets tough.

- ✔ **Handing out:** When things are particularly bad something needs to be done right now. And that's when humanitarian workers would resort to food distributions or giving out seeds and tools. But these handouts should only go on for a short period of time, and they should be part of a plan for the future.

- ✔ **Helping out:** Sometimes all you need is a little support to get back on your feet. Maybe all you need is help getting your goods to the next town to sell or some advice on how to help your crops survive the drought. Perhaps some veterinary help to vaccinate your livestock would go a long way towards making you self-sufficient. Sometimes aid is just about a gentle helping hand.

- ✔ **Feeding up:** Malnutrition isn't just about having too little food. It's also about having too little of the right food. So food is often given to supplement a diet, filling in the nutritional holes. Food supplements can be critical for young children and pregnant or nursing mothers. Supplementary feeding can be done in schools — it gets children into the classroom and keeps them healthy.

Good emergency relief programs — whether they provide shelter, health care, food or sanitation — should slot into long-term development aims so that the effects are long-lasting. For that reason, relief workers also often find themselves:

- ✔ **Training up:** Disasters like droughts, floods and earthquakes have been going on for longer than humans have been around. So there's always someone who's been there done that when disaster strikes. Many communities can benefit from very simple training in how other groups have coped with these traumas. Development issues such as education on how best to sell goods for a fair price can also be part of ongoing training programs.

- **Working up:** Food aid should build long-term food security, rather than provide handouts that only last a few meals. Food's often given out in lieu of cash to help people get back on their feet. Sometimes it's exchanged for work, like building a well, a road or a school. The aim of this approach is to improve the long-term ability of the community to cope better in the future.

- **Adding value:** Food aid projects will often include little extras that add real value. They could be cooking utensils, oral-rehydration salts, shelter or education. For example, malaria infects more than 220 million people a year and kills more than a million. The disease is particularly devastating in Africa, where it is a leading killer of children. If you can knock it on the head by handing out a bunch of mosquito nets while you help people eat, then it's a few bucks well spent.

TECHNICAL STUFF

Checking out the food parcels

Ever wondered what goes into a parcel of emergency food aid? Here are some of the usual suspects:

- **CSB (corn soy blend):** This brown paste certainly isn't delicious. But it is nutritious, and that's what counts when it comes to food aid.

- **Cereals:** We're not talking corn flakes here, but grains in general. Cereals could be anything from maize to wheat to sorghum.

- **Rice:** In many parts of the world people would rather chow down on rice than other cereals.

- **Salt:** Sodium chloride. Try adding it to food. You'll never look back.

- **Fortified vegetable oil:** Good for cooking but great for eating. This oil adds much-needed calories and a range of nutrients to your basic gruel.

- **Pulses:** Annual leguminous crops yielding from one to twelve grains or seeds of variable size. Oh, sorry. That's peas, beans and lentils to you.

- **BP5:** A high-energy, high-protein biscuit. You don't need many of these to fill you up; you don't want 'em either!

- **Canned fish:** A great source of protein. You'd better hope you have a can opener though.

- **Sugar:** The readily digestible powerhouse that is glucose. It might send your kids into a tizz, but it's a great way to get malnourished people onto their feet, quickly.

- **Country-specific items:** It might be some yoghurt, some tea or something else that forms part of your regular diet. Something to remind you of home.

Relief workers are the aid world's real-life heroes and heroines. They fly into disaster areas or conflict zones at the drop of a hat to assist the locals to recover. These guys are cool under fire and experts in coordinating emergency relief and aid from all over the world. Relief workers are usually highly trained in specialist fields. The kinds of skills you need are ones that help remove immediate danger and simultaneously provide life's necessities like food, clean water, sanitation, shelter and medical treatment. Relief workers can be engineers, doctors or IT gurus.

Even with those skills, relief workers usually have to do more training in how to behave in emergency situations. Relief work is not as easy as it looks on TV. You actually have to learn to do things like drop to the ground if you hear guns go off. The natural instinct for most people who have grown up in safe societies is to stand around open-mouthed and wide-eyed. Dropping to the ground and crawling to safety takes practice. Relief work is also one of the most psychologically and physically fatiguing jobs. Emergency relief agencies make it mandatory that relief workers take time out for post-emergency downtime, de-briefing and counselling.

Development workers

If you imagine yourself working with people to help them build better lives, you're heading down the career path that in the trade is called a *development worker*. Your mental picture might involve building schools, roads and power plants or helping communities pull together to demand their rights or impoverished women to set up small businesses. There are as many types of development as there are human activities.

While you imagine yourself helping people build better lives, remember that the right development is the development that someone needs, not the development you've been dreaming of. Development programs are more successful if the people who have to live with them get to participate in the design and delivery. Most people have a pretty good idea about what would make their lives better, but don't have the resources to make it happen. Your job as a development worker is to help them make their dreams come true.

Typical development projects tackle problems like water and sanitation, health, food insecurity, education and human rights. New approaches to solving economic problems include microfinance initiatives. These programs lend enough money to local people to get on their feet and start their own enterprises. In international terms, the amounts of money are tiny but the impact can be huge.

Development workers need a wide range of skills. They need to be able to

- ✔ Find out what communities want

- ✔ Help a community come up with workable, sustainable solutions

- ✔ Pull in technical expertise to make things happen

- ✔ Coordinate with governments and other organisations

- ✔ Ensure that members of the community are empowered to control a project

- ✔ Train people in the community to build, manage, staff and maintain a project after completion

If you can achieve all of these points, there's a much better chance of development being self-sufficient and sustainable long after you leave.

To be a development worker you need technical skills, but you also need the ability to listen and build relationships with people on the ground, and empower and enable those in poverty to help themselves. What you need to offer is a hand up, not a hand out. Most people who work in an aid agency have more than one degree, often with a master's in something like international development. It's a pretty competitive field and if you want to work in it, a university degree is usually mandatory. It also pays to specialise.

Advocates

If you're good at winning arguments, carrying out remarkable research or inspiring people to take action, you could make a great advocate for the poor. Cast off that ridiculous-looking wig, young lawyer friend, and help convince governments, multinational corporations and transnational organisations to make poverty history!

There are a few different types of advocates.

- ✔ **Researchers and policy writers:** These gems pull together all the data, world trends and best practices from a variety of different sources to create alternate, development-friendly policies. Lobbying and campaigning would be shallow and quite impossible without the work of researchers and policy writers. A famous example of an anti-poverty policy writer is American economist Jeffrey Sachs, who became Director of the United Nations Millennium Project and adviser to United Nations Secretaries-General Kofi Annan and Ban Ki Moon.

- ✔ **Lobbyists:** A rare species of lobbyist does not try to push a self-serving economic agenda like tobacco, uranium mining or agricultural subsidies. Some aid organisations lobby politicians in order to influence policies and budget decisions that affect the poor. The lobbyist's chief weapons are credible alternative policies and proof of popular, electorate-based support. Oxfam International has had a lot of success lobbying governments and even multinationals to implement fairer trade practices on behalf of the world's poor.

- ✔ **Campaigners:** Campaigners educate, inspire and mobilise large audiences to take action that will convince those in power to adopt better policies. There's nothing like the threat of thousands of people not voting for you or boycotting your product to give a politician or company the incentive to change its policies. Campaigning is about giving a voice to the voiceless. Nelson Mandela, Ben Affleck and Gwyneth Paltrow are some of the famous campaigners responsible for moving millions to take up the Make Poverty History campaign. The Make Poverty History campaign itself is a coalition of different aid and social justice organisations.

Advocating for a very good outcome

Advocacy is increasingly a crucial part of development work in poor countries. In this context some aid organisations send advocates to train local communities to ask the right questions of their elected officials. After all, they're entitled to services that have been promised by their national governments, like education and health care. The aim is to build the capacity of communities to advocate for their rights and participate fully in their country's democratic processes to ensure that they receive what they're entitled to.

The Community Scorecard was developed to get around problems like low literacy levels and fragile democracies. The scorecard is a constructive tool for communities to continually monitor, measure and vocalise their (dis)satisfaction with public services and makes providers of services — like governments — accountable.

Community Scorecards have been widely used by governments and non-government organisations around the world to better understand how people feel about the services available to them and use that understanding to improve services. The World Bank has a number of presentations about developing and using Community Scorecards. You can find this information by going to the World Bank Web site at www.worldbank.org and typing 'Community scorecard' into their search engine.

The scorecard allows local communities to nominate and rate public services on a scale of very good to very bad. The system also helps the advocate to facilitate a public meeting with the service provider (for example, local government) to negotiate possible reforms to those services that the locals feel need improvement.

Support staff

If your skill set doesn't lend itself to advocacy, development or emergency work but you're still interested in becoming an aid worker, a support role may suit you. Aid activities can only happen if they have financial and logistical backing. This takes communication specialists, call centre staff, IT gurus, designers, copywriters, fundraisers, marketers, event organisers, accountants, lawyers, managers, human relations specialists and public relations experts.

Getting the Street Smarts

Hundreds of different specialty skills are needed by organisations carrying out humanitarian work in developing countries. Some professions are incredibly complex and require years of study and experience. In fact most aid workers in the field have one or two university degrees and years of experience in the organisations they represent.

Other jobs can be quite simple and require only on-the-job training. Aid workers in the field note that practical knowledge of education, health, IT, agriculture, engineering, psychology and finance are all areas of specialisation that help on the ground.

No single recipe for success exists for going from a student to a paid professional helping people escape from poverty. In the section 'Commitment Comes First' earlier in this chapter, we point out that the one thing you do need is passion and persistence.

It's a matter of degree

Pretty much any degree will have an application in the developing world, but it helps to think through what qualifications match specific positions. The sections that follow list some of the degrees that are useful in the headlined positions:

Development worker

In the aid business, development means the development of a community, society or nation. That's the province of — how'd you guess? — development workers.

✔ A degree in international development is a good way to start your career as a development professional. You learn all about development theory, what works and what doesn't.

✔ Any kind of profession — medicine, business, education, engineering, agriculture, forestry — has its applications in this field.

✔ Community development involves the processes that many aid agencies use when they do development. Community development workers know all kinds of ways to make sure that development is what people in communities want and need, and is delivered in a way that's sustainable and appropriate.

Advocates

Convincing the authorities to allow aid to flow and, even more importantly, to let people help themselves is the work of advocates.

✔ You can't walk into a room of advocates without bumping into a few lawyers. A lot of advocacy is about creating change to laws, so it helps if you understand them in the first place.

✔ Knowing how political processes work is also a big plus for advocates. A degree in politics gives you a good grounding.

✔ Some advocates have an academic bent and know how to research and write an 80 (or 300) page report. Some kind of academic specialisation in fields like global trade, aid, international politics or human rights is useful.

✔ Campaigners are another kettle of fish entirely. They combine a lot of the other skills of advocates with PR and marketing skills. Campaigners often have to engage a wide audience and motivate them to take action.

Support staff

The full range of professional services that keep any organisation going are active behind the scene in aid organisations.

✔ Dealing with the media is a complicated business, so it helps to hire professionals. Lots of aid agencies have media and PR specialists to get their message out to a wide audience.

✔ Most aid agencies depend on donations from the public to do their work. The marketing and fundraising professionals are the ones who help them bring in the big bucks.

✔ Who's going to manage that money? Yep, you guessed it: Finance people and accountants.

Emergency relief workers

Those heroic types that fly in to provide emergency services after a disaster or conflict come from all walks of life. Really.

- Remember the television show *M*A*S*H*? Well, like the 4077th, the people emergency relief workers deal with are caught up in or fleeing conflict or disasters. That means injuries and ill-health. Any kind of health degree — doctor, nurse, psychologist — really comes in handy.

- We know it's hard to believe that they let information technology (IT) people out of the basement, but the IT specialist is a vital member of any emergency relief team. They set up the computer networks and phone systems, so that the relief effort can coordinate and communicate.

- Journalists or communications specialists tell the world what's happening in trouble spots.

- Ever thought about where 5,000 people who have turned up in a refugee camp will go to the toilet? Engineers have and they come up with quick, easy and safe solutions (going behind a bush doesn't count). They also do useful things like build shelters and provide clean water.

Trading your trade skills

University degrees are not the only useful qualifications for aid workers. All kinds of trades are valuable when it comes to development. If you can build, grow, make, design or repair stuff, then you could find a niche somewhere in the aid sector. Check the Web sites in the section 'So you want a job, now?' later in this chapter, because jobs do come up for people with trade skills. It might be a good idea to do a 'train the trainer' course along with your trade, because it means you're able to pass on the skills you have so that people in developing countries can become more self-sufficient.

Even if you don't have any further education, there's still a place for people who have a passion about ending poverty. All big aid agencies require support staff who don't necessarily have higher degrees. If you're sick of working for a call centre dealing with disgruntled customers, why not try for a job in a call centre with people who care.

Development without borders

Following the high-profile success of *Médecins Sans Frontières* (Doctors Without Borders), a range of professional associations with similar aims has emerged. The diverse list of professional associations offering their skills directly show that you don't have to work for a traditional aid organisation or charity to fight poverty.

☑ **Architects Without Borders:**
`www.awb.iohome.net`

☑ **Artists Without Borders:**
`www.art-without-borders.org`

☑ **Builders Without Borders:**
`www.builderswithoutborders.org`

☑ **CEOs Without Borders:**
`www.ceoswb.org`

☑ **Clowns (and Magicians) Without Borders:**
`www.clownswithoutborders.org`

☑ **Diplomats Without Borders:**
`www.diplomatswithoutborders.org`

☑ **Engineers Without Borders:**
`www.ewb.org.au`

☑ **Knitters Without Borders:** `www.yarnharlot.ca/blog/tsffaq.html`

☑ **Lawyers Without Borders:**
`www.lawyerswithoutborders.org`

☑ **MBAs Without Borders:**
`www.mbaswithoutborders.org`

☑ **Médecins Sans Frontières:**
`www.msf.org` (including all medical or paramedical professions)

☑ **Musicians Without Borders:**
`www.musicianswithoutborders.nl`

☑ **Reporters Sans Frontières:**
`www.rsf.org`

☑ **Teachers Without Borders:**
`www.teacherswithoutborders.org`

These associations help members to apply their specific skill set to solve development problems. These networks might also be able to provide you with great volunteer or paid employment opportunities.

Experience: Getting your hands dirty

In any job, the academic theory you learn at educational institutes will only get you so far. Jobs working in emergency relief, foreign aid and development are especially tough to get unless you have some field experience, too.

So, the job application says you need experience, but how do you get experience if you can't get the job? By experience, aid agencies mean that you've lived in a poor country and know the challenges of working in the region and delivering aid. Field experience in developing countries is an awesome way to give you that edge. It shows the employer that you know what you're talking about, you've lived it! So the million-dollar question is 'How do you get field experience in the first place?'

The best way to go is to volunteer your skills overseas through an accredited aid agency. Some are specifically set up to send volunteers overseas. For example, Australian Volunteers International or the Peace Corps in the United States match your qualifications with skills shortages in a developing country. These volunteer postings usually involve a commitment of at least a full year. Check out the section 'So you want a job, now?' next in this chapter for Web sites that will help you find where you can help others.

So you want a job, now?

Today, many aspiring aid workers get their foot in the door of an aid organisation however they can. This may involve starting out working in the support area and making the right connections after you're in.

Those who've been down this track stress the importance of having a clear idea of what you want to do. Working for an aid agency is not an extended backpacker's holiday and the reality of the work will certainly not involve romantic interludes in little villages in the middle of Africa. For more on the expectations that aid organisations require of employees, refer to the section 'Commitment Comes First' earlier in this chapter.

If you have the bug to get out there and get working, Table 4-1 lists some aid industry Web sites that publish job vacancies.

Governments also have aid programs, so it's worthwhile checking out their Web sites to see what kind of skills they need. Many governments provide an umbrella service that links to many different programs, companies and service providers involved in aid work across the world.

The United States government delivers aid from American people through www.usaid.gov.

The relevant department of the British government goes by the name of the Department for International Development. Its Web site is www.dfid.gov.uk.

The Australian government service is known as the Australian Agency for International Development (AusAid) and is online at www.ausaid.gov.au.

The Canadian International Development Agency is available at www.acdi-cida.gc.ca.

Table 4-1	Key International Professional Groups	
Site Name	*Web Address*	*Focus*
AlertNet	www.alertnet.org	A function of the Reuters organisation that links humanitarian organisations to news services, AlertNet offers a comprehensive job database.
Australian Volunteers International	www.australian volunteers.com	Australian Volunteers International is dedicated to helping Australians like you find 'your place in the world'.
Cross-Cultural Solutions	www.crosscultural solutions.org	This international organisation has branches in Canada, United Kingdom, United States and Australia.
Global Vision International	www.gvi.co.uk	Based in the United Kingdom, GVI helps connects volunteers to volunteer programs.
Peace Corps	www.peacecorps.gov	The Peace Corps places American volunteers in organisations around the world.
ReliefWeb	www.reliefweb.int	ReliefWeb focuses on emergency work but lists vacancies across the entire sector.
The United Nations	https://jobs.un.org/	The United Nations job server lists all the jobs advertised by various branches of the United Nations.
Volunteer Abroad	www.volunteer abroad.ca	An independent organisation owned by Canadian students to help them volunteer overseas.
Volunteer Service Overseas	www.vso.org.uk	VSO has been sending volunteers overseas since 1958.

Saving the World from Home

There are many things you can do to make the world a better place without dedicating your career to solving world poverty. This section outlines some of the ways you can help while maintaining a life of your own.

Using your consumer power

One thing you can do every day is be a more conscientious consumer. Sure, the next coffee you buy won't make a huge difference to poor farmers in developing countries but imagine the value of a lifetime of wise coffee choices! Even more importantly, imagine the effect of all your friends' lifetime of coffee decisions, influenced by your decision.

Currently, commodities such as coffee and chocolate pay the primary producers only a fraction of what you pay. For example, for every $3 coffee you buy, the farmer gets only 3 cents! If you support companies displaying The FAIRTRADE Label, shown in Figure 4-1, you can be sure that a fair price has been paid to the primary producer in a developing country. (For more information on Fairtrade, visit the Web site www.fairtrade.com.au.) The FAIRTRADE Label guarantees consumers that their purchase of the product will benefit the families and surrounding communities in the developing country where the product originates.

Other considerations can come into play when you're shopping, like whether garments have been produced in sweatshops — either in your country by migrants or in developing countries. Search for Web sites committed to listing 'FairWear' suppliers or shaming companies with unethical practices.

Of course, another power you wield as an individual is your vote. You don't have to wait for an election to get involved in your democracy. Write to your local elected federal representative and ask what his or her policies are on alleviating the burden of unpayable debts, making trade more just and increasing the quality and quantity of aid to the world's poorest nations.

Figure 4-1:
The FAIRTRADE Label appears on products that meet internationally agreed standards.

Guarantees a **better deal** for Third World Producers

FAIRTRADE ®

Demanding responsible behaviour

Big global problems like poverty can't be resolved unless all sectors of the community get involved. That includes consumers, governments and corporations. You can talk to the team in charge of your work's corporate social responsibility and see what they're doing to help people living in poverty across the world. There should be an ethical protocol for your company if it does business in developing countries. Other ideas that you may have already applied at home, like buying Fairtrade Certified coffee and tea, could be so much more effective if implemented across your entire organisation's tearooms.

Larger corporations have established *matched giving schemes* where they match the donations made by employees every payday to a charity selected by the employees and corporation together. Some employers give *volunteer leave* to employees who want to work for aid organisations. Ask your employer what support it can offer if you do some pro-bono work for an international aid organisation.

Schemes like these help corporations lift their public profile and achieve positive results for the triple bottom line. The *triple bottom line* measures a company's social and environmental performance along with its financial results. Various forms of social and environmental reporting are discussed in Chapter 17.

Going pro-bono (volunteering)

If you don't want to give up your day job, then you can always volunteer in your local community. It's not hard to find a need in the developing world to support — organise a group of friends, colleagues or fellow church-goers to volunteer a few hours to help. You're guaranteed to feel fantastic about your contribution. Alternatively, you can volunteer your arms and legs or professional head hours to an international aid organisation.

Most nations have a volunteer register where you can register your interest in volunteering and specify what kinds of work you'd like to do.

In the United States, you can start at www.usafreedomcorps.gov the Web site of the Freedom Corps.

The British government has Partnership Program Agreements with a range of non-government organisations that support volunteers. The Department for International Development Web site at www.dfid.gov.uk has a list of them that you can find by typing *volunteers* into their search engine.

In Australia, Volunteering Australia, at www.volunteeringaustralia.org, is a great place to start. Find out more about volunteering and the opportunities available. Volunteering is a great way to get experience that could help you get jobs in the aid and development sector later on.

The Canadian government supports a variety of private sector organisations through the Canadian International Development Agency but does not publish a list of them on its Web site.

A friend of one of the authors recently volunteered a few hours on a Sunday to pack birthing kits for African women living in poverty. She was shocked at how basic the supplies were — things such as gloves, a mat, a sterilised scalpel. It wasn't only a good deed, it was also a great learning experience and it inspired her to become knowledgeable about the subject of maternal and infant deaths. Without setting out to do so, this woman contributed towards the Millennium Development Goal to reduce the number of mothers who die in childbirth. Huzzah!

Part II
Poverty's Building Blocks

Glenn Lumsden

'On the plus side, you guys eventually inherit the earth.'

In this part . . .

What causes poverty? In this part we begin by examining the historical dynamics that have helped shape the world today, outlining how colonisation, wars and other big events have taken their toll on populations around the globe.

Today, though, little has changed for many people. Living in a danger zone, whether the region is prone to disaster or embroiled in conflict, creates a cycle of poverty that's hard for people to escape. We explain how poor people are more at risk when disaster strikes, and how it's much harder for them to recover after one. Corruption within societies is yet another factor that undermines livelihoods. Corruption feeds off vulnerability. The wheels that get greased at all levels of life kick people when they're down. But cultures of corruption can be reversed, and even you can help make a difference.

Chapter 5

Shadows of the Past

You know enough history to know that human beings make the same mistakes over and over again. Studying the past can help people avoid the repetition of those mistakes. In this chapter, we take a look at some of the historical forces that have shaped the massive poverty that confronts the world today.

The bad news is that these historical forces are fundamental — they appear in all cultures, on all continents, at most points in human history. They're part of the worst side of human nature. The good news is that during some periods in history the forces that create poverty have been pushed to the background.

This chapter outlines these historical trends. It's sobering to recognise these old-fashioned, bad behaviours whenever you open the daily newspaper.

Rigging the Scales: Institutional Inequality

Money begets money. If you have money, making more is fairly easy. The children of today's rich are likely to be tomorrow's rich, and the poor of today are likely to have children who remain poor. Very few actually bridge the divide. Sure, some lucky poor individuals do win the lottery or some rich folks may fall on hard times and lose their fortunes. For the most part, though, the rich stay rich and the poor remain poor.

Is this because the poor aren't as clever as the rich or don't work as hard? No. Social and political structures keep the rich where they are and make sure the poor don't rock the boat. Chronic and enduring poverty is structural. The development of these structures can be traced historically. In the following sections, we look at some of the processes that have weighted global systems against the poor.

The slave trade

Pretty much every civilisation in history has used slaves. Ancient Rome, Greece and Egypt did, so too did the Vikings, the Persians, the Mayans and the Aztecs (to name just a few). Africans themselves practised slavery and an organised trade carted off African slaves to Middle Eastern countries while Europeans were still huddling in caves. The Arabs and the Ottomans (Turks) conquered much of North Africa in the seventh and sixteenth centuries respectively, and began taking slaves from the continent. But the impacts of previous slave trades were nowhere near as widely felt as those of the transatlantic slave trade that began 500 years ago.

In that time, well over ten million Africans were subjected to the terrible voyage across the Atlantic. Some estimate as many as 40 million people may have been shipped from Africa, although disease, malnutrition and abuse ensured that nowhere near this many arrived in the Americas. Not alive anyway.

The actual impact of the transatlantic slave trade is still debated. Some people claim that the slave trade brought much-needed investment and capital into many African countries at the time. A more realistic interpretation of this human trade takes these facts into account:

- **Political turmoil:** Slavery didn't involve a bunch of Europeans jumping off a boat, grabbing the nearest black man and sailing off with him. Slavery was a well-organised system that relied on some Africans selling others into slavery in exchange for goods and cash. Some Africans involved in the enslaving got very rich from the trade. Slavery fuelled tribal conflicts and cemented ethnic inequity. What better way to get rid of your enemies than to ship them off to some faraway land, and get paid for it?

- **Economic turmoil:** Some Africans got richer, but others got poorer. Shipping huge numbers of people out of the continent had a destabilising effect on local economies. Suddenly, many of the most productive members of those economies were carted off across the oceans as slaves.

✔ **Social turmoil:** The slave trade involved the one-way migration of people out of inland Africa to the coast and off the continent. This had a negative, and long-reaching, impact on cultural, social and military relationships between African nations. It is not just the current generation of children in Central Africa who have grown up with armed conflict and seen their parents raped, killed or carted off by neighbouring tribes. This history dominates Central African society.

A Wilberforce to be reckoned with

After 24 years of campaigning, British politician and evangelical Christian William Wilberforce died within three days of seeing the Slave Trade Act passed into British law in 1807. It was to be another 24 years before the Slavery Abolition Act was passed, but he had completed the hard work of convincing both sides of British politics that slavery was inhumane and that humanitarian considerations should be placed above commercial ones. The British Navy was employed to police the Act on the high seas. Wilberforce also founded the Society for the Prevention of Cruelty to Animals and was responsible for a number of missionary associations being established in Britain and across its colonies.

Colonialism

Colonialism is a particular form of imperialism. Instead of simply ruling a conquered country as an extension of the empire, the colony operates somewhat independently with its own administration. The term colonialism is applied when the region being governed is not connected geographically to the rest of the empire and has some political autonomy.

Colonisation was predestined to go global when European countries first became mad keen on securing sea trade routes to reach Asia's booty. At the time, the Ottoman Empire controlled the land routes. From opening the sea routes to India, countries like Portugal, Britain, Spain, France and the Netherlands went on to criss-cross the globe, colonising countries everywhere. (For more details, see 'A mad scramble for the world' later in this section.)

Colonialism isn't unique to Europeans, though. The Vikings, the Ottomans, the Greeks, the Romans, and just about every people in history half decent with a sword, have tried their hand at colonising someone, somewhere, sometime.

The impact of colonial rule depends on many factors. One is the function of the colony in the overall scheme of the empire. Settler colonies, such as the Roman towns of London or Cologne, the British colonies in Virginia, Australia and New Zealand, or the Chinese settlements in South East Asia, have gone on to play significant roles in world affairs. Similarly, trading posts such as Alexandria, Mumbai, New York, Hong Kong and Singapore were established as imperial outposts but evolved as an integral part of their own region.

Today, colonialism has a bad rap because European colonial powers left behind all sorts of problems when they retreated to Europe at the end of World War II. Many of the nations once ruled by colonial powers face the worst poverty today.

A mad scramble for the world

Until the nineteenth century dawned, colonialism was a relatively laid-back affair. You can symbolise eighteenth-century colonialism using the odd flag stuck in the sand, and a bunch of forts and settlements strewn around. By comparison, the 1800s was a gold rush for European colonisers. From the 1870s to the outbreak of World War I, the mad scramble by European powers for Africa added one-fifth of the globe to the overseas colonial possessions of Europe. Figure 5-1 shows a map of Africa prior to 1900.

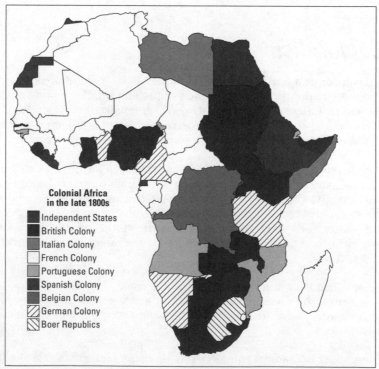

Colonial Africa in the late 1800s
- Independent States
- British Colony
- Italian Colony
- French Colony
- Portuguese Colony
- Spanish Colony
- Belgian Colony
- German Colony
- Boer Republics

Figure 5-1:
The African map before the 1900s.

Divvying up the Dark Continent

In 1884 a conference in Berlin, known in German as the Kongokonferenz, divided up the African continent between the European powers. The discovery of the upper reaches of the Congo River a decade earlier had largely completed the mapping of Africa, and a race for control of vital resources led to many skirmishes between European powers. The Portuguese called for some organisation because they were losing valuable ground in the free-for-all, and the emerging power, Germany, gladly hosted the conference.

In addition to drawing lines on the map, dividing up great swathes of the continent between the European royal families and the Ottoman Empire, the Kongokonferenz also dictated rules of engagement, establishing free trade zones, a system of notifying signatories to the agreement when new protectorates were established and an end to the formally approved slave trade. It also introduced the requirement that any nation claiming ownership of a colony actually had to govern it (as opposed to letting it fall into ruin and creating problems for neighbouring colonists).

Ethiopia (known as Abyssinia) and a small nation called Liberia, set aside for returned slaves from the United States, were the only independent zones on an entirely colonised continent. A number of colonies settled by Dutch immigrants (Boers) were also politically independent nations governed by European settlers. Britain and France took the lion's share of the landmass, and Germany gained significant possessions.

The land-grab reached Asia and Latin America, too. Of all the countries in South East Asia, Thailand is the only one never to have been colonised by a European power. Ethiopia can make the same claim in Africa, despite a short period of accommodation with Italian interests in the area.

Colonialism's legacy

You can thank the Europeans for many things: The Scots for TV, electricity and the steam engine; the Germans for cars; the Swiss for watches, banking and chocolates; and the French for revolutions, republics and fine food. But Europeans have a lot to answer for, as well. Colonisation is at the top of that list.

For a few hundred years, Europeans publicly promoted colonisation as a benevolent act designed to 'civilise' and 'save' people they considered as poor, primitive heathens in Africa, Asia and Latin America. The sidebar 'Divvying up the Dark Continent' details this approach. Colonisation was also branded as a way to bring technology, religion and culture to those who lacked them. In hindsight, colonialism was wholly selfish. The section 'Machines, slaves and world domination' later in this chapter details the reality of trade under colonialism.

Here are some of the other notable effects of nineteenth-century colonialism:

- **Up to the eyeballs in debt:** Colonisers reaped the rewards by controlling the resources in their colonies; some charged their colonial subjects for the privilege as well. When Haiti finally won independence, France demanded 150 million francs for the favour. That's the equivalent of around $20 billion today. It took more than a century for this tiny Caribbean country to pay back the debt.

- **At each other's throats:** Legend has it that Queen Victoria had the borders between Kenya and Tanganyika redrawn to present her cousin Kaiser Wilhelm with Mount Kilimanjaro for his birthday. The story's only a myth, but it perfectly sums up the colonial lack of regard for people, language and culture. Enemies were lumped together, communities and families split down the middle. Colonial map drawers fuelled the ongoing fires of African violence for decades, if not centuries.

- **Looking after number one:** The colonial practice employed favouritism, bribery and corruption. After all, the population had to be convinced to rule in the interests of the colonial power, rather than of their own people. And if that sounds a bit like the regimes of Zaire's Mobutu or Indonesia's Suharto, it's more than just coincidence!

- **Here now, gone tomorrow:** Another well-taught lesson was going after short-term profit instead of investing in the nation's future. Colonial powers were great at shipping a country's wealth overseas, but rather lousy at helping to build up that country's people and infrastructure. English speakers tend to think that British colonialism was relatively benign, but when Tanganyika was granted independence from Britain in 1961 the country was left with just 12 doctors. Some legacy!

- **Trading down:** Trade is supposed to be something that helps you enrich your life. It's supposed to be a way of expanding and moving on to bigger and better things. But the global trade imbalance of today has its roots in colonial times when resources flowed freely out of the colonies and into Europe, and nothing of much value flowed back.

Machines, slaves and world domination

Factories and machines are pretty new in the big scheme of things. If you go back just 300 years or so, most people were still labouring in the fields. That may seem like a long time to you, but when you consider that humans have been around for one quarter of a million years, and labouring in fields for 10,000 years, 300 years may as well be yesterday.

The growing Europe of the nineteenth and twentieth centuries was pretty much self-sufficient — with the exception of rubber and some textile materials, Europeans didn't need their colonies. And they certainly didn't rely on the colonies to buy their products. Total exports from Europe to the colonies were less than 1 per cent of the total value of production. Colonies were not a significant market for colonial powers.

At the peak of the slave trade, Britain was earning less than 5 per cent of its annual income from the slave trade and slave-operated plantations: Slavery wasn't a significant building block in the economies of many of today's rich countries. However, colonisation formed the backbone of a deliberate and ongoing campaign to concentrate power in the financial and industrial complexes of the world's leading economies.

It's also important to understand the rise in importance of manufacturing during this period. In 1750 Britain manufactured 1.9 per cent of the world's total output of manufactured goods, and India 24.5 per cent — primarily fabric, especially cotton. The cotton fields of Virginia, run using slave and convict labour and the mills of Manchester run by the new machines were not only competitive with Indian manufacturing, they were protected by cotton laws made in Britain to control the growing and manufacturing of cotton in India. By 1880 the statistics were reversed: Britain manufactured 22.9 per cent of the world's manufactured goods, and India 2.8 per cent. The British, as India's coloniser, simply destroyed India's place in the global economy and took it for themselves.

The West is still reaping the benefits of being the first out of the gate. Not only do Europe and North America enjoy a trading system that's weighted in their favour, but many poor countries have to pay back huge amounts to the West as interest on debts amassed under unfair conditions. The major civilisations of India and China are only now beginning to recover from the ravages of European colonial rule.

Twentieth-Century Blues

Wars throughout the twentieth century concentrated economic power in a small number of hands, which has resulted in enormous global poverty. One message you can take away from a century of global conflict is that backing corrupt regimes to fight for global economic interests is a humanitarian disaster. Poverty in many parts of the world has been exacerbated, or created, by the interference of dominant powers. One way to reverse this is to strengthen independent governments capable of ruling in the interests of their people.

The Great War (aka World War I)

History is rife with war and conflict. People have been raiding, pillaging and killing each other since the dawn of time. But nothing prepared Europe for its Great War — World War I, which took place between 1914 and 1918.

You might imagine doing something significant to change the world. But you probably don't want a legacy like Gavrilo Princip's. In the summer of 1914 the 19-year-old Bosnian Serb knocked off the Archduke Franz Ferdinand Karl Belschwitz Ludwig Josef von Habsburg-Lothringen, imperial prince of Austria and Prince Royal of Hungary. That's when the proverbial excrement hit the fan. According to many school texts this was the catalyst that started World War I. The traditional story is outlined in the sidebar 'Archduke Ferdy — what a guy!'

Another interpretation points out that the world's navies were shifting to oil-powered ships, and that Germany had no oil of its own and had nearly completed an oil pipeline to Baghdad. The week before the Archduke was shot, the Germans celebrated the connection of Berlin to Serbia as the first link in this vital military supply line.

World War I brought an end to the European expansion throughout the Southern Hemisphere. Colonial conquest was pretty much put to rest with the onset of war in Europe. As a result, the United States model of expansion through economic dependency began to supplant European colonialism.

What did not change was the use of modern technology to dominate the countries of the world in the interests of a small number of rich countries.

Gluttons for punishment: World War II

World War I had halted European colonial expansion but World War II caused it to actually collapse. Part of the reason was that the power had shifted to Japan, Germany, Russia and the United States. Japan's armies dominated the Asian landmass and the United States had interests across the Pacific. Japan and the relatively young USSR had already carved up north-eastern Asia, and the USSR was expanding across Europe.

Archduke Ferdy — what a guy!

A war responsible for the death of nine million soldiers and ten million civilians over four years was sparked by the murder of Archduke Franz Ferdinand, heir to the Austro-Hungarian throne. Austria–Hungary retaliated with attacks against the homeland of the assassin, Serbia, and the dominoes began to fall. The Russian Empire geared up to help the Serbs.

The German Empire, allied with the Austro-Hungarians, declared war on Russia for interfering in Serbia. Russia was allied with France and the British Empire, so Germany decided it might as well fight them too. The Canadians came to help their Commonwealth buddies across the pond. Then Turkey, who had been secretly in bed with the Germans, joined the fray.

The British, backed by their imperial possession, India, took on the Turks in the Middle East. The South Africans, Australians and New Zealanders signed up to fight alongside the Brits. The Italians were feeling left out, and so with promises of first dibs on a carved-up Austro-Hungarian Empire, they too saddled up and joined in. The Americans were late to the party, but when they got on board in 1917 they helped deliver the final blows that led to an allied victory. By the end of 1918 World War I — the Great War, the War to End all Wars — was over.

Germany rebuilt itself from the ashes of World War I, determined to create an indestructible Reich. German, Russian and American interests in the Middle East and Africa displaced the comfortable agreements made between France, England and the other European powers.

Another factor was the shift in economic power from governments to corporations. This went hand in hand with a political shift from the divisions in hereditary class structures to economic ones. The economic disaster of the Great Depression sped up this social upheaval. In Europe, especially Germany, economic hardship encouraged the development of a militaristic government.

Germany's expansionist plans alarmed the other European powers. France and Britain (along with its Commonwealth allies) declared war on Germany. Japan also seized huge areas of South East Asia and the Pacific, even after the United States entered the war following the Japanese attack on Pearl Harbor in Hawaii.

Eventually all of Europe became consumed by the war that was to last another six years. Fighting spread across North Africa, Asia and the Pacific, as Japan and the United States came to blows. This time round it really was a 'world' war.

Europe suffered greatly. Violence, disease, starvation and genocide left more than 60 million dead across the world. The economies of Europe were again in tatters. The United States now had a military presence around the globe with major centres of power in Japan, the Philippines and Germany. The map of the Middle East was redrawn and the modern state of Israel created.

Colonial armies found themselves fighting wars in the interests of their oppressors. The Indian troops in Burma, for example, died to keep Burma British. Across Asia, local people found themselves fighting on one side or the other (or both) as the Japanese and European forces fought to control their countries. Not only were their resources and homes destroyed by the war, but there were often reprisals when the fortunes of the war shifted and local people found themselves in enemy territory . . . without ever leaving home.

Decolonisation: Europe retreats

By the time Hitler and Mussolini were overthrown in Europe, it was clear that the colonial powers were not the invincible titans they had once appeared to be. Colonies across Africa, the Middle East and Asia were getting restless. Tired of foreign rule, independence movements found new supporters.

The response by most European powers to the spread of nationalism was violent repression:

- In 1947, fierce fighting between the French and independence fighters in Madagascar lasted a year and left up to 90,000 dead.
- India was partitioned in 1947 and Pakistan was created by British bureaucrats drawing a line on the map.
- Nearly a decade of brutal conflict in Algeria ended in 1962, marking an end to French rule in North Africa.

Hey dude, where did my country go?

Palestine had been governed by Rome, Greece, the Ottomans and the British before World War II. In 1947 United Nations resolution 181 cut the British Mandate of Palestine in half to give the displaced European and Russian Jews their own nation, giving away lands that Palestinians had considered their own.

This is one of many actions that has made Israel/Palestine the powder keg of the Middle East. The history of the Middle East is dealt with in detail in *The Middle East for Dummies* (Wiley Publishing Inc., 2003).

The more Europeans tried to keep a grip on their crumbling empires, the more they fuelled resistance. Ten years of fierce fighting by the Vietnamese forced the French to eventually grant them independence in 1954. Most of the rest of Asia followed suit over the following decades. By 1980 virtually the entire continent of Africa was free from colonial rule (with the exception of a couple of Spanish enclaves, Ceuta and Melilla, on the coast of Morocco). Some of the stragglers were the trading post colonies of Hong Kong, which was returned to China in 1997, and Macau, which the Portuguese handed back to China in 1999.

Many countries were handed back debt-ridden and broken. They suffered because control was handed over to corrupt rulers and many nations were bankrupt and war-torn. Some colonial powers even had the gall to demand payment in return for independence.

Colonialism's last-ditch effort

In a final attempt to retain control over their commercial interests in their dwindling empires, European colonial powers tried every trick in the book to prevent strong independent governments from ruling in the interests of the local citizens. They tried the old 'divide-and-conquer' routine, or they resorted to outright violence and repression. When all else failed, they murdered leaders who presented significant threats.

Here are some of the many assassinations and murders of anti-colonial leaders that European powers were involved in:

- Ruben Um Nyobé, an anti-colonial Cameroonian leader, was killed by the French army in 1958. Nyobé was replaced by Félix-Roland Mournié, who was in turn assassinated in Geneva by the French secret service two years later.

- Patrice Lumumba, also an anti-colonial nationalist, was the first democratically elected Prime Minister of the Republic of the Congo (now the Democratic Republic of Congo). He was assassinated in 1961 with Belgian officers present.

- Eduardo Mondlane, a Mozambican political leader, was assassinated in 1969 by a secret military group that had originally been set up within NATO (the North Atlantic Treaty Organisation).

- Outel Bono, opponent of the Chadian president, was assassinated with suspected French involvement (in 1973).

Not all of Africa's murdered leaders were killed directly (or indirectly) by European powers. But colonialism's legacy certainly played a part. Between 1960 and 2003, 107 African leaders were overthrown. Two-thirds of these were murdered, jailed or exiled. Not one was voted out of office, and only three retired peacefully during these four decades.

Facing Mutually Assured Destruction

The second half of the twentieth century was a period of unparalleled growth. The world was remarkably stable, the rich grew comfortably richer and the poor just kept on starving to death. Most of you reading this will have lived through times of more or less continuous economic growth and faced very little hardship. At the same time, the world has faced a new danger — annihilation due to man-made weapons. This was the period when Russian and United States military advisers seriously considered using nuclear weapons, risking the complete destruction of human life on planet earth. MAD (mutually assured destruction) is possibly the most appropriate acronym ever coined.

The cold war

A *cold war* is one where there's no fighting. It's a conflict where there's tension and political rivalry, but without the violence that normally accompanies it. Except the twentieth-century cold war wasn't cold. Not for everyone, anyway.

When the dust settled over the ruins of Europe after World War II, two great powers were left standing: A communist Soviet Union and a liberal capitalist United States. A political standoff between the two countries had been brewing for years. But after 1945, and without any other opponents, the Soviet–US rivalry began to grow. By the late 1940s the cold war had well and truly begun.

Presented to the world as a clash of ideologies, each of which vehemently opposed the other on economics, religion and politics, the cold war can also be seen as being about economic self-interest — carving up the world between them. The United States supported a weak South Vietnamese government, supposedly to oppose the spread of the communist scourge. After more than a decade of military involvement, nearly 60,000 dead American soldiers and the equivalent of US$662 billion dollars down the drain, the capitalist superpower retreated.

The Soviet Union had its own Vietnam too. In 1979 Soviet troops invaded Afghanistan to support a communist regime on the brink of losing control to rebels. But the Soviet Union was forced to pull out after nearly a decade during which the US government poured more than $10 billion into arming Islamic fundamentalists. More than 15,000 Soviet troops died, but well over a million Afghans perished in the violence.

One lifetime of radical change

Co-author Ash's great-grandmother lived to see the world change more dramatically than it ever had before. When she was born the streets of her home city of Cardiff were filled with horse-drawn carriages. By the time she died, not a horse was in sight. She lived to see Neil Armstrong walk on the moon, and she flew across the oceans in a passenger plane. She also saw Europe tear itself apart in two world wars. And she died while the world watched Reagan and Gorbachev play their great game of chess that was the cold war. In the twentieth century a lot was going on, and a lot of it was violent.

Many of the countries in which the hotter moments of the cold war were played out suffer today from the aftermath. For example, the billions of dollars of CIA arms sent to Afghan rebels in their fight against Soviet troops helped create the terrorist networks that were later held responsible for the September 11 attacks in 2001.

The fall of the Wall

All things come to an end. After more than four decades of macho posturing across Europe, the cold war finally ended. The symbol of the cold war, the Berlin Wall, was brought crashing down by angry crowds in late 1989 just 25 years after it had been built to separate East from West. The Soviet Union had been imploding from within due to economic pressures and by the early 1990s Mikhail Gorbachev led a new Russia towards democracy. Western Europe, the United States and liberal capitalism had won the ideological battle for the hearts and minds of Eastern Europe.

The first year of university is notorious for drunken and rowdy teenagers. For many, it's their first opportunity to party and drink without the watchful eyes of their parents to keep them in check. That's what it was like for many countries that had been caught up in the cold war — when it ended, they went nuts.

Without Soviet or American aid, many countries tumbled back into petty conflicts and power struggles. The end of the cold war saw the fragmentation of many states and the revival of past ethnic tensions. Liberia, Somalia, Sierra Leone and Rwanda all degenerated into bloody violence or genocide.

Yugoslavia falls ... apart

Communism had been the glue that held Yugoslavia together. But Yugoslavia was made up of many different ethnic groups, all of whom had different ideas for what should happen next. As communism retreated, independence movements sprouted up across the country. The republics of Slovenia and Croatia declared independence from Yugoslavia in 1991.

Slovenia managed the transition without too much drama, but Serbs had other plans for Croatia. A bloody war broke out that lasted until 1995. The war ended with a victory for the Croats, but thousands had died and hundreds of thousands had been forced from their homes.

The people of Macedonia were next to jump ship in September 1991. But they got away scot-free.

The following year, Bosnia and Herzegovina decided it was time to control their own destiny and declared independence. But once again, ethnic Serbs were not content to stand aside and see their republic disintegrate. More than three years of fighting saw more than 100,000 dead and close to two million displaced.

About the same time, Serbia and Montenegro decided to hold hands and form a new Federal Republic of Yugoslavia. But the largely Muslim region of Kosovo didn't want to be included in this new republic. From 1995 tensions continued to build between ethnic Albanians and Serbs, before erupting in violence and ethnic cleansing in 1998. Up to 15,000 people were killed and a million forced from their homes. Until recently, Kosovo has been a province of Serbia but under United Nations control. On 17 February 2008, Kosovo declared itself independent. At the time of writing, Serbia refuses to recognise the declaration, and Kosovo remains administered by the United Nations.

Even Serbia and Montenegro couldn't stay together long. In 2006 Montenegro decided it too would go it alone and split from Serbia. So what had been one country just 15 years earlier has fractured into six or seven separate and autonomous states. But the costs were high!

Have weapons, can sell

When you're gearing up for a global war you need a lot of weapons. And the Soviet Union knew this all too well. It came up with a winner in the AK-47 assault rifle — a compact, cheap-to-manufacture, durable and accurate machine gun that can fire up to 600 rounds a minute and hit something 300 metres away. The AK-47, or Kalashnikov, is the world's most popular gun.

More than 100 million of the weapons have been produced during its 50-year lifetime. And the Soviets were generous, allowing the gun to be manufactured without any licensing fees.

During the cold war the Red Army of the Soviet Union at times topped more than five million troops. But when Communism collapsed, hundreds of thousands of their weapons were no longer needed. These weapons flooded every corner of the globe. Even children were able to use the notorious Kalashnikov. In Sierra Leone four out of five combatants were between 7 and 14 years old. Many were armed with the AK-47. The gun continues to fuel conflicts in Sudan, Colombia and Uganda.

Have money, don't need weapons

Ah, economic conquest. From Ancient Rome to Portugal's grab in the Americas, the colonisation of remote regions involved taking resources at gunpoint. Just because colonialism didn't last, though, doesn't mean it's not worth another try. But this time the game has changed. New tactics are the order of the day.

Do you know what is one of the world's most widely recognised phrases? No, it's not 'thank you' or 'bye'. It's *Coca-Cola*. And better known than the cross of Jesus or the crescent of Mohammed is the symbol of commerce, McDonald's *Golden Arches*. Colonisation is no longer about physical control. Economic and cultural dominance are the order of the day.

The first President of Tanzania, Julius Nyerere, once said, 'It seems that Independence of the former colonies has suited the interests of the industrial world for bigger profits at less cost. Independence made it cheaper for them to exploit us. We became neo-colonies.'

For more information about economic factors that affect countries, see Chapters 16, 17 and 19. To find out more about geographical factors and understand which nations are worse off and where most poor people live now, refer to Chapter 3.

The power of oil

The reshaping of global politics since the fall of the Berlin Wall has had a lot to do with oil. The 'axis of evil' countries all began trading oil in euros, not dollars. Venezuela and its president, Hugo Chavez, created a South American trade zone opposed to US interests. China became the powerhouse of Asia. These are the economic realities that underpin the current geopolitical manoeuvring.

Dominance of the world economy depends more than anything else on a source of energy, and the cheapest energy source in the history of the world is oil. Saudi Arabia, Iraq and Iran have the largest known reserves; with the United States, Russia, the Ukraine and Venezuela in the second tier. The oil industry and Russian, Chinese and US manufacturers all see the war in the Middle East as the key factor determining who will control the flow of oil in the coming century.

Since the Russians lost control of Afghanistan, Georgia and Chechnya, they can no longer build a pipeline to China and sell Russian and Ukrainian oil to the Chinese. Instead, interests in the United States plan to pipe oil from Iraq and Iran to the Mediterranean for the benefit of Western industry.

Chapter 6

Conflict and Disaster

. . . .

. . . .

*W*hen disaster strikes — for example, during wars or natural disasters — the poor suffer most. It's then that the global effort of the world's well-off to ameliorate their suffering has the most dramatic benefits. This is called emergency aid and is compared with other sorts of aid in Chapter 4.

In this chapter we look in detail at the nature and impact of conflict and extreme weather that might descend suddenly on a community and turn it upside down. It reviews the actions that aid agencies and foreign governments take to help those most affected by natural disasters and war.

The violence that descends on communities when human conflict and natural disasters strike:

✔ Destroys accommodation, water and food supplies

✔ Creates opportunities for disease, crime and other secondary problems

✔ Interrupts income, education and development (sometimes permanently)

✔ Displaces people, making them vulnerable and reducing opportunities

There are significant differences between man-made and natural violence and the impacts they have on communities. One of the most significant differences is that it is much more difficult for outsiders to intervene in conflict situations. Because of these key differences, the two types of disaster are dealt with separately in this chapter.

At Each Other's Throats

War, what is it good for? Almost every country on earth has been to war at some time in its history. Whether fuelled by racial, ethnic or religious animosities, ideological fervour, or a simple lust for land and wealth, war and conflict cause economic and social destruction, and widespread death and misery.

Hundreds of years ago, when two armies lined up on a field and charged each other, virtually all casualties were combatants. During World War I, civilians accounted for less than 5 per cent of all deaths. But with today's modern warfare, the tables have turned. 'Smart bombs' and 'targeted strikes', combined with asymmetrical warfare, mean that more than 75 per cent of those killed or wounded in wars today are civilians.

Poverty, conflict and war are cosy bedfellows. In the last 50 years Africa has been more affected by conflict than any other continent, with more than 20 major civil wars in countries like Rwanda, Somalia, Angola, Sudan, Liberia and Burundi.

When is a war not a war?

Not all conflicts are wars. According to the Heidelberg Institute for International Conflict Research's 'Conflict Barometer' (gee, those Heidelberg boys come up with some wacky titles) there are five types of conflict ranging in intensity from non-violent to violent:

- **Latent conflict:** A pretty heated argument between two parties. Language your mother probably wouldn't approve of, but non-violent.

- **Manifest conflict:** Threats to settle this argument outside in the car park! Still non-violent.

- **Crisis:** The situation is tense. One side uses sporadic violence — another brick through your window. The Basque separatists in Spain, for example, have engaged in this kind of violence for decades, occasionally ramping it up a notch into a severe crisis.

- **Severe crisis:** Violence is repeatedly used in an organised way. Think militia groups in Sudan and the Democratic Republic of Congo using violence to grab political power.

- **War:** Continuous, organised and systematic attempts to wipe your opponent off the face of the earth. The destruction is massive and lasts and lasts. Think Iraq, the Vietnam War, World War II.

FLOODLIGHT

Civilised nations fight with fish knives

The only 'war' between two liberal, western, democratic states, ever, was the 'Cod Wars' of the 1950s and 1970s between the United Kingdom and Iceland. During these decades of tension, two ships were rammed and some shells were fired. Although this should reassure you that democratically elected governments only fight in a civilised manner over essential resources, it does put the news that the world's fisheries are declining due to over-fishing in a dramatic context.

That's the extent of open hostility between such states. The widespread destruction of Europe, twice in the last century, was due to the failure of democracy and the emergence of military dictatorships in their place. Similarly, the Falklands War between Britain and Argentina doesn't meet the criteria because the military dictator General Galtieri ruled Argentina at the time. Argentines who feel that Britain's Prime Minister Thatcher was the aggressor find this selection criterion slightly prejudiced.

The number of conflicts around the world is increasing in all five violence categories. Seventy-four conflicts were recorded in 1945 and 278 in 2006. Here are a couple of things to keep in mind about the situation right now:

- Most conflicts are low-intensity and non-violent. In 2006 there were 160 non-violent conflicts versus 118 violent ones.

- It seems that as the number of high-intensity conflicts falls the number of medium-intensity conflicts rises. This is because ceasefires don't bring an end to conflict. Just because people stop killing each other, doesn't mean everyone suddenly starts playing Happy Families.

- In 2006 most high-intensity, violent conflicts were in these regions:

  - Sub-Saharan Africa (13 severe crises and 2 wars)

  - Middle East (6 severe crises and 3 wars)

  - Asia (8 severe crises and 1 war)

  - Russia was the only 'rich' nation in 2006 to record a violent conflict (Chechnya secession). The Basque conflict makes Spain a borderline case.

  - The Americas and Europe were relatively peaceful, not even recording one conflict per state on average. (Peaceful to live in, if not nations of peace — some of these states were deeply involved in conflict in other parts of the world.)

Civil strife: Fighting at home

You might think the number of conflicts seems a bit high. You certainly don't hear about them all, not even on war report headquarters, CNN! Maybe that's because your idea of conflict is one country (or state) going at another one. However, that type of high-intensity, inter-state conflict is relatively infrequent. Since 1945, the number of international wars at any one time has never risen above ten. Most violent conflicts happen inside countries — they're known as *intra-state* — like civil wars, coups d'état or militia skirmishes.

The trend in the numbers of violent civil situations is also bad news: The number of intra-state, high-intensity conflicts has risen from five in 1945 to 40 conflicts in 2004 and 30 conflicts in 2006.

Mary Kaldor is a professor at the London School of Economics. She believes that the break-up of the Soviet Union spawned a new style of war:

✔ United States hegemony and the increased importance of NATO and the United Nations means more international interference, leading to slow-boiling, lower-scale conflicts like Pakistan vs India, Yugoslavia, East Timor and Sudan.

✔ The proliferation of arms from the dismantled Soviet war machine has made huge quantities of weapons (mostly small arms, AK-47s) available to the world at knock-down prices.

✔ Independence struggles in former Soviet states have also added to the total number of conflicts.

✔ Former cold war struggles taking place by proxy (such as in Mozambique, Laos, Vietnam, Cambodia, Angola and Latin America) now take on a different character.

✔ It's also possible that the collapse of the Soviet Union means that some governments might be more prepared to fight because there's no longer the threat of Mutually Assured Destruction by a massive nuclear war.

You get the idea . . .

The evidence is that governments work hard to avoid conflict with their neighbours if possible. Non-violent conflicts between different states outnumbered intra-state ones, 35 to 24.

Fifteen minutes of media interest

Western media aren't really interested in civil unrest in Africa and Asia (unless, of course, Western interests are involved). Everyone has an opinion about the troops in Iraq, and hardly a day has gone by since the March 2003 invasion when the conflict in Iraq hasn't garnered media attention. By contrast, the most heinous intra-state conflicts get buried on page 13!

The most telling case of Western ignorance of high-level violence in the developing world is the Rwandan genocide of 1994. It slipped by largely unnoticed, until the violence was largely over and millions of refugees flooded border camps unable to cater for them. Then President of the United States, Bill Clinton, wrote in his autobiography that while he blamed no-one more than himself for this oversight, 'there was no particular call for the United States [to do anything about the slaughter] . . . not much clamour in Congress or the editorial pages.'

What are you fighting for?

Like it or not, violence is a fundamental part of human history. Clausewitz said that 'war is a continuation of politics by other means', and Chairman Mao argued that 'political power grows out of the barrel of a gun'. Empires have been built on violent conquest throughout history. The archaeological record indicates it was the case in prehistoric times as well.

One hundred and sixty years ago, Henry David Thoreau wrote an essay called 'Civil Disobedience', which outlined reasons why citizens should not support violence by governments. A large number of Americans had fled religious persecution and violence in Europe and agreed with his non-violent stance. His views were taken up in the last century by Gandhi and Martin Luther King.

Today, a growing peace movement seeks alternate ways for civilisation to resolve disputes and move forward. Getting involved in this movement is as simple as typing 'Henry David Thoreau' into a search engine like Google and starting to read. Before you know it, you'll be communicating with local members of the peace movement.

Despite such enlightened thinking, wars continue. A billion years of genetic evolution means that people are hardwired to fight. It seems so simple. One side's right and the other mugs are wrong. At a certain stage, words don't cut it anymore, and nothing else matters.

The Devil's Garden

The Sahrawi people in the north-west of Western Sahara were entrapped by Morocco in the 1980s after it surrounded their lands with a huge wall and an army of roughly the same size as the entire Sahrawi population. Western Sahara appealed to the United Nations and a peace resolution was passed. Despite this, since the 1991 ceasefire the Sahrawi have held their collective breaths for a fair referendum.

Meanwhile, between 90,000 and 160,000 people (the number is in contention) have been living in poverty in refugee camps in neighbouring Algeria. The area is known as The Devil's Garden because of regular sand storms and 50 degree Celsius (122 degree Fahrenheit) days.

There's little or no vegetation; and firewood has to be gathered by car tens of kilometres away. Only a few of the camps have access to water, and the drinking sources are neither clean nor sufficient for the entire refugee population. Basic life can't be sustained in The Devil's Garden, and the camps are completely dependent on foreign aid. Food, drinking water and materials for tents and clothing are brought in by international aid agencies.

Here are some examples of real world conflicts waged in the name of a specific cause.

A quick raid on the neighbours

In 1990 Iraq invaded and annexed Kuwait over disputed port access and oil drilling practices. It took only a little over 1,000 hours for a coalition led by the United States to force Iraq to withdraw. You have to wonder if the speed of this liberation was somehow linked to the developed world's need for a certain black runny resource.

Wars for the clear wet stuff

If you were playing Monopoly in Bolivia you wouldn't want to land on 'Water Works'. The privatisation of Bolivia's water by an international consortium called *Aguas de Tunari* on the instructions of the World Bank led to huge increases in water prices, riots and the eventual cancellation of the contract by the Bolivian government.

Onward religious soldiers, marching as to war

Since most religions pray for peace, you may be forgiven for thinking a 'holy war' is a pretty big contradiction in terms. In fact, you know war is hell, so why do religions still bless battleships and advocate 'just wars' when the end result keeps its flock poor?

Teaching terror at poverty school

In Pakistan there are around 45,000 madrassahs. Between 10 and 15 per cent of these religious schools are associated with extremist religious or political groups promoting a radical political agenda. The graduates of these schools have become recruits for transnational Islamic militants.

As Pakistan becomes poorer, the government is less able to provide basic services to its people. So the madrassahs are filling a void in basic areas of social services such as education, food and clean water.

Unfortunately, some schools have an extremist political message to deliver as well. People who might not normally be sympathetic to radical voices may, in times of distress and extreme poverty, be open to their message.

Without state supervision, it's up to the individual schools to decide what to teach. This leaves the radical schools free to teach a distorted view of Islam that promotes hatred and martyrdom. Many of the radical religious schools also include weapons and physical training.

Both the Christian crusaders of the fourteenth century (who set out to save the Levant from Islam) and the militant Islamic fundamentalists funded by the CIA to defeat Russia in Afghanistan in the 1990s fought their battles in the name of God. Even the United States Commander-in-Chief, George W Bush, claimed he was 'driven with a mission from God' to invade Iraq. The medieval crusades and the mujahideens' battle against the USSR were both funded by the rich and powerful to ensure access to critical resources.

Ethnic hatred

Ethnic or racial differences (read hatred) have sparked many inter- and intra-state conflicts. Some of these involve ancient grievances that may have once been economic, but now defy simple logic. For example, there are different groups within the small Russian state of Chechnya who are only united by their common hatred of the Russians. Some of their differences can be traced back to the 1940s when the Russian army forced the entire population to relocate to Siberia. This resulted in the death of approximately a quarter of the Chechen population. It's hard to imagine a better reason for a relationship of hate and revenge.

Freedom fighters

Is one man's terrorist another man's freedom fighter? Maybe it just depends whose newspaper you're reading. 'Terrorists' and their guerrilla warfare tactics aren't new. French revolutionaries storming the Bastille in Paris on 14 July 1789 were considered terrorists by those in power, but are now regarded as heroes of modern democracy. The British labelled

Menachem Begin a terrorist in the 1940s. As Prime Minister of Israel in the 1970s, Begin applied the same label to Yasser Arafat.

During World War II the United States considered Ho Chi Minh a freedom fighter, and he drew on the American Declaration of Independence when declaring Vietnam's freedom from the colonial French. Ten years later he was labelled a terrorist, and the United States backed a puppet government in the South. Today, there are differing opinions about whether Hezbollah is a 'terrorist organisation'. The United States, United Kingdom, Canada, Australia, Israel and Netherlands consider it to be one, but Japan and the majority of European nations don't. People laying down their lives in the fight for freedom is clearly honourable if it doesn't threaten your commercial interests, but it's immoral when it does.

Children caught up in war

In some countries, children are forced to run through minefields to clear the way for soldiers, or work in diamond and gold mines to fund rebel armies, or act as sex and domestic slaves for adult soldiers.

In many cases these societies have long histories of violent culture. Or there may be very few adults as a result of recent conflict. Sometimes the children are not actually forced to fight, but willingly volunteer. If a child's family has been murdered, abused or mutilated, the feelings of revenge, guilt and fear make a military life seem attractive.

In Uganda, the National Resistance Army (NRA) took control in 1986. It had 3,000 children in its ranks, including 500 girls. The defeated army of President Obote had orphaned most of these children as it rampaged through the country, killing 200,000 people in four years. These children looked at the resistance army as their surrogate parents.

In Guatemala, joining the rebel army was an attractive alternative to being forcibly recruited into the state army. The guerrillas did not beat the children nor force them to kill, but fed them and respected their indigenous cultural values. The children were allowed to leave the rebels at any time.

The business of war

When we said earlier that war is good for absolutely nothing, it wasn't strictly true. Some people make billions of dollars of profits from selling the tools of war.

The five permanent members of the United Nations Security Council — the United States, the United Kingdom, France, Russia and China — are collectively responsible for 88 per cent of reported conventional arms exports. Agreements to limit the production and export of arms are supposed to make the world a safer place, but seem a bit pointless when the guys at the top are so embroiled in their manufacture.

United Nations officials say that in 2005 small arms were responsible for the death of half a million people around the world. Currently, about 25 per cent of the US$4 billion annual trade is either illicit or not recorded as required by law. There's currently one gun for every ten people on the planet.

'The time for us to succeed in stopping arms transfers is now,' said Liberian President Ellen Johnson-Sirleaf. 'I plead with the governments of the world, arms manufacturers, brokers, and traders not to deny Liberia and every other country this great chance to consolidate peace for our children and ourselves.'

Often the people who created the arms in the first place are embarrassed by the fruits of their labour. The inventor of dynamite, Alfred Nobel, founded the international peace prize that bears his name so that the royalties from his destructive invention could do some good. A group of scientists working on the creation of the atom bomb in the top secret Manhattan Project signed a letter to President Truman, urging him not to drop the bomb on Japan. Mikhail Kalashnikov invented the world's most popular gun but regrets it. 'I would have preferred to have invented a lawnmower,' he said.

Former United States President Jimmy Carter said it beautifully in his 1976 presidential campaign: 'We can't have it both ways. We can't be both the world's leading champion of peace and the world's leading supplier of arms.' The role of the United States in Nicaragua under his leadership knocks Carter's halo a little askew.

Kiss and Make Up

When nations want to settle disputes without going to war, they reach into a toolkit of techniques almost as old as war itself. A range of modern variations on this theme exists but the basic models are simply formal expressions of instinctive behaviour to avoid battle, whenever the stakes are not high enough to endanger life and limb.

It's worth remembering that many of the techniques discussed in the following sections depend on the implicit threat of violence. They're part of a tradition that incorporates war and differ markedly from new approaches to non-violent conflict resolution. In the day-to-day world of global politics, the tried and true traditions get employed more often.

Diplomacy: Talking heads

Remember those fantastic photo opportunities, er, we mean peace talks, between the United States, Israel and Palestine that always seem to climax with a three-way handshake on the lawns outside the White House? They're a great example of using diplomacy (and media) to try to resolve violent conflict.

Nearly every country has a group of diplomats representing its interests in nearly every other country in the world. Behind the cameras there are lots of different types of diplomacy taking place around the world all the time. These can include:

- ✔ **Multilateral diplomacy:** Many countries talk about and come up with international agreements, resolutions or treaties — often through the United Nations or other multi-state bodies like the Organisation for Economic Cooperation and Development (OECD). Good examples of multilateral diplomacy to affect the poor in a positive way include the 1999 Ottawa Treaty, which banned the use and production of anti-personnel mines.

- ✔ **Shuttle diplomacy:** A third party brokers peace talks or helps in the negotiations in some way, as in the United States, Israel and Palestine example.

- ✔ **Cowboy diplomacy:** A description of brash risk-taking, intimidating, military deployment or a combination of such tactics. Overly provocative language like George W Bush's 'You're either with us or you're with the terrorists' is a prime example.

Sanctions: You are so grounded!

Sanctions can range from stopping an entire country's imports or exports to the freezing of assets of a select few individuals. Sanctions can be legislated by the United Nations Security Council, coalitions of countries or single nations to try to bring an end to conflict. Recent examples include the UN's resolution to impose sanctions on rebel armies in Sierra Leone and Angola that traffic diamonds and recruit child soldiers for their wars. Another example is the arms embargo, travel ban and asset freeze in place on North Korea as a result of their resumption of nuclear testing in 2006.

The United Nations: Bigger than any government

Perhaps the most visible role of the UN is its peacekeeping operations. The peacekeepers are thrown into the fray to protect the innocent and keep warring factions apart. But it doesn't usually go that smoothly. Peacekeepers have been accused of rape, torture and spreading diseases like HIV everywhere from Haiti to Sierra Leone, Sudan, Liberia and Somalia. Poor peacekeeping behaviour hasn't done the UN's reputation any favours.

Despite knowing how difficult establishing a lasting peace can be, until recently no part of the UN was directly responsible for helping countries make the transition. In December 2005 the UN Peace Building Commission was established to help fill this gap by focusing on reconstruction, institution-building and the promotion of sustainable development in post-conflict countries.

Peacekeeping, for example, is a type of operation aimed at keeping combatants apart using an independent military deployment. *Peace building*, on the other hand, refers to a full range of measures required to help warring parties move from a state of conflict to a state of peace; a peacekeeping operation can be a central part of a peace-building effort.

It's All Completely Natural

This planet is always dishing up horrible, jaw-dropping disasters. The impact of these events on rich and poor alike serves as a terrifying reminder that although you may be on the top of the food chain, you're still small fry when it comes to the climate.

The good news is that the number of lives lost due to natural disasters has declined over the past 20 years — 800,000 people died from natural disasters in the 1990s, compared with two million in the 1970s. But the bad news is that the number of people affected by disasters has actually risen. Now, 75 per cent of the world's population lives in areas that have been affected at least once in 20 years by an earthquake, a tropical cyclone, a flood or a drought. That's a lot of people living in the danger zone!

Unnatural side effects

One of the key reasons for the greater frequency of disasters is the effect of human activity on the environment. On one hand the environment is less stable and more extreme because of global warming. On the other, it is more fragile because the damage inflicted on it makes it less resilient.

For example, deforested land is more likely to flood severely because heavy rains on newly bare land moves much faster than on forested areas. With too few trees to hold the soil together, landslides and mudslides occur with greater ferocity. Not only are lives and property at stake, but fertile topsoil is washed away, leaving farmers with poor soil from which to grow new crops.

Pollution can have far-reaching effects too. An Australian study showed a link between aerosol pollution in Europe and changing cloud formations leading to increased drought in central Africa. Once emission controls were introduced in Europe, there was a corresponding increase in rainfall in the drought-stricken African region. So put down that hairspray, sister!

Co-author Ash remembers a few days in the spring of 1986. He was living in Switzerland when the meltdown of the soon-to-be infamous Soviet nuclear power plant, Chernobyl, caused his family to spend a few days huddled under ground in their Swiss-built, regulation bomb shelter. A radioactive cloud from the disaster paid a visit to more than 30 countries across Europe. Still, he says, 'I did get a few days off school'.

Global warming is also changing weather patterns around the world. As the earth's average surface temperature rises, owing to the increase of carbon dioxide in the atmosphere created by human activity, the earth's climate is changing. The icecaps are melting, rainfall patterns are changing and storms are becoming more frequent.

The yellow yin and yang of life (and death)

The Yellow River is the second-longest river in China. It's also the most sediment-laden in the world, making the surrounding land rich and fertile. Because it's the most prosperous region in Chinese history, the Yellow River has earned such honorifics as 'Birthplace of Chinese Civilisation', 'the Cradle of Civilisation' and 'Mother of China'. However, it's prone to constant flooding, with 11 major floods in the past century, each causing tremendous loss of life and property. The Yellow River is also known as 'China's sorrow'.

Risk and reward: Where disasters strike

No-one in Luxembourg has died as a result of a savage hurricane, volcano, earthquake or indeed any other type of natural disaster. And chances are, no-one will. Some places on earth are just more dangerous than others — Luxie, if you're listening, you're as safe as Fort Knox.

Ninety per cent of the world's earthquakes occur in what's known as the *Pacific Ring of Fire* — a 40,000 km horseshoe shape that stretches from New Zealand to South East Asia, Japan and around the west coasts of North, Central and South America. It includes a nearly continuous series of oceanic trenches, island arcs, volcanic mountain ranges and shifting tectonic plates. This disaster zone hosts 30 volcanoes, including Krakatoa — an island that was turned into dust by a massive volcanic explosion in 1883, dimming sunlight around the world — and has recorded thousands of deadly earthquakes.

It's not just poor people who live with risk because of a convenient location. Scientists predict that it's only a matter of time until an earthquake shakes California into the Pacific. Until then, Californians are willing to take their chances and enjoy the sunshine. Despite the threat of coastal erosion and rising sea levels, coastal land around the world is still sought after to the extent that land prices continue to rise.

It's Elemental, My Dear Reader

The four elements of classical times — earth, water, fire and air — all have the power to nurture and to destroy life. That's one of the reasons they occupy such an important place in the scheme of things. This section details the variety of disasters that each element causes when it gets up and gets going.

Earth: Unexpected movements

Right now gigantic plates of the earth's crust are pushing and grinding against each other — usually at those trendy nightclubs called *fault lines*. Eventually, one plate buckles under the pressure of its partner, creating a violent displacement of the earth's crust, radiating seismic waves, triggering the earth to literally move, tsunamis, volcanoes, death and destruction. Doooooom!

Buried in mud

In February 2006, an entire village was buried by a major landslide in the central Philippines following heavy rains and a small earthquake. Approximately 1,000 people died in the disaster. Five hundred houses and an elementary school were completely buried under a mud layer up to 10 metres thick. All the school's 246 children and the seven teachers were buried in a few seconds.

Survivor Dario Libatan said: 'It sounded like the mountain exploded, and the whole thing crumbled.' Another spoke of boulders bigger than a house sweeping into the village amid the torrent of mud and earth. While the rains and earthquake triggered the mudslide, it's thought that a combination of mining and deforestation made the region unstable. It's still uncertain to what extent human activity made the disaster worse.

Earthquakes

Earthquakes are sudden large-scale disasters acting on a geological level. There are much more local events as well, known as *mass wastings*. These include avalanches, landslides, rockfalls and mudflows. Mass wastings are usually caused by human activities such as mining, drilling and logging or can be natural side effects from earthquakes, volcanic eruptions, heavy rainfall or flash floods. They come in two speeds:

- ✔ **Fast:** The earth simply moves rapidly downwards destroying everything in its path.
- ✔ **Slow:** The earth gradually moves or creeps over months, years or decades, damaging buildings, moving roads and causing land values (if not the land itself) to plummet.

Volcanoes

Volcanoes are openings in the earth's crust that allow hot molten rock, ash and gases to escape from deep below the surface during an eruption. Volcanoes are a favourite topic for Discovery Channel and nature documentaries. You've probably seen those dramatic rivers of fiery lava burning their way through, well, everything. Very destructive, sure, but oh so fascinating to watch.

Just as threatening are the massive plumes of volcanic ash that can blanket populated areas. People suffer irritation to their eyes, intestinal infections and breathing difficulties. The ash also covers crops, destroying sources of food for decades. Of course, in the very long term — thousands of years — that same ash and lava is one of the best sources of nutrients for the very same crops. You have to look at things from a geological timescale to see a volcano's good side.

Water: The fluid of life . . . and death

People complain when it rains. People complain when it doesn't. Two of humanities greatest challenges, drought and flood, are usually brought on by variations in rainfall.

Floods

Floods are sudden and disastrous, requiring emergency response. They're not always caused by a deluge from the heavens, though. Sometimes events at sea — tsunamis, hurricanes or rising sea levels — can flood coastal areas. The result is the same; land is swiftly submerged under lots of water, destroying property and sweeping people away, sometimes never to be seen again.

A flood is also a disaster that continues to evolve. Once the initial deluge is over, all that water lying around is bad news. Untreated sewage can get into water supplies and cause gastric diseases like diarrhoea and cholera. Wherever there's stagnant or still water, there are mosquitoes. The risk of catching some kind of mosquito-borne disease like malaria or dengue fever increases dramatically after a flood.

But wait, there's more. If crops survive the initial onslaught of rain and flood, but the water hangs around, it's likely that the crops will rot under the water, leading to famine.

So, with floods you get a wall of water sweeping through your home and mud covering your possessions; you suffer from sewage in the water supply and disease-carrying mosquitoes. Then there are the rotting crops and imminent starvation. Finally, there is this really scary thought: One of the commonest causes of death during floods is snakebite.

You know that global warming will probably raise sea levels and flood billions of people living on the coast. As well as the people whose homes will actually go under water, everyone in low-lying areas will find themselves exposed to larger and more frequent floods. The Bangladeshi coastline is one of the most densely populated places on earth. It's estimated that 10–15 million people will lose their homes as a result of global warming. That's the entire population of Michigan or more than half the population of Australia.

Preparing for a rainy day

If you wonder why developing countries suffer more from natural disasters than developed ones, compare the flood-control defences along the rivers and shorelines of the United Kingdom and the United States with those of Bangladesh.

London completed construction of a £1.3 billion flood control structure called the Thames Barrier in 1984. The United States government has committed about US$5.7 billion to strengthen the New Orleans levees after Hurricane Katrina flooded the city in 2005.

By comparison, the Bangladeshi government spends a few million a year on flood control out of its total annual budget of US$6.4 billion. Bangladesh contains around 150 million people living in the Ganges river delta less than five metres above sea level. They face the twin threats of floods from large snow- or rainfalls in the Himalayas or its foothills and rising sea levels in the Bay of Bengal.

Drought

A lack of water can kill in so many ways — it's definitely a disaster. Chapter 9 deals in detail with the interaction between food, water and other issues surrounding poverty.

- Subsistence farmers in developing nations rely on what they can grow to feed their families, so are at the mercy of the rain.
- Farmers on the borderline of poverty eke out a modest income growing cash crops, so are completely broke if those crops fail.
- A lack of clean drinking (and washing) water causes endemic health problems for many societies.

You could probably survive a drought on the planet's driest inhabited continent — Australia — because it's a G20 country, which means it's rich. Australian governments and communities can afford to pipe, desalinate, treat, recycle and find other engineering solutions for water shortages in the major cities. Australians have the luxury of flushing more water down their toilets in one sitting than many people in developing countries have to drink, clean, cook and wash with for the whole day.

Tsunami

A *tsunami* is a wave created when a body of water (such as an ocean) is rapidly displaced on a massive scale by an earthquake. The sheer weight of water is enough to pulverise objects in its path, often reducing buildings to their foundations and scouring exposed ground to the bedrock.

Over 200,000 people died on 26 December 2004, after an earthquake registering 9 on the Richter scale in the Indian Ocean triggered a huge tsunami. One and a half million people lost their homes and livelihoods in what has become the most notorious natural disaster in living memory.

Fire: Man's red flower

The animals of Rudyard Kipling's *Jungle Book* believe the supremacy of humans over animals is a direct result of humanity's mastery of fire; man's red flower, as they call it. It may be the basis of our civilisation but, when it gets out of control, fire is also one of the greatest threats to it.

Firestorms, wildfires and bushfires are all names for an uncontrollable fire that burns everything in its path and is not easily contained. They are a menace to rural communities, destroying forest plantations, livestock and crops and occasionally killing people. The effect of fire on farmers — rich and poor — is catastrophic. Prevention requires good fire-fighting preparedness and communication infrastructure as well as long-term approaches to forestry management, appropriate land use and availability of water to manage the fires when they break out.

Air: The importance of atmosphere

You can't see it or taste it, but boy oh boy can you feel it when it starts moving around. Air wraps you completely, every moment of your life, and you can't live without it for more than a few minutes. When it gets going, though, it can wreak havoc.

Hurricanes, tropical cyclones and typhoons

These are different names for the same phenomenon: A cyclonic storm system that forms over the oceans and creates enormous damage when it reaches land. This phenomenon goes by the name

- ✔ Hurricane in the Americas
- ✔ Tropical cyclone in the South Pacific
- ✔ Typhoon in Asia

It doesn't really matter what they're called. When they're picking up your house like a toy and throwing it across the road, you can call them anything you like, just treat them with considerable respect. They're deadly and increasingly common, causing long-term destruction to property and livelihoods every year.

Meet the Mongolian dzud

In Mongolia they have regular blizzards and then they have *dzuds*. A dzud is a summer drought followed by early and heavy snowstorms with temperatures falling way below average. The dzud freezes to death already malnourished animals. It differs from other natural disasters in that it's slow to become evident and takes months to form, as opposed to 'rapid onset' disasters that usually happen with little warning. A dzud may not have an easily identifiable beginning and its impact may not be immediately visible on the human population. Therefore, a dzud is also described as a *creeping disaster*. However, it can be triggered or aggravated by rapid onset hazards like snowstorms and blizzards, and Mongolian herders watch helplessly the suffering and death of their animals from starvation and freezing.

Global warming

Climate change, climate chaos and *global warming* are names for the impact on the atmosphere of two centuries of industrialisation. A relatively simple cause — the release of 70 million tonnes of carbon dioxide into the atmosphere every day — is having very unpredictable results. Chapter 15 offers a more detailed account of the causes and impact of global warming. Suffice to say, now that the two-thirds of the world's fresh water locked up in ice is melting, earth's inhabitants are all in deep water: Seven metres, in fact, if all the ice in Greenland melts, almost ten times that if it has the same effect on the Antarctic.

Heat waves

Heat waves are becoming more frequent as a result of global warming. Defined as lengthy periods of unusually high temperatures (for that geographical area), heat waves cause droughts, crop failure, firestorms and bushfires. They can also cause electric power outages when too many people use their air-conditioners.

Heat waves are responsible for a surprisingly large numbers of deaths from heat stroke, especially in urban centres that effectively create and retain heat. In the European summer of 2003, a heat wave caused the deaths of 22,080 people in England and Wales, France, Italy and Portugal. Most victims were old and poor, a reminder of how vulnerable the poor are, even if they're living in rich countries.

Living In a Danger Zone

The sheer scale of natural disasters means that no society, regardless of its standard of living, can completely avoid suffering from their impact. There is no doubt, though, that a liberal sprinkling of cash helps avoid the worst effects of wild weather. The World Bank's Global Risk Analysis puts it this way: 'Poorer countries are more likely to have difficulty absorbing repeated disaster-related losses and costs associated with disaster relief, recovery, rehabilitation and reconstruction.' Being poor sucks. When fire or flood destroys your home, you have nowhere to go and have to start again, with nothing.

Not only are the world's poor more likely to die in the disaster itself and lose more money afterwards, but the long-term consequences will almost certainly be more severe for them as well. Development in poor countries is slow and uncertain, so rebuilding infrastructure and the economy after a disaster can take decades.

The following sections outline the key components required to avoid the harshest impacts of natural disasters. They all require well-developed, and expensive, infrastructure.

BEEP BEEP BEEP Tsunami!

The *Tsunami Alarm System* service illustrates how wealthy people have a better chance of surviving a disaster than poor people. According to the Web site www.tsunami-alarm-system.com you can 'Forever take the fear out of visiting the coast anywhere in the world, for you and your family, by turning your mobile phone into a reliable Tsunami Alarm System'. The service, which you can subscribe to with your trusty credit card via its Web site, costs US$39 annually and will SMS you if a tsunami is heading your way. Not so handy for the Acehnese fisherman whose entire family struggles to survive on US$3 a day.

The Pacific Tsunami Early Warning System cost tens of millions of dollars to install and was paid for by the United States government. The United Nations built a similar system covering the Indian Ocean.

Pakistan earthquake 2005

An aid worker in Pakistan at the time of the earthquake in 2005 provided an eyewitness report of how the effects of the earthquake rippled through the community, weeks before the onset of winter.

It took just 35 seconds for the quake to heavily damage or destroy 90 per cent of the buildings in Bagh. The newly constructed hospital came crashing down, killing doctors, nurses and patients. The police station also crumbled, reducing the force from 300 to just 50. At the boys' college in Bagh, recovery efforts seemed futile as men with picks took turns to hack through layers of concrete floors that had fallen on about 200 students.

The usual four-hour journey from Pakistan's capital Islamabad to the Bagh district, home to some 500,000 people, in Pakistan-controlled Kashmir on 14–15 October 2005 extended to nine hours. This was due to the congestion of aid vehicles travelling to and from the district, primarily belonging to grassroots Pakistani groups banding together to help their fellow nationals.

The primary need was shelter. Winter normally comes in earnest (with sub-zero temperatures) to the heights of Kashmir by the end of October, but this year it had arrived early. There was food, water and medical help there but not adequate shelter for tens of thousands of people.

Many left the area immediately, seeking refuge in the big cities such as Islamabad. Others remained in refugee camps and suffered through a freezing winter that raised the death toll even higher.

Bracing for the blow

Tsunami early warning systems currently service nations bordering the Pacific, the Atlantic and — since the 2004 disaster — the Indian Ocean. However, an early warning isn't as useful to a poor region as it is to Europe or the United States. The time it takes from detection of an earthquake to a tsunami hitting surrounding coastlines is measured in minutes. The message 'A tsunami is coming, run for your lives!' is much more effective when most people own TVs, radios and cars. Many countries also suffer from cultural problems such as mistrust of the authorities and ethnic divisions that prevent equitable sharing of available resources. While these may be more acute in the developing world, Hurricane Katrina is a powerful reminder that such inequities exist in developed societies as well.

Heavy equipment to the rescue

Poverty exacerbates the toll of a disaster at every level — rescue and recovery become longer and grimmer. After an earthquake, for example, a shortage of heavy moving gear means fewer people can be rescued from the rubble of fallen buildings. If buildings are of poor quality in the first place, more of them are likely to collapse. Poor roads, ill-equipped ports, corrupt officials and geographic isolation can all hamper rescuers and international aid efforts.

The problems are exacerbated by overcrowding in the world's megacities where poor people living in slums and shantytowns suffer the immediate and long-term effects of natural disasters most acutely.

Dealing with the knock-on effects

Obviously the immediate impact of a disaster is the most dramatic and sudden set of problems in an affected community. It can be the tip of the iceberg, however. Here are some of the ways that the disaster can be compounded in the days and weeks after it occurs.

- ✔ **Health emergencies — adding illness to injury.** Waterborne diseases and the destruction of stores of safe water and food can kill at least as many people as the initial catastrophe, doubling the death toll. In poor countries, not only do the victims find it difficult to deal with the disaster, but they do not have the money to buy themselves appropriate medicines.

- ✔ **Looting and opportunistic crimes.** Amid the chaos of death and disaster, human vultures see an opportunity to swoop on the survivors at their most vulnerable. Children separated from their parents are cajoled or coerced by child traffickers and sold, sometimes across the border, into slavery or prostitution. Other opportunistic crimes include theft and rape.

- ✔ **Economic woes flow in the wake of disasters.** The economic impact of a natural disaster or violent conflict is just as straightforward as the physical one — devastating. All business and consumer activity can collapse immediately. Following the 2002 and 2005 bombings in Bali, for instance, tourism to the rest of Indonesia slumped along with tourism to Bali. On the flip side, it sure helped tourism (and tuk-tuk drivers) in Thailand.

Finding appropriate responses

The world, especially the world's poor, needs super humans able to fly at will to the most remote locations on the planet. Those heroes need to quickly acclimatise, survey the situation and start helping to save lives with the available resources.

There's no doubt that these heroes do a lot of good; however, they're not perfect and sometimes they come under fire for being too much like, how would you say . . . Rambo Reliefers? Being in tune with a community's culture can be as important as helping provide basic survival needs. For example, in Kashmiri Muslim society, males and females are segregated and so require separate rooms. However, after the 2005 Kashmir earthquake many emergency shelters constructed by agencies consisted of one room only. They remained unoccupied as men and women could not share a single room.

Trusting in local know-how

The tendency for many commentators and armchair aid workers in the face of disaster is to concoct grand schemes where the rich foreigners come to the rescue of the poor locals. In fact, there are often great local strategies already in place.

- ✔ **Local knowledge:** Through stories and general familiarity with their environment, local people can often be far more astute about what's going on — and how to avoid problems — than the urbanised folk flown in to help them. The sea gypsies of the Thai islands, for example, were prepared for the 2004 tsunami by centuries of folklore. The moment the sea began to retreat, they all ran for high ground, unlike everyone else.

- ✔ **Social structures:** In comparison to individualistic Western societies, many societies in developing countries place a far greater emphasis on the family. This means there's somewhere to turn when the going gets tough. Oh, and more children to support you in your old age as well.

- ✔ **Planning:** Keep a spare goat around, maybe as something that can be pawned off in hard times. You could say, 'Cashmere is as good as mere cash in the bank.' On the other hand you might think corn is better kept to feed people.

These traditional survival mechanisms often break down as a result of poverty, or the integration of these people into the global economy. Indebtedness (resulting in child labour, sex work, indentured servitude), and migration (fuelling urbanisation) both lead to the collapse of traditional cultures that had an inbuilt resilience.

Chapter 7

The Cult of Bribery, Corruption and Theft

*H*ow much money do you think is paid in bribes every year around the world? Go on, have a guess. Try over US$1 trillion! An aircraft flying at the speed of sound, reeling out a roll of ten-dollar notes behind it, would take over one year to get rid of the US$1 trillion that the World Bank says is paid in bribes each year. By any measure, that's a lot of moolah. And that doesn't even count the cash that goes on embezzlement and theft!

Up to five cents in every dollar spent by the governments of poor countries goes missing to corruption. This makes corruption one of the greatest obstacles to economic and social development faced by these countries.

This chapter explores what corruption is and what it means for the world's poor, and examines the widely held view that corruption is just the cost of doing business in developing countries. Perhaps most importantly, it discusses the mistaken assumption that poverty leads to corruption, or vice versa. Obviously corruption impacts on the poor, and some of the worst corruption occurs in poor countries, but the relationship just ain't that simple.

Who's Greasing the Wheels?

When you think of corruption, you may imagine the dictator of an impoverished developing country siphoning off funds into a Swiss bank account. And not without reason; ruthless dictators becoming wealthy at the expense of the people they rule have been a recurring nightmare for many struggling nations.

This is just the popular comic book image of corruption, though. Corrupt practice starts with plain and simple bribery, extortion, embezzlement or graft. It runs to dubious back-scratching with cronyism, nepotism, clientelism and patronage. To complete the corruption repertoire you can include fraud, influence-peddling and kickbacks as well.

When one person happily engages in bribery or extortion, you can describe this person as corrupt. But how do you describe an entire government that's on the take? The word you're looking for is 'kleptocracy'. *Klepto*maniacs are people who can't help themselves from stealing. And *cracy* — as in demo*cracy* — is about governing. So *kleptocracy* describes rulers who are so corrupt that no-one bothers to pretend they're innocent anymore. Check Table 7-1 for a list of unbelievable kleptocrats.

Corruption's repertoire

Perhaps you're too honourable to know the meaning of all the bad words that describe the nefarious range of corrupt practices? Here's a rundown on the shadier types of corrupt activities that people and governments get involved in:

✔ **Bribery and graft:** Offering something — usually cash — to gain an advantage.

✔ **Extortion:** Scaring or bullying someone into forking over something that you want from them.

✔ **Embezzlement:** Nicking something that's been entrusted to your care.

✔ **Cronyism, clientelism and patronage:** Showing favouritism to your friends.

✔ **Nepotism:** Giving jobs or promotions to your undeserving relatives.

✔ **Fraud:** Intentionally fooling someone into doing something that hurts him or her.

✔ **Influence peddling:** Cosying up to someone in authority to get your way.

✔ **Kickbacks:** Under-the-table fees paid for your help.

Table 7-1	Top 10 Most Corrupt Leaders of the Twentieth Century			
Ranking	*Leader*	*Nation*	*Years*	*Amount (US Dollars)*
1.	Suharto	Indonesia	1967–1998	$15 to $35 billion
2.	Ferdinand Marcos	Philippines	1972–1986	$5 to $10 billion
3.	Mobutu Sese Seko	Zaire	1965–1997	$5 billion
4.	Sani Abacha	Nigeria	1993–1998	$2 to $5 billion
5.	Slobodan Milosevic	Yugoslavia	1989–2000	$1 billion
6.	Jean-Claude Duvalier	Haiti	1971–1986	$300 to $800 million
7.	Alberto Fujimori	Peru	1990–2000	$600 million
8.	Pavlo Lazarenko	Ukraine	1996–1997	$114 to $200 million
9.	Arnoldo Aleman	Nicaragua	1997–2002	$100 million
10.	Joseph Estrada	Philippines	1998–2001	$78 to $80 million

Source: Transparency International

Rulers on the take

No country, rich or poor, is immune from corruption. Recent examples of red-faced, scandal-tainted politicians are all too easy to come by. In the United States, for example, the fall of the energy giant Enron in 2001 showed the world just how cosy the George W Bush administration was to big business. And in 2005, Australia discovered that its squeaky-clean Australian Wheat Board (AWB) had been secretly paying kickbacks to Saddam Hussein in exchange for permission to peddle grain to his hungry masses.

Examples of corrupt practices can be found in any country, but it's an unfortunate fact that the most flagrant acts of wholesale corruption have occurred in the developing world.

By the time Zaire's President Mobutu was overthrown in 1997, he had stolen almost half of the $12 billion in aid his country had received from the International Monetary Fund. But even the scale of Mobutu's graft can't top the list of the twentieth century's most corrupt leaders (see Table 7-1). Above him on the ladder are two others: The Philippines' Marcos and Indonesia's Suharto. Together, Suharto, Marcos and Mobutu ripped off between $25 and $50 billion. That's getting close to the entire global aid budget for a full year.

When the shoe fits the illegitimately rich

The wife of the number two most corrupt political leader of the twentieth century (refer to the Table 7-1) and the former First Lady of the Philippines, Imelda Marcos, was so outstandingly corrupt that she has entered the language. Her excessive collection of footwear has inspired the term 'Imeldific' and shoe shops around the world bear her name.

On a real estate shopping trip to New York in the 1980s, Imelda considered buying the Empire State Building but eventually rejected it as being 'too ostentatious'. Mrs Marcos settled instead on the Crown Building, the Herald Centre and a couple of other prime slices of Manhattan.

After the Marcos family was deposed, Imelda was found to have hoarded the world's largest collection of jewellery, as well as a collection of 3,000 pairs of shoes — she admitted to owning only 1,060 pairs. She also had a bullet-proof bra among her clothing collections — probably not a bad idea considering how intensely she was hated!

Many allegations of corruption against Imelda and her family were dropped during the 1998–2001 rule of her friend and ally Joseph Estrada — himself responsible for embezzling an estimated $78 to $80 million. Estrada appears at number ten on the list of most corrupt leaders.

The Marcos family wealth was alleged to have peaked at round $35 billion in a country where eight out of ten people live on less than $2 a day. Eager to bolster her ill-gotten fortune, Mrs Marcos has recently released the *Imelda Collection*. Coming to a store near you, her collection covers low-cost glitzy jewellery, bags, accessories and sports shoes.

As long as the mega-corrupt enjoy the protection of a government in some corner of the world, there is an implicit acceptance of the practice. Because you are only a bystander, the most effective action you can take is to pressure your governments not to provide refuge for corrupt leaders escaping the wrath of their own people.

Nations on the make

Measuring *actual* levels of corruption is very difficult. Any attempt to get an idea of the number of bribes changing hands is more likely to measure the openness and social acceptability of corruption than the real extent of it. Some people brag more than they do it; others do it but keep quiet.

To get around this, some studies have instead looked at the number of prosecutions and convictions in cases involving corruption. But this has its own problems. These studies probably indicate the quality of the legal system or the political pressure to combat corruption, rather than the level of corruption itself.

In an attempt to resolve this problem, Transparency International examines the *perception* of corruption. The Corruption Perceptions Index is based on asking people in government and business to evaluate the level of corruption that they are exposed to. The index is produced annually and ranks countries by the amount of corruption that people report is present among public officials and politicians. You can find the latest version on the Web site at www.transparency.org by selecting Surveys and Indices and looking under Policy and Research. Table 7-2 summarises the best and worst results of the 2007 survey.

Table 7-2	Corruption Perceptions Index (2007)
Squeaky Clean	*Dodgy Dealers*
1. Denmark	1. Somalia
2. Finland	2. Myanmar (Burma)
3. New Zealand	3. Iraq
4. Singapore	4. Haiti
5. Sweden	5. Uzbekistan
6. Iceland	6. Tonga
7. Netherlands	7. Sudan
8. Switzerland	8. Chad
9. Canada	9. Afghanistan
10. Norway	10. Laos

Source: Transparency International

The 2007 study looked at 179 countries. Finland, Denmark and New Zealand were jointly perceived to be the least corrupt nations. The world's diplomatic lepers Myanmar (aka Burma) and Somalia were perceived to be worst; followed closely by the United States' current basket-case, Iraq, and the chaotic and chronically corrupt Haiti.

Obviously, corruption is a widespread problem. The worst offenders in the Corruption Perceptions Index sprawl across five continents — about the only group not on the list are a handful of the world's richest countries.

Bearing the brunt of corruption are the poorest countries in the world. In 2002, the former Nigerian President Olusegun Obasanjo claimed that as much as $150 billion each year — 25 per cent of Africa's combined national income — is lost to corruption. Obasanjo's figure is a lot more than the World Bank's estimate, but theirs didn't count theft and embezzlement.

Regardless of the absolute figures, the reality is that the most extreme cases of political corruption take place in countries with some of the world's poorest people. Places like Zimbabwe or the Philippines undeniably show a relationship between corruption and poverty.

Leadership and the Politics of Poverty

A quick scan of the Dodgy Dealers column in Table 7-2 shows that none of the most corrupt nations are rich democracies. Why is this so?

Poor countries have fewer resources to control corruption. So you may think they are the most corruption-prone. But some of the world's poorest countries — Burkina Faso, Ghana, Mali and Rwanda — have relatively little corruption. Conversely, China, Vietnam, Greece and Italy — countries which are clearly not poor by global standards — exhibit relatively high levels of corruption. Even more telling, the richest countries in the world do not dominate the Squeaky Clean column in that table, either.

Although the worst corruption usually occurs in the poorest countries, the relationship is not as straightforward as 'poverty leads to corruption'. The political framework of the country seems to be almost completely irrelevant — dictatorships, democratically elected socialist governments and capitalist economies appear on both sides of the table.

The following sections outline some of the factors that come into play.

Applying censorship

When information flows readily through a society, levels of corruption are lower. With freedom of information, you have the capacity to inform yourself of what's going on and have the opportunity to react when you don't like what you see — often by voting or protesting. Free speech and a free press tend to go hand in hand with manageable levels of corruption.

The prolific investigative journalists across Europe and North America actually help weed out corruption. A free press is likely to mean less corruption. So, in a roundabout way, your fight against global poverty is linked to the struggle for freedom of the press. The Committee to Protect Journalists ranks the level of press censorship by country. Table 7-3 lists the worst offenders of 2006.

Table 7-3	Nations with Worst Free-Speech Records
Rank	*Nation*
1.	North Korea
2.	Myanmar (Burma)
3.	Turkmenistan
4.	Equatorial Guinea
5.	Libya
6.	Eritrea
7.	Cuba
8.	Uzbekistan
9.	Syria
10.	Belarus

Source: Committee to Protect Journalists; 2006

Gagged!

States use censorship to maintain power and control over their citizens. They do it by controlling what goes on the TV, what appears in newspapers and even what you can search for on the Internet. Try to search the Internet in China for information on the Tiananmen Square massacre, human rights or the Falun Gong, and you'll get booted off. It's part of a systemic censoring of the Internet — a combination of 30,000 public servants monitoring searches and software known as the Golden Shield. Combined, they create what's known as Great Firewall of China. Blogs, email, Web sites and even SMS messages are also scrutinised for comments that 'threaten national security'. Consequences for disobedience are severe and people end up in prison or in re-education labour camps. This means that citizens also censor themselves.

Legal systems

Experts in the field believe that the major safeguard against corruption is an effective legal system and the safeguards it provides. Modern democracy is based on the rule of law. All the people, even (or perhaps especially) the rulers, fall under the jurisdiction of the law — just the same as you do. Leaders in a democracy have to 'answer for their actions'. They're 'accountable'.

In countries ruled by despots who put themselves above the law, this system breaks down. In a dysfunctional democracy or a country with a weak legal system, corrupt officials are rarely punished. In some of the more authoritarian states — Myanmar and North Korea, for example — accountability is literally non-existent. Corruption goes on unabated.

If you want to know how easy it is for a leader to forget the rule of law, have a look at the comments Richard Milhous Nixon made during his interview with David Frost. There's even a Broadway play named after the famous interview but you can read a summary of the transcripts at www.landmarkcases.org/nixon/nixonview.html.

A strong, independent and trustworthy police force is necessary to bring corrupt rulers to justice. Independence is the key word; many corrupt politicians have come to power through close personal relationships with the military.

Once corruption becomes endemic in the system it requires the combined efforts of non-government organisations, such as Amnesty International, an organised opposition in society and the press to identify and expose it. These organisations usually require the support of international agencies to bring pressure to bear on those officials exposed as being corrupt. Without international pressure, the efforts of the press and protestors who put their lives on the line may come to nothing.

Social conditions

Corruption doesn't simply pop up overnight. And the phrase 'one bad apple is all it takes to spoil the barrel' doesn't summarise the spread of corruption either. The rot of corruption will spread more quickly or slowly depending on the external conditions.

Crime is largely opportunistic. You see a chance — you take it. The reality of human nature is that many people who lack strong moral convictions will behave selfishly if they're given the opportunity. A large part of why corruption is so rampant in some places is simply the lack of any checks and balances to discourage it.

The countries listed as Dodgy Dealers in Table 7-2 earlier in this chapter are characterised by many of the conditions in the following list. You may recognise some of these characteristics from personal experience in your workplace or dealings with bureaucracy at various levels.

- **Sprawling bureaucracy:** Each layer of the bureaucracy offers another chance for a corrupt official to siphon off a little for themselves. Often there are only minimal safeguards in place to make sure the funds are spent correctly. And these can be easily bypassed by greasing the right palms.

- **The nod from the top:** In all organisations, the values at the top set the tone for the staff below. The faintest whiff of approval, or the sense that senior officials have their noses in the trough, and everyone in the organisation will take the opportunity to get something for themselves.

- **Bonus fever:** When public officials are poorly paid, corruption breeds. A policeman struggling to feed his family is more likely to demand bribes and kickbacks to supplement his meagre pay. If salaries are adequate in the first place, it reduces the incentive to engage in corruption.

- **Divided we fall:** Corruption can spread when a 'them' and 'us' climate exists. Countries with social cliques or an 'old boy network' are the perfect breeding ground for corrupt relationships. Religious, racial or tribal favouritism often leads to endemic corruption.

- **Little education, lotta trouble:** Low levels of literacy and education are also conducive to corruption. When people are poorly informed and unaware of the nature of the problem, open discussion is constrained. As a result, leaders are not held accountable for their actions and the poor are more easily hoodwinked.

Just because someone (or a country's people) is not literate, it doesn't mean he or she is not perfectly capable of being politically active. It's more difficult, but still possible. Take Mexico, for example. In this country comic books are as popular as newspapers and cover politics and economics as well as the usual comic book heroes. Comics allow even the illiterate to be politically engaged.

Druglords, warlords and Malalai Joya

Malalai Joya has been called the bravest woman in Afghanistan. At 27, she was the youngest person ever to be elected to the Afghan parliament. She's a staunch defender of human rights and a powerful voice for Afghan women.

She came to international prominence in 2003, at a national meeting convened to ratify the Constitution of Afghanistan. There, she spoke against the warlords and drug smugglers who were in attendance as representatives of their local regions.

She became enormously popular with the Afghan people and won her seat in the National Assembly in 2005. Since her election, Joya has continued to be an outspoken defender and promoter of the rights of Afghan women and children and publicly calls for accountability for war crimes — even those perpetrated by fellow parliamentarians.

She has won many awards for her efforts to bring justice to the people of Afghanistan, including the International Women of the Year Award in 2004. But Joya has also made very powerful enemies. On 21 May 2007, the Lower House of the Afghan parliament voted to suspend Joya for comments she made during a television interview the previous day. Joya has survived four assassination attempts, travels with armed guards and reportedly never spends two nights in the same place.

What's a little graft on the side?

Corruption is usually about money — getting more of it. But the effects of corruption aren't limited to the wallet.

- ✔ **Bureaucratic incompetence:** We won't claim this is unique to corrupt countries but, when the overriding motivation for political office is personal profit, it's unlikely you're going to see any dramatic welfare reforms or changes to labour relations — not good ones anyway!

- ✔ **Democracy for sale:** If you pay for everything else, why stop short of paying for votes? Corruption offers the unscrupulous rich marvellous opportunities in the world of politics.

- ✔ **The rule of cash:** Rules and regulations can be troublesome burdens if you don't have the cash to bypass them! Corruption throws the rule of law out the window and replaces it with the rule of cash.

✔ **The end of trust:** Trust is the foundation of any good relationship. Corrupt practices break the trust that should exist between any two individuals or groups, including a government and its people. No-one will work for the common good when the rewards are constantly stolen.

✔ **No consequence, no responsibility:** Bribery, extortion, graft — they're all stages on the slippery slope to large-scale organised crime. The sex and drug trades thrive in corrupt societies. And that isn't good for anyone — well, except for the successful criminal.

Kicking the poor when they're down

It can be easy to dismiss the profoundly destructive effects of corruption because it can be very hard to see a victim. Money changes hands, a contract is awarded. It's all done in the shadows, and often it's not obvious who actually loses from the deal. But the biggest victim is usually the poor. Corruption hits the poor hardest. Here's why:

✔ **Uneven purchasing power:** A $5 bribe costs relatively more for the poor than it does for the rich; $5 means little to someone pulling in 50 grand a year. But if your income is less than $5 a day, it really hurts! The cost of living with corruption is borne more heavily by the poor.

✔ **Draining the public purse:** There's no profit in social services. Corruption skews public spending away from health care and education. And it's the poor that feel it most. Those with money have alternatives. But the poor simply go without.

✔ **Left on the sidelines:** When you're poor you've got less to bribe with. You're out in the cold. The poor don't have the money to participate in corruption; so they don't have the influence. They don't have the bargaining power, so they can't get things done. The poor get left out.

History and the Causes of Corruption

If you've ever been to a shrink to talk over your woes, the doctor may have approached the problem in one of two ways. The doctor can look at the obstacles you're facing today as the cause of your problems — like relationship trouble or job worries. Or the doctor can put you on the couch to look further back into your past to dig up something like childhood trauma or bad parenting. In the following sections we put the world on the couch and go back, looking for the cause of the problems it faces.

Human nature or nurture?

Europeans doing business in Africa and Asia often consider corruption a part of the culture. People in countries where corruption is widespread often accept it as 'the way things get done'.

Of course, it ain't just about the cash. Sure, corruption is easier to identify when a financial transaction occurs, but a lot of corruption is also about favours and influence. It's often thought to have its roots in tribal and clan-based structures in Africa. And in Asia the Confucian family dynamic is regularly said to lead to nepotism and other practices that are considered corrupt in Western countries.

Remember how levels of corruption are not simply correlated with a country's income? Well it's the same for culture. Across countries with similar cultures, corruption can vary enormously. So, one way that you can be part of the solution instead of part of the problem is to remember that corruption is not cultural — developed countries face exactly the same challenges as the rest of the world.

Here are some examples of downright shoddy behaviour affecting nations in the West:

- ✔ The name on everyone's lips a few years ago was Enron — the tsunami of corruption scandals.

- ✔ France was rocked to the core when three former executives of their beloved oil giant, Elf, were convicted of 'misappropriating' €350 million that were used to buy political favours abroad and at home.

- ✔ United States President 'Tricky Dicky' Nixon is an example of a ruler who put himself above the law. Even after he resigned, rather than be impeached, he did not admit to wrongdoing. He told interviewer David Frost, 'Well, when the president does it that means that it is not illegal.'

- ✔ What of the near-total control that Italy's Silvio Berlusconi exerts over his country's media? Or the laws he passed in his first stint as prime minister exempting him from prosecution on existing corruption charges?

The bottom line is that corruption is not a racial or a cultural trait. It's not even unique to poor countries. It's simply the result of a combination of factors that are more common in poor countries than rich ones.

Colonial influences

Colonisation is a factor in corruption because it was a system of government that rewarded those who were of most use to the colonial power, rather than those with the best skills or the greatest integrity. By encouraging the bureaucrats to govern on behalf of a small elite rather than in the national interest, colonisation made corruption endemic.

Often the policy from Europe was as overt as *divide and conquer*. Tribal or ethnic groups were pitted against each other so that the colonisers had an easier time of ruling.

Of course, corruption may well have been present in many of these countries before the arrival of colonialism. It may even have been widespread. But colonial systems served to institutionalise corrupt practices, which have often survived independence and, in many countries, continue today.

Don't get bogged down pointing fingers at the past, though. Colonialism is just one of a many factors that contribute to corruption.

Dealing with the wild West

So you're skimming a respectable few hundred million a year off your impoverished country's budget. What do you do with it? Easy. You find a tight-lipped Swiss banker or helpful Jersey-based financial adviser to stash it overseas for you. Hey, you may even receive 10 per cent interest!

And where does all this money come from? It's not the average guy in the street that you're taking it off. It's the foreign companies, dying to set up shop and take advantage of cheap wages.

By 1997, as much as US$80 billion a year, according to Susan Rose-Ackerman in *Corruption and the Global Economy*, was paid in bribes by international companies just to get governments of developing countries to turn a blind eye to employment conditions or to offer lucrative contracts. That's only a fraction of the total amount that disappears through corruption, but it's more than all the international aid that's spent on the poor. Business is big business for corruption.

And it's not just businesses. Western governments are in for their share of the blame as well. It was Western governments that propped up Indonesia's Suharto, the Philippines' Marcos and Zaire's Mobutu, who star in Table 7-1, earlier in this chapter. They were given cash, political support and even arms. Why? Because they were prepared to take bribes and commit to infrastructure projects that served the interests of Western businesses and the governments they supported.

Often these regimes were supported on the basis that they were anticommunist. The theory was that totalitarian, tyrannical kleptocracies are better than socialism, right? Better dead than red! History shows how dangerous such oversimplified rhetoric is.

Zaire and cold war rhetoric

For most of your life a rather large patch of central Africa has been engaged in a civil war that has cost the lives of millions, and left millions more starving and impoverished. The name of this country has regularly changed — from Belgian Congo to the Republic of the Congo to Zaire to the Democratic Republic of the Congo (DRC) — but the one constant has been the suffering of its people. The UN describes the current situation in the DRC as the world's 'worst humanitarian crisis'.

When independence came and the country's first elections were held in 1960, Patrice Lumumba was elected by a popular majority. But he was overthrown and imprisoned in a coup d'état within weeks of the election. The Soviet Union put forward a UN Security Council resolution calling for his release, but it was defeated in an 8–2 vote. After a failed escape attempt, scenes of the former prime minister being beaten by soldiers were televised.

One evening, within months of having taken office, Lumumba was secretly executed along with two of his colleagues. Belgian officials were present at the execution and later exhumed his body and dissolved it in sulfuric acid. Weeks after his death, Congolese radio reported Lumumba had escaped and had been beaten to death by angry villagers.

It has since been revealed that both Belgian officials and the CIA had plotted to kill Patrice Lumumba on a number of occasions. United States President Eisenhower reportedly called for his execution personally, believing him to be a Communist (despite Lumumba's statements that he deplored Communism as much as colonialism). The CIA and Belgium supported Mobutu before and after he took power.

Zaire is far from an isolated case. This cold war mentality was repeated again and again over the decades that followed; across Central and South America, across Africa and Asia, from Guatemala to Laos, Angola to Vietnam, Cuba to Mozambique, Korea to Indonesia. When governments use general sweeping terms to divide the world into 'us' and 'them', it is important that voters analyse critically the motives for providing military support to any particular regime.

Despite the widespread recognition that rich countries must take some responsibility for the level of corruption in developing countries, almost nothing is being done. Until 2002, the UK didn't even have anticorruption laws that covered its own businesses operating abroad.

Governments make decisions that appeal to their constituents. This means that foreign policies that make those constituents wealthier are more likely to be adopted than those that fit with a particular moral framework. Three times British Prime Minister W E Gladstone (between 1868 and 1894) followed the rule that 'there is no such thing as foreign policy, only domestic policy applied abroad'. This is a two-edged sword for governments, as it gives voters the power to influence foreign policy. The success of recent campaigns in Australia concerning refugees, Guantanamo Bay and climate change demonstrate how effectively this power can be applied.

The commerce merry-go-round

If you open the financial section of any daily newspaper, you'll probably find news stories discussing the profits made by companies who have shifted their manufacturing overseas. Executives of these companies talk about 'kick-starting' the economies, or 'bringing them into the global market'. The assumption behind this talk about global trade is that it's good for everybody.

You are a potential shareholder in these companies and a consumer of their products so you can bring your morals to bear on the company. The fact is that capital itself does not have a conscience. It simply seeks to lower operating costs. You have to answer this question: If it takes a little bribery to get these deals going, is the world really worse off? The answer is simple. Well, yes. Actually it is.

The trickle-down effect

Corruption doesn't cause poverty directly. But it certainly can make poverty worse. The general rule is that the money for bribes has to come from somewhere, and that ultimately means less money for the people who need it most. Here are some of the ways this mechanism works.

- **Wasted resources:** Unnecessary projects receive funding to line someone's pockets — a road to nowhere or a school with no pupils; a tourism development makes money for an international hotel chain at the expense of the local economy. Bribery and corruption means money goes down the drain.

✔ **More red tape:** It's expensive to do business in a highly corrupt society. That cost is low to an international company, but high for the locals. They become second-class citizens in their own country.

✔ **The rigged playing field:** When you can bribe your way out of economic or legal trouble, the market stops working. Capitalism is supposed to encourage the survival of the fittest. This is no longer true when corruption kicks in: Corruption breeds inefficiency.

✔ **Scaring the investors:** Who's going to sink their money into a corrupt country? Corruption may smooth the path to short-term profits, but it's a gamble. It scares off cautious investors, and with them the cash that should fuel long-term economic growth.

✔ **Skewing government spending:** Who needs hospitals when you can have tanks? Official decisions are distorted by the scale of arms deals and large industrial projects. The graft is far more lucrative than the pocket change that a corrupt official can make out of a new school.

✔ **The poor pay more:** The last thing that the poor need is to pay more for everything. But that's exactly what corruption leads to. The cost of everything goes up for those who aren't getting the kickbacks.

✔ **Playing without protection:** Those pesky international agreements on deforestation and labour standards! How's a chap supposed to get by? Simple; bribe your way out of it. Now your underage factory workers can do 30-hour shifts producing all those World Cup soccer balls.

✔ **The resource curse:** The discovery of oil or diamonds in poor countries has generally brought nothing but sorrow and misery to the local poor. The 'easy money' undermines healthy development, and tempts unscrupulous politicians to bolster their retirement funds at the expense of national development. Check out the sidebar 'Oil for blood: Global economics at work' for an example of this paradox. Chapter 16 discusses it in more detail.

✔ **Capital flight:** Where do you hide billions of dollars of ill-gotten gains? The obvious solution for corrupt officials is offshore banking. Keep it out of reach of rivals in an account overseas that no-one can touch. Sure, your own country desperately needs schools, but you can send your 30 kids to a British boarding school for their education.

The amount of capital fleeing the countries that create it is staggering. It's estimated that 40 per cent of African savings are held outside the continent. That compares with around 6 per cent in East Asia and 3 per cent in South Asia. Every year, tens of billions of corruption-tainted dollars are sent overseas from Africa. Aid is now small relative to the international movements of private capital to and from low-income countries.

Oil for blood: Global economics at work

Equatorial Guinea recently became a massive oil exporter. The oil reserves discovered in 1996 now bring billions of dollars into the country each year. With a population of just over half a million people, average incomes are some of the highest on the continent. But 'average' doesn't tell the whole story; 65 per cent of the population lives in extreme poverty. Nearly half of children under five are malnourished and most cities lack basic public services like water and sanitation. In the decade since the discovery of oil, health spending is down, and spending on education has roughly halved.

This has taken place against a backdrop of three decades of brutal rule by the Nguema family. The current president, Teodoro Obiang Nguema Mbasogo, executed his uncle in a palace coup after the uncle had killed or exiled nearly a third of Equatoguineans. Many of his victims were tortured in a football stadium while he played Mary Hopkin's 'Those were the days' to drown out the screams.

In 1999 Obiang paid US$2.6 million cash for a home in Washington, DC, and US$3.75 million for a condo in California and bought one of his 40 or so kids his own rap label.

Oil companies ExxonMobil, Halliburton, ChevronTexaco and Marathon Oil work closely with the White House to bring Equatoguinean oil into America as cheaply as possible. A weekly direct flight between Texas and the Equatoguinean capital, Malabo, lovingly called the 'Houston Express', flies American bankers, oil executives and members of the Nguema family in and out of the country.

United States Secretary of State Condoleeza Rice welcomed President Obiang to Washington in 2006 with the words, 'you are a good friend and we welcome you'. Barely a month earlier, her own State Department released a report on Equatorial Guinea that detailed torture by security forces; judicial corruption; severe restrictions on freedom of speech; violence and discrimination against women; widespread human trafficking; and forced labour and child labour.

This is a clear example of how global economic interests can support a corrupt regime. It raises the question of how you can act to counter global events. Some effective actions in the past include boycotting particular companies, lobbying government to remove support for particular governments, and concerted action to influence shareholder meetings.

Stepping Towards Solutions

People have different opinions on how corruption affects poverty. One side blames poverty on the people themselves, believing that it's their own fault for engaging in self-destructive, corrupt practices. The other side of the debate treats corruption as nothing more than a symptom of poverty, something that will go away once the real causes of poverty are dealt with.

People on opposite sides of this fence don't usually agree on what solutions to poverty will work when it comes to corruption.

This debate affects the policies in place on giving aid to impoverished countries and on addressing corruption itself.

Band-aid solutions

When it comes to giving international aid, many people think it's just throwing good money after bad. But does aid really get through? Here are some arguments against continuing to give aid to countries with excessive levels of corruption:

- **Siphoned off:** How do you explain to the old lady giving half her pension to aid agencies that a percentage is going on Ferraris for crooked politicians? Even if it's not a large percentage of aid, it's still pretty disheartening for prospective donors.

- **Ulterior motives:** Aid can have hidden and undesirable consequences. Like when it's used to prop up a politician's own business or help out his relative.

- **Political back-scratching:** Rich countries use aid as a way to get what they want too. Japan is notorious for using aid to leverage support that keeps its whaling fleets pillaging the oceans. 'You let me plunder your waters, I'll help your children go to school.' You've gotta love politics!

- **Legitimising crooks:** When aid is channelled through a crooked government, it can be seen as giving them credibility. Aid can offer underserved legitimacy to its recipients.

Then there's the other side to the debate. Here are some of the compelling arguments to be made in favour of continued aid:

- **Do it for the children:** A tug at the heartstrings — the moral argument. Aid makes a difference and it's the morally right thing to do!

- **Reform:** Change from the inside is more effective than trying to make changes from the outside. Engage with corrupt regimes and work to reform them.

- **The cost of *not* doing it:** Where to begin? Illness, disease, terrorism, organised crime, conflict, cross-border environmental problems. Face up to globalisation. The problems of the poor become the problems of the rich in time. So be selfish. Donate today.

There's definitely some truth to the claims by the 'tough lovers' who say aid can be redirected for corrupt purposes. But removing aid doesn't force corrupt governments to reform their evil ways. They still get plenty of what they're after from business and from extracting it from their own populations.

On the other hand, when monitored and controlled by competent and experienced professionals, aid does get through. It has been shown time and time again that when it's effectively targeted, aid does improve the lives of the poorest. If you're not convinced, then skip on over to Chapter 18 to see how aid can make a difference.

Reversing the slide

Rich countries need to recognise that they and their companies are often complicit in corrupt practices in poorer countries. Governments must do more to clamp down on corruption. You play a critical role in getting them to tackle this global problem. Here are some first steps you should encourage your government to take:

- **Hit 'em where it hurts:** Start prosecuting. Prosecute the money launderers operating within rich countries. Freeze the assets of those suspected of engaging in corruption.

- **Roll out the lawyers:** Make sure there are no loopholes for businesses based in rich countries to get around anticorruption laws. Improve domestic legislation to ensure companies based in your country behave ethically overseas and sign agreements with other countries to share information. Most importantly, take action when violations occur!

- **Clean up house:** Encourage major businesses based in developed countries to smarten up. Any large company that works in developed countries should fall in line and uphold anticorruption agreements.

- **Don't just criticise:** Do something. Rich countries need to be prepared to offer advice to poor countries on how best to fight corruption. And back it up with the cash to make a difference.

- **Carrots and sticks:** It's not all about the blame game. Offer rewards and incentives to good performers. Increase aid and economic ties in exchange for successful anticorruption measures.

- **Don't turn a blind eye:** Don't do business with corrupt regimes and companies. Boycott them. Refuse to buy from them. Don't turn a blind eye.

Rich and poor countries have to be willing to discuss the issues of corruption and work out ways to limit its impact. Aid and trade are two of the ways to do this, but openness, freedom of information and education are also necessary components in the fight against corruption.

Part III
Poverty Under the Microscope

Glenn Lumsden

'Water? Now that's an idea. This one just pumps weapons and fancy cars to the guy that runs this place.'

In this part . . .

Who are the world's poor, how do they live and why are they likely to stay poor? In this part, we look at the poverty-stricken in detail.

First we discuss the plight of females. From the moment they're born, women and girls are worse off than men. Worldwide, women are more likely to be poorer, have less to eat and have less education than men. They spend more hours working in both paid and unpaid labour and are more likely to suffer gender-based violence. Next we look at hunger — the scourge that's a disgrace to the West — and show you why so many people don't even have the basics. Being hungry and thirsty are day-to-day realities for most of the world's poor. Finding nutritious food to eat is a struggle, and billions are forced to drink dirty water that makes them sick.

Similarly, reading and writing is a privilege that many people in the West take for granted. In this part, we also discuss why education is fundamental to development — even a basic education gives people an enormous advantage to overcome poverty. We then look at what effect poverty has on a people's health. In essence, why they get sicker and die younger.

Chapter 8

Women: The World's Poor

. . . .

In This Chapter

▶ Identifying the role of women in poorer societies

▶ Understanding gender discrimination

▶ Living with oppression and violence

▶ Addressing women's rights

. . . .

*W*omen are the poorest of the poor, the oppressed among the oppressed. In almost all cultures, they do more work than men and most of the child rearing and food preparation. This imbalance is reinforced by gender-based violence, which is common and serious. In many societies, female children are still considered a liability; in some, they're regularly sold as sex slaves. The victims of armed conflict are mainly civilians — that often means women and girls.

These factors mean that not only do the women themselves suffer, but the whole society suffers as a result. The women are discriminated against, and that discrimination forces them to the margins where they can't make the positive contribution on which society depends. Nutrition and health suffer, culture and knowledge suffer, and social systems break down further and faster.

Empowering Women and Girls

One of the most effective ways to end poverty is to work directly with women. Because women run the households in almost all societies, any improvements in their lives flow on directly to the lives of their families. Helping women helps entire communities.

Putting women at the centre

Many development efforts focus on the big picture. Some development agencies assume that if a nation builds ports, railways and power stations and attracts international companies to do business, then the people will be better off. Unfortunately, the statistics indicate that this approach rarely works.

It makes a much bigger difference to get down to grassroots and improve the way people live at home. Projects that specifically help women are especially important. If women have more money to spend, then families eat better, kids have better clothes and the health of the community improves. If women have access to education, then that knowledge is shared in the community and everyone benefits.

Half the world population — 80 per cent of the rural population in developing countries — use solid fuel fires to cook with. Campaigns to provide cleaner, more fuel-efficient cooking stoves reduce the effort required to collect fuel. This gives women more time to work on income-producing activities, and allows girls to get to school. In turn, that increases the family income now and in the future. The reduction in fumes and smoke particles in the homes also reduces pulmonary diseases and eye infections. The World Health Organization estimates that 1.6 million people each year die from conditions relating to toxic indoor air.

The statistics indicate that efforts that address the fundamental issues of how people eat, work and live and that empower people to have more time and better choices, have long-term positive effects on society. Freeing women from discrimination, giving them the right to control their own money and choose the timing and nature of their sexual activity and child bearing are fundamental building blocks of a better future.

The strategic health of women

As summarised in Chapters 2 and 12, the medical attention received by mothers and pregnant women is critical for the wellbeing of children. A few simple things make a huge amount of difference to the number of women who die in childbirth and the number of children who die before they reach five years old.

- Nutrition for the mother during pregnancy and while breastfeeding
- Access to clean water and sanitation

- ✔ Attention of medical expertise (traditional or otherwise) during pregnancy, birth and infancy
- ✔ Access to information about the health care of children

When set out like this, these factors seem self-evident, but it's only after considerable research that the importance of each item has become evident. The sidebar 'Comparing bony babies' in Chapter 12, for example, relates how mothers in southern India thought their malnourished children were normal, because they had never seen a healthy child. Foreign aid workers were unaware of this problem because it had never occurred to them that such a problem could exist.

In 2000, members of the United Nations signed up to end poverty by focusing on eight Millennium Development Goals. Separate millennium goals specifically focus on maternal health and infant mortality. These are separated from the first goal (to eradicate extreme hunger) and the second goal (to eliminate discrimination in primary schools). The precious gift of life that a mother gives to her child establishes many aspects of that child's wellbeing into the future. By nurturing mother and child at this critical phase, the health of the entire community is significantly improved.

Empowering through education

One of the Millennium Development Goals is universal education; another is the ending of gender discrimination. Both these goals have received a huge boost in Bangladesh, where a concerted effort to lift the education rate for girls has seen considerable success.

In 1991, only 20 per cent of females in Bangladesh could read and write — they were among the least educated in the world. Today more than 50 per cent of girls in Bangladesh go to secondary school. The World Bank partnered with the Bangladeshi government to provide small cash stipends to ease the financial burden of schooling for girls. Under the first project, enrolment in the project areas more than doubled from 462,000 in 1994 to slightly above one million in 2001. The project is such a great success story that we include it in Chapter 21.

The project in Bangladesh provides more than just money to encourage girls to attend school. It also aims to improve the quality of teachers, school management and even basic school facilities. Many schools are in regions where the girls drop out of the education system simply because there are a lack of toilets. So, providing separate latrines along with safe drinking water are key elements of the project.

In many countries, legal discrimination against women has been virtually eliminated. The next challenge is to address social and cultural discrimination that holds back the entire society and its economy.

The Convention on the Elimination of All Forms of Discrimination against Women (CEDAW) is the second most widely ratified human rights treaty in the world. Nevertheless, 32 countries have not submitted reports on their progress to implementing it, and a further 8 have refused to be a party to it. The United States is the only developed nation not to have ratified or acceded to CEDAW.

Sisters, doing it for themselves

One of the biggest success stories of the last couple of decades is setting up small-scale banking schemes with women in the community.

It works like this. Poor women don't have access to commercial banks. They simply couldn't qualify for a regular loan. That's where an organisation such as the Grameen Bank (also discussed in Chapter 21) comes in. The bank brings a bunch of women in a particular community together, dispenses small loans to help those women set up micro-businesses or grow their existing businesses. The loans may be as little as US$100 and are used to buy things like a sewing machine or livestock.

This approach is known as a microfinance project. It trains the women to run the business and, if necessary, teaches them basic skills like reading and writing. Each month, the women in the group pay back a portion of the loan (with a tiny interest rate) and also save a portion of the money they have earned. All profits from the scheme go back into the group so that more people can benefit. These microfinance programs have much lower rates of loan defaults than are experienced by large commercial banks. And they work. It's been proven that with a tiny injection of cash in the right place, whole communities can work their way out of poverty.

Working for the Man

Over the last century, anti-poverty campaigners have realised that women are severely discriminated against in most societies. This discrimination is a powerful obstacle to overcoming poverty. It's no accident that three of the eight Millennium Development Goals deal with ending gender discrimination in various ways. Goal 2 is to end discrimination in schools, Goal 3 is to end discrimination against women, and Goal 5 is to improve mothers' health.

Women are worse off than men in a particular society because the rules in that society make it that way. Every society and culture has expectations about the way men and women behave, what kinds of work they do and how they relate to each other — Mars and Venus and all that. Often these roles are seen to be a result of biology — they're seen as natural differences. The differences between men and women might be natural, even the roles they play in society tend to be similar across societies, but the relative importance or status of those roles is a social invention.

Where the attitude to women gets ugly is when it comes to who has the power. Lots of social rules hinge on whether a person is a man or a woman. Girls and women in many societies get less nutritious food to eat, don't get as much education and earn much less. Some women around the world can't legally own land or other resources and don't get to participate in decision-making in the home or community.

Progress towards equality is painfully slow. But it's not just about who's ruling, it's about who's doing the rest. While women have entered the paid labour force in great numbers, they're grossly over-represented in unpaid work and precarious work outside the system. When they're in paid employment, women earn less than men and women do the bulk of subsistence work. That leads to higher rates of poverty.

Working hand to mouth

Women are concentrated in work associated with low and unstable earnings and with high risks of poverty. The lower you slip down the food chain, the more women you will find. It's not just about how much women and men earn, but how they earn it and for how long. Poor women work in some of the worst jobs in the world.

Many women around the world are engaged in what's known as subsistence agriculture — that's the kind of farming a person does to survive, not to make a profit. In almost all cases, subsistence agriculture is conducted by women who work for hours on family plots for no pay, growing food to keep their families alive.

Besides managing their own households and families, many women around the world work for other people as domestic workers, cooking, cleaning and caring for families. This makes them vulnerable to violence and exploitation because they're isolated from their families and communities by distance, culture and language. Migrant women are even more at risk and many women who have been trafficked work as domestic workers.

Many women work in unregulated factories where they earn meagre wages. The industrial boom in places like China and India mean that many women move to cities to find work in factories. What seems like an opportunity to become self-sufficient and to provide for their families, often results in poverty and ill-health. Many factory workers are forced to work long hours, in dangerous conditions, for tiny pay. If you think that's bad enough, many end up owing factories for food, board and equipment. It's a modern-day form of slavery. The mechanics of this type of slavery are described in detail in Chapter 11.

Rights to land, livestock and property

Land ownership brings with it wealth and security. It provides somewhere to live, and working the land can provide a living and help sustain a person's family. But for many women even the possibility of land tenure is a dream. Women own less than 2 per cent of all the titled land in the world.

Entrenched discrimination against women means that they're often not registered as landowners because traditionally only men are viewed as heads of households. Inheritance is one way for women to acquire or gain access to land. However, women are often considered or treated as legal minors so their inheritance, whether it be land or valuable livestock, gets handed over to their menfolk.

Ensuring women's equal rights to property and access to resources is critical in the fight against poverty. When women don't have title to land or housing they have much fewer choices about how they can make a living and support their families. They may become homeless or forced to engage in risky activities, such as offering sex in exchange for food, housing or education. This can drive them and their families deeper into poverty. On the other hand, women with secure land tenure are more likely to invest in their land and increase its value. This can greatly increase poor people's wealth.

A World Bank study into rural poverty in Cambodia found that well-defined property rights raises crop yields, land value and household consumption. Because owners have secure land titles, they're more willing to invest in higher-risk and potentially higher-payoff activities, such as planting perennial trees and diversifying into vegetable and cash crops. Something as simple as a formal land title in the form of a certificate had a significant impact on wealth. In this case it increased the:

- Rental value of the land by 57 per cent
- Sale value by 38 per cent
- Crop yields by 63 per cent
- Household consumption by 24 per cent

Violence Against Women

Violence against women is a universal problem and is one of the most pervasive human rights violations in the world. One in three women will be beaten, coerced into sex or otherwise abused in her lifetime, usually by someone she knows. Half the women who are murdered in the world are killed by their current or former husbands or partners. More often than not, perpetrators go unpunished. The consequences for women, their families and their communities are enormous.

As traditional societies break down, the role of men as hunters and protectors is often destroyed. Women continue to do the majority of the work, but they might lose the respect and protection of the men.

Women who suffer violence are more likely to suffer from depression and anxiety, and have much higher levels of general ill-health. Violence is the main cause of death and disability for women aged between 15 and 44, affecting more women than cancer, car accidents, war and malaria. There's also an economic cost. Not only does violence against women put a huge burden on health systems, but women who suffer violence are less likely to be able to work and earn significantly less than other women.

Here's how Kofi Annan, the former United Nations Secretary-General, summarised the situation during his tenure: 'Violence against women is perhaps the most shameful human rights violation. It knows no boundaries of geography, culture or wealth. As long as it continues, we cannot claim to be making real progress towards equality, development, and peace.'

Tackling violence against women globally

One of the most significant achievements by the United Nations and a growing number of governments is making violence against women a human rights issue. The UN Declaration on the Elimination of Violence against Women was adopted in 1993. It recognised that

violence against women is a manifestation of historically unequal power relations between men and women, which have led to domination over and discrimination against women by men and to the prevention of the full advancement of women, and that violence against women is one of the crucial social mechanisms by which women are forced into a subordinate position compared with men.

Trafficking of women and girls

The trafficking in human beings is a multi-billion-dollar industry. Women and girls from impoverished and low-income households in rural areas and urban slums are especially vulnerable. Women and children are trafficked because there's a demand for their labour or their bodies. In many cases, victims of sex trafficking are promised lucrative jobs in the country of destination, but instead are sold into sexual slavery. Many are forced to work in the sex industry, in pornography, prostitution or sex tourism. Some end up as labourers in factories or agriculture, as domestic servants or in industries like mining. Others are used in armed conflict as child soldiers, porters, landmine clearers or sex slaves for rebel soldiers.

Trafficking happens in every region of the world, but Asian countries, particularly Cambodia and Thailand, are recognised as hubs for trafficking and sex tourism. Wealthy countries are part of the problem because their citizens provide demand for trafficked children. For example, Australians have been identified as sex tourists in 25 countries and United States citizens account for an estimated 25 per cent of child sex tourists worldwide. Places like Bali and East Timor are emerging as 'easy targets' for child sex exploiters.

You can take action to help people in the field address this issue. World Vision in the United States, for example, has a range of online activities and ideas for actions that you can take in your life to help address the sex tourism industry and the impact that AIDS has on society. Visit the Web site at www.worldvision.org and look under the Get Involved tab.

Rape as a weapon of war

The kinds of tactics used in modern warfare to terrorise and control civilians make an ugly list: Torture; mutilation; abduction; amputation; execution; systematic rape; the destruction of crops, villages and towns; and the poisoning of wells. Rape is used in conflicts to hurt and terrorise women, to humiliate their men and to tear communities apart.

In the last twenty years, rape as a weapon of war has reached epidemic proportions. In the 1994 genocide in Rwanda, it's estimated that up to 500,000 women were raped, many at gunpoint. It's also been a brutal feature of conflicts in Sudan, Iraq, Democratic Republic of Congo, Sierra Leone, Rwanda, Kosovo, and Bosnia and Herzegovina.

In some cases, women are raped then killed. In others, women are used as sexual slaves to service troops, as well as to cook for them and carry their loads from camp to camp. Survivors suffer trauma and physical injuries, and many are exposed to or purposely infected with HIV.

These devastating tactics make peace-building and reconciliation exceptionally difficult and serve to deepen poverty. Many victims are unable to cope with the trauma and have no reserves to start rebuilding their lives.

Refugee and displaced women

More than 75 per cent of people who are displaced as a result of conflict are women and children and in some refugee populations the number is as high as 90 per cent. From the time they flee their homes they're vulnerable every step of the way. While they're on the move, they're vulnerable to indiscriminate attacks. Even after they arrive in refugee camps, it's a precarious kind of safety and many women suffer from violent attacks as they care for their families.

Taking Power, Making Decisions

Empowering women at all levels of society is an essential component of eradicating extreme poverty. Within the family, in the community, government and international organisations, allowing women equal access to power is essential.

Women in parliament

At the beginning of the twenty-first century over 95 per cent of all countries, both rich and poor, had granted women the two most fundamental democratic rights: The right to vote and the right to stand for elections. But this formal recognition has not translated into equal participation or decision-making power. Women around the world at every socio-political level find themselves under-represented in parliament.

There are almost 44,000 members of national parliaments in the world. Of the 43,210 whose gender is officially recorded by the Inter-parliamentary Union, only 17 per cent are women (see Table 8-1). It's encouraging that Rwanda tops the list with the highest ratio of female MPs in the world. The dramatic gains for women in Rwanda are a result of deliberate strategies to increase women's political participation. They include a constitutional guarantee, a quota system and innovative electoral structures.

Table 8-1	Top Ten Nations by Female Representation		
Rank	Country	Women MPs %	Women Senators %
1.	Rwanda	48.8	34.6
2.	Sweden	47.3	-
3.	Finland	42.0	-
4.	Costa Rica	38.6	-
5.	Denmark	38.0	-
6.	Norway	37.9	-
7.	Netherlands	36.7	34.7
8.	Cuba	36.0	-
8.	Spain	36.0	23.2
9.	Mozambique	34.8	-
10.	Belgium	34.7	38.0

The term 'MPs' is used for Members of Parliament (lower house members — as in the US Congress).
'Senator' is used to represent members of the upper house.
Source: Inter-parliamentary Union.

Women on the world's stage

Despite the low numbers of women in politics, they play an increasingly visible role on the world stage. This is partly because of the strong recognition of women's rights in the developed world and the gradual opening of the institutions of education, employment and political representation. These individuals offer an inspiration to other women around the world. Their example encourage women to strike out, overcome the pressures on them and refuse to submit to a second-class future.

Some women who have been recognised in recent times for the significance of their contribution include:

- **Heidi Kuhn,** who founded Roots of Peace, an organisation dedicated to removing landmines from agricultural land so it can be productive again.
- **Lynne Twist,** cofounder of the Pachamama Alliance, dedicated to empowering the indigenous people of southern Ecuador and protecting their rainforest.
- **Marie C Wilson,** head of The White House Project, an international organisation that encourages and supports women in positions of political power.

The following women have been singled out as deserving special attention.

Wangari Maathai: Nobel Peace Prize 2004

The first woman from Africa to be honoured with the Nobel Peace Prize, Wangari Maathai courageously stood up against the former oppressive regime in Kenya. Her actions show that sustainable development can embrace democracy, human rights and women's rights in particular.

She founded the Green Belt Movement and has mobilised poor women to plant 30 million trees in 30 years. Her methods have been adopted in other countries. Using forests to protect against desertification is a vital factor in the struggle to strengthen the living environment.

The Nobel Prize Committee wrote that, 'through education, family planning, nutrition and the fight against corruption, Maathai is a strong voice speaking for the best forces in Africa to promote peace and good living conditions on that continent'.

Irene Zubaida Khan: Amnesty International Secretary General

Taking the helm in Amnesty International in 2001, Khan is the first woman, the first Asian and the first Muslim in charge of the world's largest human rights organisation. She personally led high-level missions to Pakistan during the bombing of Afghanistan, to Israel and the Palestinian territories just after the Israeli occupation of Jenin, and to Colombia before the Presidential elections in May 2003.

Deeply concerned about violence against women, Khan called for better protection of women's human rights in meetings with President Musharraf of Pakistan, President Lahoud of Lebanon and Prime Minister Khaleda Zia of Bangladesh. In Australia, she drew attention to the plight of asylum seekers in detention. In Burundi, she met with victims of massacres and urged President Buyoya and other parties to the conflict to end the cycle of human rights abuse. In Bulgaria, she led a campaign to end discrimination of those suffering from mental disabilities.

Shirin Ebadi: Nobel Peace Prize 2003

Shirin Ebadi is a lawyer, judge, lecturer, writer and activist. She has spoken out clearly and strongly in her own country, Iran, and far beyond its borders. Her principal arena is the struggle for basic human rights, and the belief that no society deserves to be labelled civilised unless the rights of women and children are respected. In an era of violence, she has consistently supported non-violence. It is fundamental to her view that the supreme political power in a community must be built on democratic elections. She favours enlightenment and dialogue as the best way to change attitudes and resolve conflict.

Vandana Shiva: founder Navdanya

Dr Vandana Shiva is a physicist, ecologist, activist, editor and author of many books. In India she has established Navdanya, a movement for biodiversity conservation and farmers' rights. She directs the Research Foundation for Science, Technology and Natural Resource Policy. Her most recent books are *Biopiracy: The Plunder of Nature and Knowledge* and *Stolen Harvest: The Hijacking of the Global Food Supply.*

Chapter 9

Hunger and Thirst

Few people in rich countries know what going hungry for weeks feels like. Or what it's like to have no choice but to give your children dirty water to drink, knowing it might make them sick. Compared with that, the water restrictions now commonplace in Australia, the western United States and some parts of Europe are little more than a slight inconvenience.

This is partly because farming has come a long way over the past few centuries. Rich countries currently have an abundance of food, and throw away tonnes of it each day. You have to ask yourself why, then, do so many people continue to suffer from malnutrition and hunger? Why do shocking images of starvation continue to plague your television screen?

This chapter is about the dynamics of hunger and thirst. It describes the impact on the individual and the community, and the reasons so many people starve, and it outlines some of the solutions that have been proposed.

Living Hungry

Starvation is not an event; it's a process that takes months. The body slowly breaks down muscle and tissue to maintain vital systems. Then fat is broken down to keep the nervous system and heart from failing. Eventually, the system shuts down or is so weak it succumbs to disease.

But starvation is only the tip of the iceberg. A conservative estimate puts the number of people suffering each year from chronic malnutrition at 850 million around the world. That's more than the entire population of Europe! Malnutrition (or under-nutrition) doesn't necessarily lead to death. The effects can be as varied as stunted growth, sleep disorders, diarrhoea, constipation, muscle weakness, fatigue, depression, social withdrawal, psychotic episodes or other mental problems.

Working with the hungry

If you've worked with the hungry, dispensing medicine or food, you know that the most harrowing aspect is the grinding hopelessness. People line up everyday for the small amount of relief on offer, and if they don't get what they need they come back the next day. The alternative is death.

For the hungry, the reality is like a grim gambling game, in which the currency is human life and Death runs the casino. Everyday, another portion of the available lives is used but the rest keep playing for the chance to win the next round and stay alive for one more day.

Aid workers find work in such circumstances very grim, and it's difficult to forget the quiet acceptance of those people waiting for their turn. Perhaps the ultimate injustice is that as you're living and working with these people, in the back of your mind you know that you're not one of them: You can go home to a world where you can turn on the tap or open the fridge.

That knowledge makes it possible to keep going but, at the same time, underlines the awful reality that by virtue of their birth, millions of people on this planet are condemned to death.

The United Nations Food and Agriculture Organization uses the term *food security* to describe a situation where people don't live in hunger or fear of starvation. It estimates that two billion people, almost a third of the world's population, don't have the food security that is a basic human right.

Food revolutions

Guns and guillotines aren't the only tools used in revolutions. Ploughs and tractors can be part of a revolution too. They were the major tools of the green revolution that took place after World War II. The green revolution caused dramatic increases in the levels of agricultural production. It was a technology-based revolution that brought irrigation, fertilisers and high-yielding varieties of crops. This meant more food for more people.

Organic farmers view the green revolution as the application of the war machine to agriculture. They hold it responsible for the imminent collapse of our soil and water systems. Agribusiness interests view it as the logical outcome of the Industrial Revolution and the application of science to the growth of food.

Revolutions in farming began well before the green revolution of the twentieth century. Farms first appeared on the Tigris/Euphrates river basin (in modern Iraq) 10,000 years ago. Great Britain began its own agricultural revolution in the sixteenth century by throwing peasants off the land in a practice known as the enclosures. This period saw huge productivity gains that ultimately paved the way for population growth and industrialisation 200 years later. The prosperity that Europe and North America enjoy today is, in part, the result of this early agrarian revolution.

These revolutions haven't solved the food problems of the world. Hunger is not a thing of the past. Simply put, it has created butter mountains and milk lakes in the developed world that aren't equally distributed. The statistics given in the section about hunger in Chapter 2 or the role of tariffs and subsidies in Chapter 19 indicate the stark nature of the imbalance.

Looking at Hunger's Many Causes

Identifying the world's poor provides some insight into the nature of the problem. To help those poor get ahead you need to understand the reasons why they remain poor and hungry. These reasons are complex, and have resisted the efforts of many large, well-funded and well-meaning organisations. The following sections examine the underlying causes of hunger and thirst as one step towards finding solutions.

Too many people, too little space?

Want to kill an after-dinner conversation? Observe that population growth is a major problem. The topic is emotionally and politically charged for a number of reasons, the primary one being that no-one really wants to talk about the fact that there might simply be too many people for the planet to support.

If you owned the proverbial camel and wanted to make sure you didn't break its back, you'd work out its 'carrying capacity' and then load only that much straw on it. It's the same for the earth. The carrying capacity is the maximum number of people that can be fed by the planet without damaging it so that its carrying capacity is reduced. No-one agrees on what the actual number is.

The wide range of figures given for the carrying capacity of the earth is a sign of how controversial this topic is. The figures range from 12 billion at the top end, to 600 million at the low end. Even fairly cautious scientists assume that the earth will feed more than two billion people. There have been more than two billion people since World War II, so many of those scientists are afraid that we are already well past the safe limit.

Most major organisations predict that the earth can feed more than ten billion. Conveniently, that means there is enough food to go around. This raises the tricky question, 'If hunger and starvation aren't about too many people or too little space, what are they about?'

Not enough to go round?

There's plenty of food on the planet right now. You live in a country that grows more food than it needs and exports food to the rest of the world. In fact, the world's farmers produce enough for everyone on the planet to be really fat. Yet 30 million people die of hunger every year.

Each year, 20 million Australians spend nearly A$5.5 billion dollars on food they don't eat. Instead, more than 3 million tonnes of it rots in landfills. If you've ever heard the line, 'That food could feed an entire village in Africa!' you'll realise how unfair it is that rich countries bulldoze entire food crops into the ground.

Similarly, the European butter mountains are talking points in every round of global trade agreements. It's not as simple as shipping the excess food from rich countries around the world, though. Dumping cut-price food in the markets of developing countries causes instability in their economies and undermines the farming sector.

But it's not just the West that grows more than it needs. Many of the world's undernourished live in countries that actually export more food than they import. In fact, nearly 80 per cent of all malnourished children under five in the developing world live in countries with food surpluses. So even most 'hungry countries' have enough for their people to eat.

The corn curse

When poor countries begin to develop, their middle class typically is the first to grow. But what some countries have found is that with a growing middle class comes a shift towards certain imported goods. In Africa, demand for wheat has shot up alongside economic growth. But wheat can't be grown economically on the continent. It has to be imported to the detriment of local farming. Similarly, many African currencies have been overvalued in the past. This made imported food artificially cheap, undermining local production.

Imagine you could have a dish piled high with your favourite food in place of this book. Now imagine that for the rest of your life you're going to be eating this dish. Whatever you chose, our guess is you'd get sick of it pretty damn fast (especially if it's something like chocolate or ice-cream!). But more important than culinary boredom, there's no single food that fulfils all your dietary needs.

In much of Africa maize (that's corn to you and me) is immensely popular. But that's not always such a good thing. Here are some of the problems that countries like Malawi have found with the maize mania:

- Maize doesn't grow easily on the continent. Either it has to be imported or it's grown inefficiently at great cost. And that's not good for Malawi's economy. It's not very good for the soil either and can leave it barren in just a few years.

- Many Malawians eat little else. Corn makes up a large part of their diet. But the grain is nutritionally rather poor. It's filling, but not nourishing. So Malawi's kids may have full bellies, but far too many of them don't get the nutrients they need to grow up healthy.

- Because it's so difficult to grow, yields from a field of maize can vary enormously in Malawi. It's not unusual to see yields vary 20 per cent from the previous year, and sometimes by as much as 50 per cent. That's a lot of economic uncertainty and maybe even a lot of hungry mouths.

Unfortunately though, maize production is promoted by the government. Malawi encourages its farmers to grow maize by offering them subsidies.

Maize isn't the only culprit. Indonesia suffers from an over-reliance on cassava (a starchy root, a bit like a tough potato), and much of Asia's poor have a diet made up predominantly of rice.

In the 1990s India become one of the world's major food grain exporting countries. Along with wheat, India now exports substantial quantities of rice, and is in fact a leading rice exporting country, accounting for a third of world rice trade. At the same time, according to the Food and Agriculture Organization of the United Nations, nearly 50 per cent of the world's hungry people live in India. About 35 per cent of India's population — 350 million — are considered food insecure, consuming less than 80 per cent of their minimum energy requirements.

The problem's not that there's not enough to go round. It's that the existing economic systems don't deliver what's available to those who need it.

It's all the economy's fault

Chapter 19 looks in detail at the relationship between global trade and poverty. The specific impact of the economy on food security, though, is summarised here. The work done by the Food and Agriculture Organization (FAO) identifies three different approaches that it hopes can end global starvation.

- ✔ **Market forces:** You're probably not surprised to hear that the World Trade Organization (WTO) recommends free trade as the solution to poverty. The logic is that tariffs on imports, or subsidies to farmers, prevent the market operating smoothly. The regular riots at WTO talks, and the fact that developing countries, led by India, walked out of the Doha round of trade talks in 2007, indicates widespread dissatisfaction with this model.

- ✔ **Food justice:** People dedicated to eliminating world poverty are beginning to unite in the belief that governments have a duty to regulate markets so that no-one in the world starves. This view is consolidating under the banner Food Justice, a term that's almost self-explanatory.

- ✔ **Food sovereignty:** A slightly different view places the blame squarely on the multinational companies that use free trade agreements to extract maximum profits, regardless of the social and human impact. People with that view believe that giving individual nations power over global corporations is the way to address this issue.

The demon's in the detail

The global forces of trade and international policy may shape the world's economy but myriad local effects have a direct impact on the amount of food available in any individual corner or the globe. The following sections (though not exhaustive) show just how complex the issues are.

Climate chaos and natural disaster

Natural disasters have long-term knock-on effects for those who survive them. Roads, buildings, telephone lines, crops, tools and livestock are all vulnerable in natural disasters. Any damage to these is likely to lead to food insecurity. See Chapter 6 for the lowdown on natural disasters.

As the planet's climate changes, natural disasters are expected to become more common and their effects more severe. Food production will be one of the many casualties of our increasingly ferocious planet.

Rising temperatures will take their toll in other ways as well. Scientists have found grain yields to be on the decline in Asia, and fear that food production in the tropics may fall by as much as 30 per cent over the next half century.

Human and agricultural disease

The impact of disease on food production shouldn't be underestimated. Diseases like malaria and AIDS have decimated entire generations in some countries, killing the most productive members of society. See Chapter 12 for more information on disease as a cause of world poverty.

Modern farming is focused on maximising the productivity of each crop, often damaging the land and reducing the profits made by the farmer. This focus leads to the planting of large areas with single crops and exposes the farmer to variations in natural and economic conditions. If prices fall for the one crop or animal that farmers are producing, they may well be left destitute. Similarly, if many farmers within a country focus on the same crop, fluctuations due to drought or disease can damage the entire economy.

Specialisation (focusing on a small range of products) also increases vulnerability to disease. A country that relies heavily on beef is going to be particularly vulnerable to the spread of mad cow disease. Countries that depend on fowl are at enormous risk from avian flu.

Fishing practices

Approximately a billion people in Africa and Asia depend on fish as their main source of protein. But both livelihoods and diets of the poor are at risk from intensive deep-sea fishing that depletes fish stocks.

Farming practices

Fertilisers and genetic modification (GM) of crops offer previously undreamt-of levels of agricultural production. They may well offer part of a solution to the hunger and chronic malnutrition suffered by millions of people each year, but the long-term impacts of genetically modified crops are unknown.

Most people think of GM crops as being either the best thing since sliced bread or the single most dangerous development of the twentieth century. There's rarely a middle ground. The effect on crop yields, soil fertility and human health is still unknown. GM crops are costly. Farmers need to use specific fertilisers and pesticides. Most crops need to be planted from commercial seed, not from seed collected on the farm. These ongoing expenses provide profits for international companies, not for the farmers.

The costs of war

Wars and fighting get in the way of farmers trying to plant and harvest. Conflict also makes it much harder to transport produce to market. Hundreds of thousands are displaced by fighting; they're no longer growing food but someone has to feed them. In times of war, someone's got to do the fighting so farmers are drawn into the violence, the land lies fallow and fewer people are fed.

It might be hard to farm when the bullets are flying, but it can be even more difficult when they stop. Unexploded ordnance (UXOs) — landmines, cluster bombs and the like — are often left behind after violence. Around the world, 200,000 square kilometres are thought to be contaminated with landmines. These can be hidden in vegetation or even partially buried in the ground. They make otherwise good farmland useless and can take decades to clear.

Local politics

In Chad, Central Africa, an estimated 10 per cent of cultivatable land is actually being used. In the Horn of Africa, a region renowned for recurring drought and famine, the area of unused good quality farm land is many times greater than the area actually farmed today. Why then do millions of the residents of these regions suffer from drought, malnutrition and even starvation when there's more land available to farm?

Conflict's greatest influence on food production is that it uproots hundreds of thousands of people at a time. Farmers and rural populations are often forced to flee the fighting and abandon their fields. This can destroy the food-producing capacity of an entire country.

Land

In parts of the world land is inherited by the first-born male. He is expected to continue to farm the soil and produce for his family. In other traditions land may be divided among all children (well, the male ones at least). This sounds fairer, but think of the effect two or three generations down the line. A plot of land may be divided in two, three or even more parts, and then divided again with each generation. You very quickly get a plot of land that can't grow enough for an emaciated rabbit to live off.

Where land is being combined to make farming more efficient, those who lose their land become unemployed. Many of them head to the nearest city, creating the slums described in Chapter 14. Even if they get a fair price when they first sell their land, it doesn't go far once they have no income.

Feeding the Hungry

Famine and malnutrition aren't caused by too many people or too little food. The inequalities built into modern trade and production force people to go hungry. The global system for distributing food has failed two billion people.

Often journalists or politicians trace the causes of hunger back to a particular event like a war or a drought. This may indeed be the catalyst, or the last straw. People starve and suffer from malnutrition because they're poor and are denied access to food. It's the social and economic environment that causes malnutrition and hunger, not a lack of food. That's the challenge of eradicating extreme poverty.

How to support the hungry

International trading rules can be altered to prevent the world's poorest people from dying only if the changes address corruption, conflict and cultural issues that currently prevent the food getting to where it's needed.

Chapter 4 discusses the detail of delivering food as part of an emergency relief aid program. This section concentrates on the next step, helping the poor recover and establish the means of feeding themselves in the next and subsequent seasons.

All the following elements need to be part of the solution:

- **A stable political environment:** Keeping warring parties apart, preventing bandits from stealing food and preventing further damage from ongoing conflict are necessary conditions for alleviating hunger after conflict. In northeastern Africa over the last decade, United Nations peacekeeping forces have had to deal with conflict as a key cause of starvation.

- **Appropriate technology:** As well as simply handing out food, aid agencies need to deliver solutions that address the causes of hunger. The saying, 'Give a man a fish and you feed him for a day, but teach him how to fish and you feed him for a lifetime' applies. Increasingly, solutions that address climate change or desertification due to overgrazing must be part of the mix.

✔ **Economic independence:** One recurring criticism of international aid is that it creates an ongoing dependency. Whether you view this as a 'handout mentality' due to some deficiency in the recipient or a 'capitalist plot' designed to maximise profits for companies based in rich countries, the effect is the same. The hungry never get to escape the vicious cycle of poverty. If they can be provided with the means to feed themselves in subsequent years without borrowing to buy fertilisers, grain and water, then this can be addressed.

✔ **Ongoing education:** Traditional farming methods evolved through trial and error, rather than a broad study of all the possible solutions. They're often vulnerable to external changes in climate, economics and the political landscape. By combining a scientific understanding of agriculture with relevant traditional methods, robust solutions can be developed that support local communities and traditional culture in the most efficient manner possible. Permaculture methods, recycling of waste, and nutrients and water can bring the world's best practices to local agriculture.

✔ **Girl power:** Farmers aren't only men. Women farm too. In many places women are in fact the principal food producers. Yet, in many situations, women are left out of decision-making processes, with negative effects for food security. Programs like the microcredit systems developed in India and Pakistan can empower women to rebuild and preserve the means of production rather than see them being traded in power plays.

All of these solutions are gradual and specific. They're things that aid workers can do on the ground when faced with a hungry population. They go beyond the immediate relief that has to be handed out during a food emergency and help address the direct causes of a particular incidence of hunger.

Changing the system

Hunger usually isn't the result of a single event; a combination of factors builds up over many years. Conflict or drought may be the last straw, but they rarely lead to malnutrition and hunger in well-organised societies.

Societies generally organise themselves to protect the population from hunger. Widespread hunger is generally the result of a collapse in social organisation rather than a simple natural disaster. This means that preventative measures can be established to protect societies in the future.

Parisians didn't learn to cook rats, snails and frogs because they were good eating — it was a coping mechanism. Given the choice, no-one would voluntarily chow down on cockroaches or grasshoppers, yet in parts of Asia this too was a coping mechanism for food insecurity. Moving the menu up the evolutionary tree, Hindu India became vegetarian around 1500 years ago as a result of a famine caused by a shortage of cattle. The food security offered by dairy products is more important than the short-term benefits of killing the cattle.

These historical adaptations in diet can be supplemented by permanent food forests, fully closed organic farming systems and agricultural techniques that replenish the soil and recycle energy, water and nutrients. Sustainable farming techniques may or may not work as part of the global economy, depending on the political and economic environment. These techniques have the distinct advantage that they allow communities to be independent, protecting them from variations in global politics, markets and oil prices.

Many efforts to eradicate global poverty focus on ending the exploitation of the world's poor for profit. These efforts get bogged down in arguments about whether the exploitation is real or imagined. Historically, popular movements that oppose the exploitation of people by commercial interests encounter well-organised opposition but eventually prevail. The African slave trade, for example, made many Europeans wealthy and was debated for decades before the humanitarians won the arguments against the commercial beneficiaries.

Some suggestions about ending exploitation include:

- Replacing the global institutions that have bankrupted so many countries
- Cancelling the enormous debts incurred under those systems
- Establishing a fair trade system to support developing countries (as opposed to the free trade system that exploits them)

These solutions are idealistic. Those in support of them — such as the authors of this book — point out that any compromise of these ideals can be measured in human lives destroyed by hunger and starvation in the future. To us, that seems like an ideal worth pursuing.

The Scary Facts of Water Scarcity

Water covers 70 per cent of the world's surface. Why do many people still have trouble getting their hands on it? It's the most common substance on the surface of the planet after all, so what's all the fuss about?

- ✔ Over 97 per cent of the world's water is full of salt! Less than 3 per cent is fresh water that's drinkable.

- ✔ Two-thirds of the fresh water on earth is locked up in snow, glaciers and ice.

- ✔ Evaporation is responsible for the loss of between 50 and 80 per cent of the water in rivers and lakes. Global warming will increase that rate of evaporation.

- ✔ The remaining fresh water is demanded by growing numbers of people, industry and farming. Agriculture consumes 70 per cent of the water used worldwide.

- ✔ The remaining fraction is delivered to cities and towns in pipes that leak increasingly as they age. Some European cities lose as much as 60 per cent of their water through leaking metropolitan plumbing.

Luck of the draw

Some places get more rain than others. Some countries are blessed with large quantities of readily available and safe water; other countries have drawn the short straw, and struggle to find enough to keep them going. The tropics are wetter than the subtropics, but get heavy downfalls in the wet season followed by long dry periods. The eastern seaboards of the United States and Asia are both well watered, while the west coasts of all continents can be wet or dry, depending on their latitude.

Large continental areas away from the sea tend to have high rates of evaporation so even a moderate rainfall may not result in lush, fertile land cover. The deserts of Africa, China, the United States and Australia are all inland areas to the west of the continent outside the tropics. The Australian and American deserts receive around 25 millimetres (one inch) of rain each month, on average, compared with around three times that amount for the north-eastern United States and western Europe.

Africa, Asia and South America are all continents with extremes of rainfall, from monsoonal areas in the tropics that receive hundreds of millimetres of rain each month for half the year, to areas of desert that often have no rainfall for years.

But the story doesn't end with the meteorological data. Access to water varies enormously between countries with similar levels of rainfall. For example, compare Israel and the neighbouring Occupied Palestinian Territories. One could hardly claim Israelis have significantly more rain than the Palestinians next door, yet Israeli settlers on the West Bank use nine times more water per person than Palestinians living in the same area.

The consumption of water in the developing world is around 15 litres per person per day. In most developed countries it's higher than 200 litres each per day. In the United States it's as high as 380 litres per day. Flushing the toilet alone consumes between 5 and 15 litres. That's a day's supply of drinking water for many of the world's poor.

Rain today, dry tomorrow

Climate change is not about reduced rainfall. It's about changing weather patterns. In fact, global levels of precipitation are predicted to *increase* with rising temperatures and the greater evaporation they bring. Places in higher latitudes, such as Britain and Northern Europe, are predicted to receive more rainfall, whereas lower latitudes — many of the countries actually experiencing drought today — will receive less rainfall.

Adding to the troubles of the poor, water cycles are predicted to intensify. Expect more severe monsoons, harsher droughts, more violent floods. Check out Chapter 15 for more on the world's weather.

In just 40 years, Lake Chad in Africa has shrunk to less than one-tenth its former size. When it was first surveyed by Europeans in the early nineteenth century, the lake was one of the largest in the world. But today there are fears that the lake will dry up completely during the course of this century.

The lake forms the border between Cameroon, Chad, Niger and Nigeria, but draws its water from as far away as Algeria and the Central African Republic. Twenty million people depend on the water that falls in the lake's catchment basin. Not only are people and their livelihoods at risk, but plant, animal and fish life is already under serious threat. Some species have recently become extinct in the region.

Elsewhere, the disappearance of the glaciers provides dramatic evidence of global warming. In the short term, melting glaciers can make river levels rise. But within a couple of decades, these glaciers will have melted so much that some of today's most impressive rivers may actually begin to dry up. Glaciers in the Himalayas supply the waters of the Ganges, Indus, Brahmaputra, Mekong, Yangtze and Yellow Rivers. Without these glaciers, literally billions of people will lose their primary water source.

Honey, I shrunk the Aral Sea

No-one does 'big' like communists. So when they decided to turn the desert of Uzbekistan into one of the world's largest cotton-producing regions, an entire sea all but disappeared.

Once the fourth largest lake in the world, the Aral Sea and the rivers that fed it were tapped for irrigation — well, more like re-routed. Perhaps you've seen the pictures of huge fishing vessels marooned in the middle of the desert.

The Uzbek cotton-growing project of the Soviet Union began in the 1960s, and by the 1980s the sea was falling at a rate of nearly one metre each year. The Soviets described the sea in the middle of the desert as 'nature's error,' the demise of which was seen to be inevitable. By 2004 the Aral Sea was a quarter of its former glory and shrinking fast.

Not only did they tap the water source for all it was worth, but Soviet weapons-testing and industrial waste turned the waters into a chemical-infested cesspool. People living on the Aral's shores now lack a source of clean water. They suffer unusually high rates of cancer and lung disease as winds circulate the chemicals that have been left behind by retreating waters.

Even the local climate has been impacted by the grand Soviet scheme. Now that the sea has diminished, rain is lighter and less frequent, dust storms are a familiar sight, the winters are colder and the summers are hotter.

Since the fall of the Soviet Union, the decline of the Aral has come to the world's attention. Kazakhstan, Kyrgyzstan, Tajikistan, Turkmenistan and Uzbekistan — all countries that depend upon the sea — have pledged 1 per cent of their national budgets to help with recovery. The World Bank has also taken a keen interest in restoring the body of water.

In 2006 an actual increase in water levels occured for the first time in twenty years. Fishing stocks were recorded to be once again at an economically significant level. The port of Aralsk — which at the worst point was once more than 100 kilometres from the water — is now only 25 kilometres from the sea's shore. Even rainfall appears to be returning to previous levels.

Hogging the waterhole

Over the course of the twentieth century, global water consumption rose sixfold and it's still growing. About 1.1 billion people don't have access to safe drinking water. Since the Millennium Development Goal of halving this number was declared in 2000, the number of people with enough water has increased. Now, 84 per cent of people in Asia and 59 per cent of people in Africa have access to safe drinking water. The United Nations Water for Life program estimates that US$11.3 billion a year needs to be spent to achieve the goal.

The lost source of the Nile

The River Nile and its fertile floodplain have been the basis of Egypt's wealth for thousands of years. The mighty river has built an enormous delta that's home to the great seaport of Alexandria. Now, instead of its annual flood, the Nile is reduced to a trickle and it peters out before reaching the sea. Alexandria is cracking up as the delta shrinks from the lack of water.

Traditionally, the nations of Central Africa have used little of the Nile's water. This arrangement was formalised in colonial times, when treaties granted the water to the nation of Egypt. The vast bulk of the Nile's water comes from the Blue Nile, which flows through Ethiopia without being used. Now that Ethiopia has emerged from a protracted war and has the largest army in Africa it is likely to start using the river.

The demands on the Nile's water extend below the ground, as well.

Colonel Gaddafi built a major pipeline, known in Libya as Great Man-made River, that brings ground water from aquifers under the Sahara to his coastal nation. The project is an alternative to a desalination plant on the Mediterranean coast or to a proposed pipeline to bring water from Europe. Designed to irrigate 130,000 hectares of farm land, the world's largest underground network of pipes taps an aquifer containing water that's over 40,000 years old. Egyptians are concerned it could lead to seepage from the Nile.

The Pharaohs rightly believed the strength of Egypt depended directly on the regular flooding of the Nile. By that measure it appears the future of Egypt isn't too rosy. It looks distinctly as if there's demand for more water in north-eastern Africa than is available.

The following sections cover some ways in which hogging the waterhole compounds water problems.

Pollution

With more people comes more pollution. Agricultural and industrial output is growing in most countries to keep pace with population. There's more farming and industrial waste, so more water is needed to keep these systems going. Human waste and rubbish is on the rise as well, adding to the bacteria and the level of nutrients and toxins in the water.

Ground water

In many areas short of readily available water, tapping into groundwater has been the only option. But if water from watertables is extracted at a faster rate than it can be replenished, reservoirs that have accumulated over thousands of years will disappear. Watertables in some parts of the world are falling as fast as three metres a year. Pollution seeping into the ground also jeopardises underground water sources.

Increasing consumption

Countries like China and India have dramatically helped their citizens out of poverty through economic growth. But rising incomes go hand in hand with consumption similar to that of rich countries. Meat is increasingly popular in both countries among the newly affluent. Producing meat, though, requires five times as much water as an equivalent quantity of grain. The demand for meat includes a hidden increase in the demand for water.

Only 20 per cent of water scarcity in the coming decade is predicted to be due to climate change. As much as 80 per cent will be attributed to population pressures and economic development.

Urbanisation

Population pressure isn't just about more people; it's also the concentration of those people in the world's megacities (see Chapter 14). These cities can't be supported by the resources available in the immediate vicinity. Government planning is needed to make safe, clean water available. This is extremely difficult because concentrated populations mean concentrated waste, an expensive problem to solve.

Water Matters

The amount of water in the world never really changes. People drink it, people expel it; it evaporates, it rains. It's a cycle that keeps on going. But with demand for water increasing, what role will water scarcity play in the planet's future?

Even today, almost one person out of every five living in the developing world lacks access to clean water. That's 1.1 billion people across the globe! By 2025 nearly three billion humans will be living in countries that find it difficult to get their hands on enough clean water. By 2050 that could be as high as seven billion people.

The UN recommends that people have access to at least 50 litres of clean water each day for their drinking, washing, cooking and hygiene needs. But in reality, many poor people are forced to get by on less water each day.

The health hazards of H₂O

Access to drinking water is essential for good health. Foul water brings a range of diseases with it. Here are some of the usual suspects. (Warning: Don't read this if you've got a weak stomach):

- **Diarrhoea:** Diarrhoea is a death sentence for the poor. Diarrhoea is caused by a multitude of infections — most of which are waterborne — and leads to severe dehydration. It's life-threatening, particularly in the young, but can also lead to malnutrition.

  Its effects are staggering: 4 per cent of all deaths around the world are attributed to diarrhoea, most of these in children. In Africa and South East Asia this figure is as high as 8.5 per cent of all deaths.

- **Cholera:** Cholera is an acute infection of the intestines and is usually spread by drinking water that's been contaminated by faeces or vomitus. In very severe cases, the disease causes intense diarrhoea and vomiting, leading to severe dehydration that can kill within hours.

  In 2000, around 150,000 cases of cholera were recorded. About 5,000 people died of the disease, nearly 90 per cent of whom were in Africa. If untreated, up to half of all severe cholera sufferers will die, but with treatment more than 99 per cent can live.

- **Typhoid:** Spread in the same way as cholera, typhoid can be easily prevented with clean water and good hygiene. This disease leads to fever, constipation or diarrhoea, and an enlarged spleen and liver. There are around 17 million infections of the disease each year.

- **Polio:** This results in muscle weakness and even paralysis and is also caused by eating or drinking food or water contaminated by faeces. Once widespread, concerted international efforts have nearly eradicated the disease. Today, about 1,000 new cases of polio are reported each year.

- **Hepatitis A:** Hepatitis is polite enough to come in several forms — A through to G, in fact. Hep A (as well as the little-known Hep E) results from eating and drinking contaminated substances and attacks the liver, resulting in muscle aches, vomiting, fevers and other such fun items. It can also lead to jaundice. Hepatitis A is mostly found in developing countries with poor sanitation, but at least mortality rates are pretty low — the World Health Organization (WHO) records them as below 0.2 per cent.

- **Guinea worm:** This infection is caused by a large worm (well, technically it's called a nematode) that bears the fitting name of Dracunculus, meaning little dragon. You get infected by Guinea worm by drinking water that contains Guinea worm larvae.

The worm declares itself with itching and a fever and then erupts from a blister, usually on the leg. The worm can be up to one metre long and it takes months for it to be slowly pulled out of the body. The parasite is only found in a few countries in North and West Africa.

✔ **Trachoma:** This is a bacterial infection that's spread from person to person and can result in blindness if untreated. All it takes to avoid it is washing your face in clean water. Today, 6 million people are blind because of trachoma, and another 150 million need treatment.

Coming clean with water for the poor

The problems for the world's poor in accessing clean drinking water can seem unsurmountable. Fortunately, they're not. Millennium Development Goal number 7, detailed in Chapter 18, is to ensure a sustainable future. All the goals have targets and measures, so robust numbers are available that state how much this will cost. A cost–benefit analysis by the World Health Organization shows that:

✔ Every US$1 invested in improved drinking water and sanitation services at a national level can yield economic benefits of US$4 to US$34.

✔ At a domestic level these figures jump to benefits of US$5 to US$140 per dollar invested. This is an incredible return on investment.

✔ When you sum up this impact across the world, the economic payback from investing US$11.3 billion per year in drinking water and sanitation systems is estimated to be US$84 billion by 2015.

✔ The impact of reducing diarrhoeal disease alone will exceed US$700 million a year.

These figures indicate why there's such a strong focus on solving the problem of delivering water to the world's poor. Of course, you don't need an economic reason. The human misery and suffering would be sufficient on its own. Wouldn't it?

Chapter 10

The Foundations of Learning

*E*ducation is the most effective way to help people lift themselves out of poverty. Teaching people to read gives them access to a world of information they would otherwise never know. Teaching them to count, calculate and analyse gives them the fundamental tools to make sense of the complex civilisation that they share with others.

Perhaps most importantly, it gives them the opportunity to work in skilled employment or take advantage of commercial opportunities that close the gap between them and their counterparts in the developed world. If you can't get a decent job, then you can't escape poverty.

The challenge is that you can't put an education on a ship and send it off overseas. This chapter examines the challenges involved in delivering an education to the poorest people in the world.

Education for All

The English language is peppered with aphorisms that boast about the power of knowledge. You know that the pen is mightier than the sword; a little knowledge is a dangerous thing; knowledge generally is everlasting life; and knowledge itself is power. This last point is sometimes forgotten, because military and sporting triumphs dominate the front pages of newspapers. There are, however, relatively commonplace examples of how important knowledge can be.

 ✔ Explorers, or adventurers, die for the lack an up-to-date map.

 ✔ Share traders with inside information make millions at the expense of others who don't have access to that knowledge.

 ✔ Media-savvy lobbyists outmanoeuvre a major company in a local protest action because they understand the people on the ground and know how to get their message across.

The amount of knowledge required to succeed in today's world is considerably greater than in the past. In thirteenth-century Italy, Leonardo Fibonacci introduced Arabic numerals, the times table and double-entry bookkeeping to Europe. They were still novelties when Leonardo da Vinci learned arithmetic to formalise his studies on perspective 200 years later. Today, the times table is taught in primary school, and Fibonacci's contribution to commerce (double-entry bookkeeping) is used in most businesses across the world. Citizens of developed countries learn things at school that four centuries ago were available only to an elite group of thinkers.

The education that gave you those basic survival tools is not available to most people in the developing world. This section examines the reasons, and looks at the progress towards the second of the Millennium Development Goals described in Chapter 18.

The ever-receding goal

For 90 years, education has been a key element and a high priority in the mission to end global poverty. At the end of World War I, the League of Nations was established with the aim of achieving global security. One part of encouraging peace and welfare was the promotion of education in poor countries. By 1934 the League had adopted the goal of extending basic education to all children.

This focus on education was even more prominent when the United Nations was formed after World War II. Written in 1945, the constitution of the United Nations Educational, Scientific and Cultural Organization (UNESCO) states that there should be 'full and equal opportunities for education for all'. This was backed up in 1948 with the Universal Declaration of Human Rights. Article 26 begins with 'everyone has the right to education', and goes a bit further by saying 'education shall be free, at least in the elementary and fundamental stages'.

Okay, so a global agreement that education is important was made 60 years ago, but still it hasn't happened. In 1990 UNESCO had another crack at providing universal education at the world conference on Education for All. At the time:

- ✔ More than 100 million children, including at least 60 million girls, had no access to primary schooling
- ✔ More than 960 million adults, two-thirds of them women, were illiterate
- ✔ More than 100 million children and countless adults failed to complete basic education programs
- ✔ Millions more went to school but did not acquire essential knowledge and skills

In 2000, UNESCO held a World Education Forum and reported that education for all 'remains a distant goal in many countries'. In fact, while the Asia Pacific had made significant improvements, other regions, such as sub-Saharan Africa, had gone backwards. So the target dates were reset for 2015. This target was included in the Millennium Development Goals, which support universal primary education, in particular encouraging access to education for girls.

You don't have to ponder too long on that century of good intentions to wonder if these new education goals will be met this time, or if the dates will be reset yet again and the goal continues to be an ever-receding one.

Diagnosing the complaint

Lots of things have got in the way of the program to educate everyone. Wars, natural disasters and global politics all block attempts to deliver education. The main reasons, however, are poverty and government spending decisions. Poverty can have an impact at both the individual and the national level.

On an individual level, living in poverty means that parents or carers can't afford to let the kids off work, or can't pay the school fees. Yep, you read that right — it's not uncommon for children to not go to school because they're working and earning an income to assist in supporting their families. It surprises many people to know that in some of the poorest regions, parents are required to buy uniforms for their kids to attend school.

On a national level, providing education (especially if it's free), depends on government spending. If the country is poor, then funding education is tough and is made even more difficult if the government has a large international debt. Chapter 20 details the extreme debt faced by the poorest countries and how that debt has robbed many nations of services like education.

During the Education For All decade of the 1990s, several countries (Ethiopia, Honduras, Nicaragua and Zambia) had to spend considerably more on repaying debt than they spent on education.

Of course, even a little money can go a long way if spent wisely. A report to the UNESCO Forum encouraged governments to consider not only the amount of money spent on education (commonly compared with the amount spent on the military), but also how that money is being spent.

Educating a nation isn't just about providing schools and books and teachers; it's also about dealing with issues of:

- Parent/carer income
- Child labour
- School policies regarding fees and uniforms
- International debt repayments
- Government spending priorities

Missing out, dropping out

All the Millennium Development Goals established by the United Nations in 2000 have targets and criteria for monitoring progress towards those targets. The target for the goal of universal education is to ensure that all boys and girls complete a full course of primary schooling. The first criterion measuring progress towards that target is the number of enrolments in primary school. Obviously if kids are in the fields working instead of going to school, they're not getting much of an education.

The criteria set down in the millennium goals also measure the number of students going on to secondary school and the literacy of the young adult population (15- to 24-year-olds). This goes some way to answering the important question of whether they have the 'basic education' deemed necessary for doing well in the modern world.

As highlighted in Table 10-1, estimates of education enrolment and attainment published in the 2006 Human Development Report provide a snapshot of the differences in access to education around the world.

Table 10-1	Education Enrolment and Attainment		
Country	Net Primary Enrolment Ratio (%, 2005)	Net Secondary Enrolment Ratio (%, 2005)	Children Reaching Grade 5 (% of Grade 1 Students, 2004)
Australia	97	86	86
Burkina Faso	45	11	76
Indonesia	96	58	89
Mexico	98	65	94
Mozambique	77	7	62
Niger	40	8	65
Norway	99	96	97
United Arab Emirates	71	62	95
United States	92	89	No data available

Source: United Nations Development Program, Human Development Report 2007.

The figures in Table 10-1 don't provide a complete picture on their own. They compare the number of students at different levels in the same year, and include things like home schooling in some countries but not others. It is clear from the figures, though, that a lot of kids are missing out, and even more drop out of education before they acquire basic skills.

Mozambique, for example, has increased its primary school enrolment from less than half in 1991 to more than three-quarters in 2005. A huge improvement . . . except less than two-thirds of the children who start primary school stay long enough to reach Year 5, and almost no-one goes on to high school. Want a comparison between rich and poor? Take another look at the figures for Norway on the line below Niger. It's clear why Education for All has to be measured by more than simple primary school enrolments.

Quality counts

Getting kids to school is a good start to an education, but what they do when they get there is also important. Providing good quality education shouldn't be traded off against providing more seats at school. It's notoriously difficult to work out exactly what affects quality and how to measure it, but some of the things to look for are:

- **Resources:** Do students and teachers have the equipment they need for learning? It's pretty hard to learn literacy skills if you don't have books to read, or pens and paper, or even chalk and a chalkboard, to practise writing with.

- **Teachers:** What are the standard training and working conditions?

  What kind of training and professional development do teachers have? In the Congo, for example, UNESCO estimates that 43 per cent of teachers don't meet the minimum standard of having nine years of schooling before teaching.

  What are the working conditions of teachers? Do they get paid? Is it an appropriate salary? Has housing been provided for teachers working in remote areas or small communities?

  What is the ratio of students to teachers? The smaller the class size, the more time the teacher has to meet the individual needs of each student. In North America the regional average is 13 students to each teacher, in West Asia, however, it's 41:1 and in sub-Saharan Africa it's 44:1. In six countries in sub-Saharan Africa the ratio shoots up to over 60 to 1.

- **Curriculum:** Is what students are learning relevant to them? Will it help them earn a reasonable livelihood, or become global citizens? Are they being taught using methods that encourage critical thinking, innovation and curiosity to learn more?

Report card says, 'Could do better'

The Global Campaign for Education decided to give out report cards to nations for their progress in educating the world's poor. Overall, the report cards read, 'Tries hard, but could do better.'

The report card actually evaluates the achievement of rich countries in supporting the education needs of poorer countries. It holds those countries accountable for meeting the promises they made under the Millennium Development Goals to help educate the poor. In 2007 rich countries weren't doing as well as you might hope. The results are obvious in Table 10-2. For more information on this topic, we recommend you check out the Teacher's Remarks, available at www.campaignforeduction.org/schoolreport (download the 'School Report Cards' document).

Table 10-2   School Reports, 22 Richest OECD Countries, 2007

Country	Grade	Country	Grade
Netherlands	A	France	D
Norway	A	Portugal	D
Denmark	B	Germany	D
United Kingdom	B	Switzerland	D
Luxembourg	B	Spain	D
Sweden	B	Japan	D
Ireland	B	Australia	E
Finland	C	Italy	E
Canada	C	United States	E
New Zealand	C	Greece	E
Belgium	C	Austria	E

Source: www.campaignforeduction.org/schoolreport.

Australia and the United States rank poorly for their failure to meet internationally recognised aid targets, and for failing to provide their fair share of the funding required for education in the poorest countries.

The countries that need the most help with meeting the education objectives are in Africa and include the poorest countries in the world. Chad, Eritrea, Niger and Guinea are among the ten worst education performers identified by the United Nations Education, Scientific and Cultural Organization (UNESCO). These countries pop up all the way through this book because they struggle on so many fronts.

How Learning Affects Life Chances

When kids complain about having to go to school, or are caught skipping classes, you're probably tempted to say, 'You'd better go. School's important for your future'. But why? Exactly how does having an education affect someone's chances in life?

People who have not been formally educated, or have only a few or disrupted years of formal schooling, can still lead fulfilling and successful lives. However, their choices are more limited, particularly the types of work that are available to them. In an era when written communication and information technology are so important, a lack of literacy or numeracy skills is a huge disadvantage.

Education also has a big impact on people's ability to deal with and engage in government and citizenship, their health and their children's health, and the power they exercise in their daily life — the freedom and opportunity to choose.

Learning is good for your health

Better health seems like an unlikely benefit of a good education. It's easier to see the connection between education and getting a job than between education and good health. Research carried out over the last decade by the United Nations Children's Fund (UNICEF) showed, however, that there is a correlation: More years spent at school offer health benefits for the person who went to school, and for their family as well. In particular, the more years a girl spends at school, the lower the infant mortality rate of her children will be.

There are three main ways education positively benefits health:

- **Learning about health:** Health education can be a unit studied at school on its own, or it can form part of other subjects like science or physical education. Some adult literacy classes use health education documents as learning materials for students. School provides people with opportunities to learn about nutrition, sanitation and various illnesses along with information on how to prevent or manage them.

- **Institutional support:** For a variety of reasons, food programs have been successfully combined with education in many countries. The kids who go to school have lunch (and sometimes breakfast) provided for them. The improved nutrition helps maintain and improve physical health. Other services are delivered through schools as well. Kids at schools get connected to the system.

- **Acquiring life skills:** Having an education gives people skills and confidence to manage their own health and their children's. Familiarity with school helps people to use modern medical services, take medicine and use equipment correctly. In Honduras, when the government gave out rehydration kits to help with diarrhoea in young children, it was found that mothers who had gone to school were more likely to use the kits, and to use them correctly.

TIP

The literacy question

For people with good literacy skills it's hard to imagine what it would be like *not* to be able to read or write. You probably learnt these skills when you were very young, so they seem automatic to you. For people with learning difficulties or a poor education, struggling to obtain basic information is a daily reality. Important information is locked away from them because they can't read. Everything from catching a bus or going to the movies, to entering a raffle or registering to vote becomes a complex and potentially embarrassing struggle.

You can get a taste of how challenging things become when you look at information in a different language, particularly one that uses a different alphabet. An easy way to try this out is to go to a Web site like Wikipedia,

www.wikipedia.org. The home page of that site lists a wide range of languages. Pick a language you don't know, one that uses unfamiliar characters (for an English speaker this might include Russian, Greek, Japanese and Arabic — to name just a few!). Have a look at the information that comes up, try to navigate the page and run a search, or identify the link to the English Wikipedia. Feeling frustrated and left out, yet?

You might like to try an experiment in functional illiteracy (a very limited ability to read and write, but not enough to really get by) by trying to do searches and read the results in a language you have some familiarity with. It's incredibly slow going, and you know you're not really understanding what's written. Try to imagine life being like this all the time.

Lifting livelihood through learning

The most obvious benefit of education? It sets you up with the skills and knowledge for future employment and, hopefully, a secure livelihood. You know from experience how a primary- and secondary-school education provides the basis of further training required for the vast majority of jobs in rich countries. It's easy for you to see how education determines the range of jobs available and the kind of salary you'll get for doing them.

The individual benefits of employment are measurable, even in countries where agriculture is the main source of employment. A UNICEF survey shows that a basic education results in greater productivity compared with situations where agricultural workers aren't educated. As the economy develops, having more years at school becomes even more important, because employment opportunities shift from the agricultural sector, to manufacturing, and then to services and information technology–based opportunities.

Education has a positive effect well beyond the actual skills it teaches. A range of theories exist to explain why education has such a strong and broad influence, but it's clear that going to school encourages people to approach problems differently. In addition to the skill required by employers, having an education can encourage people to

- Feel confident
- Follow directions more effectively
- Behave in ways preferred by employers
- Adapt more quickly to change and challenges
- Learn to use new technologies and techniques faster

This confidence and adaptability can also help people take advantage of self-employment and entrepreneurial opportunities.

Embracing the power of citizenship

Education is as an empowering experience, particularly when children are encouraged to think critically, to question and to debate. The 2000 World Education Forum agreed that dealing with social issues and encouraging democracy relied on countries having 'informed citizens'.

Going to school helps people to participate in political processes. It teaches

- The political processes and how they work
- Values and attitudes that form political stances
- Examples (both good and bad) of justice and governance
- Awareness of social issues and the impact of government policy

Empowering women, helping men

Girls make up the majority of children who miss out on school, yet the World Bank stated in an October 2007 report on women's empowerment that 'there is no investment more effective for achieving development goals than educating girls'.

Chapter 8 explores the reasons that sending girls to school is an effective tool for battling poverty. In short, women are the backbone of family life and instrumental in keeping communities healthy and in passing on knowledge. Educating girls multiplies the effect of that education throughout the community in a number of ways:

✔ Educating both girls and boys doubles the number of people with the skills required for a wider range of paid employment, and for seeking out entrepreneurial opportunities.

✔ Girls who are educated are more politically empowered, can challenge negative stereotypes and discrimination against women, and pass on the empowerment they have achieved.

✔ Many girls will one day become mothers, and in raising their children, influence the future of their communities.

✔ The more years of education a girl has, the more likely she is to wait before starting a family and the fewer children she's likely to have. This helps to lower the population growth and enhance the economic development of a struggling nation.

✔ In many households, women typically make decisions about the children. When the mother is educated, her children are more likely to go to school themselves and to have better health care at home.

Educated people build better countries

The benefits of education on health, political engagement and gender balance go beyond each individual. Education also has a collective social impact. Low education rates right now mean less educated adults and more chance of suffering from extreme poverty in the future. Educated people have smaller families, later in life, contribute more to the economic growth of their country and participate more in the process of building a stronger nation.

Illuminating the Future

You can be forgiven for feeling that a century of failures means there is little hope for the future. In the first section of this chapter, 'Education for All', we listed some of the opportunities lost for millions of people who didn't get to go to school as children, or get basic literacy and numeracy programs as adults. Here are some reasons not to sink into despair.

Hope rises from lost opportunities

There have been some remarkable successes with education: It has lifted millions of people out of poverty, and the effort goes on. Education is still an important goal, and some rich countries give a lot of thought to education as part of their foreign aid programs and debt relief schemes.

It is good news that the Millennium Development Goals described in Chapter 18 take account of past failures and set targets and criteria to measure success. The United Nations' Human Development Report is a publicly available document that reports on that progress.

Leaping off the bottom rung

Poor countries can make remarkable accomplishments by educating their young and giving a second chance to adults who missed out the first time around. Tanzania provides a striking example.

In 1991, Tanzania had a net primary enrolment ratio of only 49 per cent. By 2004, however, it had jumped up to 86 per cent! Not only were more children going to school, but a lot of them were staying — in 2003 the number of grade 5 students was 88 per cent of those who had started grade 1.

What happened? How did one of the world's poorest countries make such progress towards national basic education?

First, came a strong internal commitment to education and literacy. The vision statement of the Ministry of Education and Vocational Training is: 'To have a Tanzanian who is well educated, knowledgeable, skilled, and culturally mature to handle national and international challenges'.

Second, the government backed up commitment with spending. In 2002 Tanzania abolished school fees for primary education. Unsurprisingly this led to a big jump in enrolments (it's been so good that one of Tanzania's main challenges at the moment is finding enough teachers, and providing sufficient education materials for all the students). Tanzania financed this through government planning and spending decisions, and with targeted support from its development partners (other governments, non-government organisations and agencies like the World Bank).

Chapter 11

Livelihoods Lost

Poverty is a trap because it reduces your options. If you're desperate, you might take a job that doesn't recognise your basic human rights, or pay you sufficiently to feed your family properly, or give you time to study so that you can get a better job. The poorest people in the world are vulnerable to exploitation and there are plenty of employers willing to take advantage of them.

Battling Exploitation at Work

The fundamental impacts of poverty — lack of water, food, housing and health — are life threatening. Compared with those fundamental issues, employment prospects tend to be treated as a secondary problem. Unfortunately, exploitation compounds the effects of poverty. You can't get ahead if your work damages your health and pays next to nothing.

The global economy employs billions of poor people. The question is whether employment offers people a decent life, or becomes a trap.

Working without rules

A characteristic of rich countries is the wide range of regulations governing safety at work, pollution, wage levels, taxation and so on. These regulations are a constant source of complaint, and humour, in most rich countries. You have probably joked about a government regulation with your friends.

Poor countries have the opposite problem. People have to work without any regulations to protect their health, safety or income.

That *unregulated economy* is also known as the informal sector or informal economy. It means what it says — there are no rules.

The *informal sector* is not part of a country's official economy. People who have jobs in the informal sector don't pay taxes or work for an official organisation or registered business. The advantages of unregulated work are that it's flexible, provides some income and can give some hope to the poorest people. In low-income countries, the informal economy can account for over 50 per cent of the entire economy compared with about 5 per cent in high-income countries.

The problem, though, is that a lack of regulation nearly always leads to exploitation, even to the indentured labour so common today it's known as the new slavery.

Frustrated by regulations in your life? An unregulated economy possibly sounds like nirvana. Problem is, it has a very big downside. Without rules, protection comes at a price. That means that the law of the jungle prevails and the tough rise to the top. Unless you're at the top of a criminal cartel, then the pay in the informal sector is a lot less, too. Some workers in poor countries work for up to 18 hours a day, but still earn too little to feed their families.

Regulations are required to guarantee that people can expect to carry out decent work. *Decent work* has a formal definition. It means that a person:

- Does some kind of productive job
- Receives a fair salary
- Works in a safe place
- Has some kind of decision-making power
- Has equal opportunities to get ahead

The International Labor Organisation (ILO) released a report in 1999 known as *Decent Work* that notes, 'All people should have full access to income-earning opportunities. Decent work marks the high road to economic and social development, a road in which employment, income and social protection can be achieved without compromising workers' rights and social standards.'

Getting nowhere on the farm

Up until the last decade, global poverty has been rural poverty. Subsistence farmers, whose traditional way of life was spartan at best, have been disrupted by modernisation, violence or the collapse of their traditional markets. These events have destabilised their traditional way of life, but not brought them the benefits of the developed world. Villagers in the rainforests of Papua or western Brazil, nomads in Africa and Asia, and the indigenous people of the mountains in South America and Nepal are examples of the world's poorest rural dwellers.

The rise in urban poverty has changed the nature of global poverty, but only by creating hundreds of millions of newly poor people. In fact, despite the vast increase in the number of poor people living in cities, three-quarters of the world's poor still live in rural areas.

Progress in reducing rural poverty has stalled. In the 1990s, progress fell to less than one-third of the rate needed to meet the United Nations' commitment to halve world poverty by 2015. Partly because of a new focus on the urban poor, aid to agriculture — the main source of income for the rural poor — has fallen by two-thirds.

The challenges to the income-earning capacity of rural communities are generally related to agriculture and include:

- Lack of support from central governments
- Inadequate employment choices
- Control of crop prices by wealthy countries (see Chapters 16 and 19 for more details)
- Exploitation by landlords, warriors or military-backed industrialists
- Inappropriate or nonexistent land ownership systems
- The introduction of genetically modified crops that forces farmers to buy seed annually instead of stockpiling it from one year to the next

The challenges facing the rural poor are mounting rather than receding. The most recent Rural Poverty Report from the International Fund for Agricultural Development includes a list of actions required to overcome the disadvantages faced by the rural poor. That list includes:

- Legally secure entitlements to assets (especially land and water)
- Technology (above all for increasing the output and yield of food staples)

✔ Access to markets

✔ Opportunities to participate in decentralised resource management

✔ Access to microfinance

Employment options for the urban poor

Living successfully in a poor city involves struggle, endurance and resilience. Very few people in developing countries get much benefit from social security systems. Somehow they have to find the resources to provide the basic needs for themselves and their families.

How on earth do the urban poor survive or get ahead?

✔ **Professional work.** This is at the top of the tree. Even in the poorest cities, an elite workforce manages business, the professions and government. Entry to these elites is limited by education, family background and connections. Also, jobs in government aren't always well paid. Because of the size of the civil service, and the poverty of the government, even comparatively high-status white-collar workers sometimes get paid too little to make ends meet. This means those workers need to supplement their main income from other sources, which consequently often leads to widespread corruption.

✔ **Permanent jobs in industry.** These are keenly sought after, but often it's the exception rather than the rule. In countries like China, India and Brazil, where manufacturing has expanded quickly, factories provide employment for many. Workers can often earn more in the city than they can on the farm or on the streets. But many modern factories are simply sweatshops.

✔ **Service jobs.** In sectors like transport, tourism and the retail trade, service jobs provide employment but, typically, these jobs aren't permanent, wages are low and the hours are long.

✔ **Domestic work.** This type of work employs millions of women and children. As the urban middle class has grown, so has demand for cleaners, gardeners, housemaids and nannies. Women from rural areas, with limited education and not many options, fill a lot of these jobs. Millions of children also work as home help. Domestic work is not always rosy for women. Read more about that in Chapter 8.

✔ **Street vending.** At its simplest, vending is just a retail business that requires very little capital. Street vending provides livelihood for millions around the world. Vendors buy a small quantity of a saleable item — newspapers, candy, drinks — and sell them at a higher price. But the competition is tough and the margins tight. Vendors can be stuck with items that can't be sold — like spoiled food or yesterday's news. A few vendors successfully build up their business and become small wholesalers, supplying other vendors.

✔ **Urban agriculture.** Small-lot farms helps people stretch their resources. Small animals, especially chickens, can be kept in many city areas, and this also has environmental benefits by reducing the amount of organic waste. Small plots of land, including otherwise unused strips along roadsides and river banks, can grow small but useful food crops. Balconies and roofs can serve the same purpose. The section on urban farms in Chapter 14 discusses this in more detail.

✔ **Begging.** One way of surviving that has become a stereotypical image of poor people in big cities is begging. It attracts moral critics at times, but in some cultures it has been highly honoured — for example among some Catholic religious orders committed to poverty and among Buddhist monks in Thailand. Mostly begging is a last resort for the poor, though some children and disabled adults are drawn into the practice through organised syndicates. Begging is also connected with human trafficking. For example, organised gangs in Eastern Europe send groups of women to beg in wealthy Western cities.

✔ **Crime.** The pressures of poverty encourage some criminal activity. Crime is a pretty risky way to make a living, but it's present in all societies. Weak and sometimes corrupt policing, inadequate legal systems, and a culture of gang violence also encourage crime. Theft is the most common crime around the world and is illegal everywhere, but enforcement is often weak. Many poor people simply see the opportunity to steal as a matter of survival. Organised crime syndicates often romanticise crime as a way out of poverty, much as other cultures might promote music or sports stars.

✔ **Scavenging.** Rag-picking or scavenging through the mountains of garbage that cities produce is another way of making a living. Rag-pickers look for anything of value or that might be useful to someone. Scavenging is a vital environmental service because it cuts down the volume of garbage and helps recycle useful materials. But the risk of disease and injury can be severe.

✔ **Prostitution.** An astonishing number of women, and also many men and children, resort to prostitution as a means of livelihood throughout the developing world, especially in cities. The State Department of the United States estimates 100,000 women work in brothels in Mumbai, for example, with tens of thousands more sex workers on the streets.

Sweatshops in the developed world

Poor countries are plagued with sweatshops but lots of developed countries have their fair share too. In the United States, many garment workers, especially in Los Angeles, are forced to work in illegal conditions for less than the legal minimum wage. The United States has few labour inspectors, and enforcement of the rules is lax.

In Australia about 300,000 people (mostly women) make clothes at home for major retailers. These home-workers get paid about two to three dollars an hour and often work 12–18 hours a day, 6 or 7 days a week. Because they work at home it's hard for them to organise into unions. They have little bargaining power with their employers, and Occupational Health and Safety protections aren't applied.

Forcing the Desperate to Work

For every person battling poverty in an underpaid job, another two are even worse off. People who are made to work against their will are rarely paid, let alone paid enough to help them to escape poverty. Because the world's focus is on those dying of malnutrition, the people caught up in a web of exploitation and oppression are largely ignored. The lives they live, though, are fairly gruesome.

Defining slavery

When you think of slavery you probably think of Africans dragged across the Atlantic to work on cotton plantations in the southern states of America in the eighteenth and nineteenth centuries. You may be surprised to know that slavery still exists, it's growing fast and has changed considerably.

Slavery in the United States was outlawed in 1865. It was easy for white slave owners to justify their purchase of people by referring to the differences between the races. This otherness could be defined in any way — different religion, tribe, skin colour, language and customs. Maintaining these differences became more difficult and led to inane justifications, but slavery was tolerated because of the money that could be made by the owners.

Even before slavery was outlawed, it had become less popular in the United States. The business of buying and selling people provoked moral outrage, but was also quite expensive. A slave owner had responsibility for the slaves he owned — the very young, the old and sick, as well as the productive workers between 25 and 50 years of age. Legal obligations were only a small part of the reason — basically slaves were a scarce commodity and had to be nurtured. This took time, energy and money.

Slavery has kept up with the times. It's still ruthless ... and profitable. Slavery is big business but slaveholders feel no need to justify, explain or defend their methods. Slaves are often from the same country, race and religion as the slaveholder. Why pay to ship people around the world? Slaves are not looked after when they are old or sick. The children of slaves are not provided for. Because the world population is so large there's no economic reason for slave-owners to care for their slaves. Table 11-1 outlines the characteristics of the new slavery.

Table 11-1	The Characteristics of The New Slavery	
Characteristic	**Traditional**	**New**
Legal ownership	Asserted	Avoided
Purchase price	High	Low to zero
Profits	Low	High
Availability of slaves	Low	High
Long-term care	Well maintained	No maintenance
Ethics	Important	Unimportant

Want to buy a bargain?

It's easy to think about slavery as something that happens in a far-off place where you can't control it, therefore can do nothing about it. If you knew of a slave being kept by a family member or friend, you would do something about it. But some slavery is hidden so deeply in the global economy that no-one sees it, although people in other countries may benefit from it.

In Brazil large-scale charcoal production is mainly based on slave labour. This charcoal has an important role in steel production. The steel is made into car parts that make up one-quarter of Brazil's exports. Britain imports US$1.6 billion of goods from Brazil each year. The car parts are used in British cars.

Slavery lowers the production costs; these are then passed up the chain, improving profits for producers and retailers. Most people love bargains and don't often ask how products can be produced so cheaply.

Types of slavery

The idea that people can be enslaved in the modern world is unbelievable to many people. It's easier to understand how it can exist if you're aware of the different ways people are enslaved. The following sections provide some clues.

Chattel slavery

Chattels are dependants, belonging to a person. A chattel slave is born or married into slavery. The whole family is indebted to the slaveholder and each family member has to work to pay off the debt.

Debt bondage

Debt bondage was established thousands of years ago. A person becomes bonded when their labour is the only way to repay a loan.

It has been estimated by Human Rights Watch that as many as ten million people are in debt bondage in India alone, although the real figure is much higher because women and children are not counted.

Contract slavery

This is slavery that has been supposedly legalised by the existence of a document, signed by the slave, agreeing to the conditions of their enslavement. A contract to work is often used to trick an illiterate worker into slavery. The contract is used to make the slaveholder look legal and above board.

War slavery

This has happened recently in Burma. Men, women and children are all used as soldiers by the government. Women and children are used as domestic help for the soldiers and move around the country with them. This kind of slavery is unique because it's committed and sanctioned by a government.

When is a worker not a slave?

It is estimated by *New Internationalist* magazine that up to 27 million people live in slavery worldwide. This is equivalent to the population of Canada. Although many people live and work in very bad conditions they're not all slaves. The criteria that differentiate slavery from other forms of oppression include:

- A slave is someone who's forced to work through mental or physical threat
- The slaveholder controls the slave
- The slave is dehumanised by being bought or sold
- The slave has physical constraints, with little or no freedom of movement, sometimes literally being tied to the workplace

Although it may appear that bonded labour is not as bad as slavery, it is insidious because it's often continuous through one person's life and on to the next generation.

Unfree labour is a collective term used to describe work performed under duress, such as the threat of imprisonment, abandonment or destruction of property. *Forced labour* describes the same type of situation but involves the threat of violence. The coercion may include the threat of killing another member of the victim's family. The United Nations definition considers forced labour to be anything where someone does work under the threat of a penalty, but excludes civil penalties such as labour as part of a prison sentence.

Anyone for a smoke?

Beedis are the small, unfiltered, low-tobacco cigarettes made in India by small children. Tens of thousands of American young people smoke them every day, although they're not legal in many developed countries.

Each child who rolls beedis in India has to complete a six-month 'apprenticeship' during which time they're not paid at all. The work is piece-based so each child will end up earning roughly 1–4 rupees a day, rolling upwards of 2,000 beedis each.

Although the work is not physically hard in the sense of heavy lifting or strenuous activity, the days are long, up to 12 hours, with no respite or days off, and the conditions are cramped, with up to 20 small children in a room with all their tobacco leaves around them.

The children often develop back, hip and neck pain, as well as infections from the leaves, because the tobacco gets under their fingernails and they're not able to wash. Sunday is given as a day off but has to be used as a make-up day if any time was spent ill or asleep during the week. These children are often cooped up together, badly fed and have no opportunity to visit their family.

Reversing the Growth of Slavery

Slavery needs economic as well as social preconditions to occur. The slaveholder knows there's a profit in slavery, and simply needs a human with no other options. Slaves have no power to defend themselves legally or physically. The current growth in slavery has come about because of the large number of extremely poor people, with no legal status, crowded into cities that are too large for governments to control.

With the population of the world's largest cities growing so quickly, the only thing that can reverse the rapid increase in slavery is the eradication of extreme poverty so that the poorest billion people have basic human rights.

Why does everyone turn a blind eye?

Slavery has been outlawed in most countries. It is outlawed under the United Nations anti-slavery convention of 1956 and by the Forced Labour Convention in 1930, as well as being prohibited by most countries by their constitutions or civil codes. Even though slavery is illegal, having access to a pool of docile, dependent and above all cheap labour is a very attractive proposition for many unscrupulous people.

Camel Jockeys

Small boys in Pakistan can fetch as much as US$500–$1000 plus $120 a month for the family while they race camels in Saudi Arabia, usually for a period of about 2–3 years. This money can lift a family out of endemic poverty.

But being a camel jockey is a dangerous business. The boys are often beaten for not working hard enough. They can be injured with broken bones from falls or even be killed from being trampled by the camels. One small broken body is flown back to Karachi airport nearly every month. The families rarely complain about their loss because the bodies are accompanied with approximately US$25,000.

The Pakistani government has not only outlawed the selling of small boys for the rich man's sport but they actively hunt out brokers and buyers. They have little luck taking brokers to court, however, because the families are reluctant to complain because of the money they've received.

How modern enslavement works

A girl is sold by her parents for 50,000 baht (US$2,000) in Thailand. The contract between the slave broker and the parent means this sum has to be repaid by the labour of the girl before she can leave or send any money home. In some case this money is given as a loan to the parents, but with such a high rate of interest that the loan can never be repaid.

Once the contract is signed the girl is taken to the city and sold to a brothel. The debt is now 100,000 baht, double the original sum. The girl realises what she has to do and now knows how she will be treated. She tries to escape. She's caught because she has no money and nowhere to go. She's told the trouble she has caused has increased her debt to 200,000 baht.

The debt is now four times the original sum, and with charges added for food, medicine and fines for 'bad' behaviour the debt grows.

Each time the girl gets a client he pays 400 baht — a higher price than usual because the girl is young and new. One hundred baht goes to reduce her debt and repay her keep, 100 baht to the brothel owner and 200 baht to her pimp.

Over time the debt increases with no hope of it ever being repaid; she is totally enslaved. Any dissent is punished with beatings and a raising of the debt. This leads to a totally controlled and compliant economic source for the people who do make a profit.

New slavery and the global economy

It is hard to work out how much money is made by slaves for the slaveholders but we can do some estimates.

If we assume there are ten million bonded workers in India, the annual profit generated (less an initial purchase cost of US$50) could be in the order of US$860 million.

If we assume 200,000 (UN figures) women and children are enslaved as prostitutes in Thailand, we could give a conservative estimate of roughly US$10.5 billion is making its way into the economy.

Under British immigration law, returning nationals are allowed to bring domestic servants with them. This includes cooks, housekeepers, maids and nannies. By law, these servants are supposed to be over 17 years old and should have been employed by the family for over a year. This system is often abused because the domestic, who's often not paid and has no choice about leaving the employment, can't speak English and the family will often produce a false contract to satisfy migration officials.

If the 'slave' escapes while in the United Kingdom, running away from the slaveholder, they're then in breach of the Immigration Act that allowed them into the country in the first place, so they become an illegal migrant. Often the slave has no other choice but to stay with the family while in Britain.

Overcoming exploitation

The organisation of the labour movement was a major feature of the political and economic landscape during the twentieth century. Social democratic governments in Europe, the United Kingdom and countries of the Commonwealth have built significant protections for workers into the legislation of most of the developed world.

The union movement in the United States has achieved great success in some industries, but tens of millions of Americans are regarded as 'working poor'. Many labour advocates feel this is why the problem of sweatshops has reappeared in the United States. Despite the uneven history of American unions, the efforts of politicians and lobbyists have maintained and improved working conditions in the United States over the last century.

Democratic governments have to protect the individuals they govern or they may not win their vote. This is one reason why there's a strong international focus on democratic elections and condemnation of dictators and oppressive regimes as a part of the campaign against extreme poverty. In some cases, commercial interests put pressure on governments to allow exploitation at the same time that the rest of the world demands an end to that exploitation. One feature of the new slavery described in this chapter is that international companies exploit sweatshops in poor countries to maximise their profits. These companies have enormous buckets of money — sometimes as big as the national governments of the country where they want to do business. That money helps find ways around the regulations that should protect workers.

Some campaigns have successfully ended exploitation of poor workers by using pressure from customers in developed countries. This pressure consists of publicity campaigns, accompanied by boycotts that destroy the profits made by exploiting workers. An example of such campaigns include the No Sweatshops campaign that has operated against Nike since 1998. This campaign targeted Nike because the company is an industry leader and experienced a high number of strikes and complaints about working conditions in factories making shoes for Nike across Asia.

Chapter 12

Getting Sicker, Dying Younger

. . . .

. . . .

Good health is central to human happiness and wellbeing. Healthy young people have a good chance of living a long and productive life. If you live in poverty, it's more likely that you'll get sicker and die younger.

In this chapter, you find out why people living in poverty have worse health than everybody else. You discover that where you live, how you live and what you know can affect your health. You find out why some common diseases can actually kill you if you're living in poverty and you also get an understanding about how different aspects of health are inter-related. Poverty, unfortunately, makes ill-health worse.

The Right to Health

Everyone in the world has the right to physical and mental health care. This means that governments are responsible for creating conditions in which everyone can be as healthy as possible. These conditions include:

- ✔ Nutritious food
- ✔ Adequate housing
- ✔ The availability of health services
- ✔ Healthy and safe working conditions

Some things influence your health indirectly; such as access to safe water, adequate sanitation and access to health-related education. Poor people in the developing world rarely have any of these advantages.

The 1948 Declaration of Human Rights describes the right to health care as part of 'an adequate standard of living'. The International Covenant on Economic, Social and Cultural Rights says that everyone has 'the right to the highest attainable standard of health'. People argue about what's adequate and what's attainable but the intention of these declarations is clearly to urge governments to provide health care to everyone in the population, not just a wealthy elite. Some people think that governments should provide a bare minimum of services, while other people think they should provide the best care possible.

What kills the poor

In both rich and poor countries, the biggest cause of death is cardiovascular disease. An estimated 17.5 million people died from cardiovascular disease in 2005, representing 30 per cent of all global deaths. This covers a wide range of disorders of the heart and blood vessels and includes:

- Coronary heart disease (heart attacks)
- Cerebrovascular disease (strokes, aneurisms and embolisms)
- Raised blood pressure (hypertension)
- Peripheral artery disease
- Rheumatic heart disease
- Congenital heart disease
- Heart failure

The major causes of cardiovascular disease are tobacco use, physical inactivity and an unhealthy diet. Poverty is a key risk factor and many poor people smoke, exercise inadequately and don't eat well. Incredibly, two out of three overweight and obese people now live in developing countries and by 2010, more obese people will live in developing countries than in the developed world.

While rich and poor countries have some causes of death in common, there are others that have far worse effects in poor countries — perinatal conditions, diarrhoeal diseases, tuberculosis, HIV/AIDS, malaria, and road traffic accidents. Most of these problems affect children more than adults and are easily preventable. A small investment in health can make a big difference to poor countries. When you compare the top ten killers in rich countries with poor countries (displayed in Table 12-1) it is obvious that simple sanitation, inoculation and medical care could save millions of lives. The solutions for AIDS, TB and malaria are discussed in the following sections. Perinatal disease responds well to simple medical care, and diarrhoeal diseases are generally caused by poor sanitation. Road traffic accidents are the result of poor regulation and infrastructure. These killers of the poor do not appear in the top ten causes of death in the developed world.

Table 12-1	Top 10 Causes of Death in High-Income and Low-Income Countries	
Cause	*% of Deaths (High Income)*	*% of Deaths (Low Income)*
Coronary heart disease	17.1	11.4
Stroke and other cerebrovascular diseases	9.8	6.4
Trachea, bronchus, lung cancers	5.8	-
Lower respiratory infections	4.3	9.5
Chronic obstructive pulmonary disease	3.9	3.4
Colon and rectum cancers	3.3	-
Alzheimer and other dementias	2.7	-
Diabetes mellitus	2.7	-
Breast cancer	1.9	-
Stomach cancer	1.8	-
HIV/AIDS	-	7.2
Perinatal conditions	-	6.2
Diarrhoeal diseases	-	5.2
Tuberculosis	-	3.5
Malaria	-	3.0
Road traffic accidents	-	2.1

HIV and AIDS

Acquired Immune Deficiency Syndrome (AIDS) is one of the biggest challenges facing the world. The Human Immunodeficiency Virus (HIV) that causes AIDS is transmitted through an exchange of body fluids, most commonly during unprotected sex. Once infected with HIV, the victim has a high probability of contracting AIDS, unless a full treatment program is implemented. AIDS causes death by weakening the victim's immune system. As a result, a range of secondary, opportunistic infections set in and the patient dies of one or more of these secondary diseases. Common examples of these secondary infections include fatal pneumonia, tuberculosis and Kaposi's sarcoma (a form of skin cancer).

AIDS is by far the leading cause of premature death in sub-Saharan Africa and is the fourth-biggest killer worldwide. Virtually no country in the world remains unaffected by HIV and AIDS, and the numbers of people infected are rising globally. AIDS has a disproportional impact on the poor.

AIDS is not only a health problem, but also a social problem, a cultural problem and an economic problem. AIDS has a profound and systemic impact on household income and sustainability. AIDS pushes people deeper into poverty as households lose their breadwinners, livelihoods are compromised and savings are consumed by the cost of health care and funerals. The death of young adults undermines the process of passing on knowledge and expertise — in land preparation, crop cultivation, handicrafts, cultural beliefs and traditions. Death from AIDS also places a greater burden on extended family and social networks. Many grandparents are the primary carers for young children who have been orphaned by AIDS.

AIDS has a significant effect on formal institutions. When trained professionals die, the capacity of institutions such as schools, universities, health services and government departments is diminished. Services are disrupted and the difficulties in meeting the needs of a population affected by HIV and AIDS are compounded.

Food security is also affected by the disease, particularly in countries where the majority of the population is engaged in agriculture. Because HIV and AIDS affect the most productive age group of the population, they threaten the food security of households, communities and nations. In turn, the lack of food also decreases the resistance of men, women and children to opportunistic infection and therefore accelerates the onset of the disease.

The effects flow to all parts of society. It's estimated that the Gross Domestic Product (GDP) shrinks by as much as 1–2 per cent annually in countries when more than 20 per cent of the population is infected by HIV. High infection rates create conditions where famine, repression or violent conflict and war occur more easily. In turn, these conditions accelerate the spread of HIV.

Learning to live with AIDS

For people in many poor countries, contracting AIDS (Acquired Immune Deficiency Syndrome) is a death sentence. But it needn't be. Treatment for HIV (the Human Immunodeficiency Virus that causes AIDS) is getting better all the time. Although AIDS is incurable, powerful drugs known as *antiretrovirals* can be used to manage the disease. These drugs strengthen the immune system and help people stay healthy for much longer. The combination of antiretroviral drugs, good nutrition and effective management of opportunistic infections has made it possible for some people to live with HIV for many decades. But this treatment is not available to everyone. The high cost of antiretroviral drugs has put them out of reach of most AIDS victims. This price barrier, combined with the lack of other medicines to treat the opportunistic infections that follow AIDS, means that AIDS victims in poor countries are dying at much higher rates than they need to.

When patent-protected antiretroviral treatments were first introduced, the cost was over US$10,000 per patient per year, putting the treatment out of reach of the vast majority of HIV patients in developing countries. Allowing developing countries to have access to much cheaper generic brands of antiretrovirals has given the opportunity of a new life to millions of poor people. In Brazil, antiretrovirals manufactured by the country's own pharmaceutical industry has kept costs low and has allowed more people to access life-prolonging treatment. From 1996 to 2002, Brazil saw a decrease in mortality rates of 40 to 70 per cent, plus a sevenfold drop in the need for hospitalisation.

Malaria

Mosquitoes are more than a nuisance — in some countries they're deadly. They carry parasites with a name that sounds like the brand of a plasma TV — Plasmodium. It's these parasites that cause malaria. Malaria is both preventable and curable, but more than a million people die of the disease every year, most of them in Africa. About 40 per cent of the world's population, mostly those living in the world's poorest countries, are at risk of malaria, and more than 500 million people become severely ill. Children are particularly affected and a child dies of malaria every 30 seconds.

Four different strains of malaria exist and not every kind actually kills. These are Plasmodium falciparum, P. vivax, P. malariae and P. ovale. Plasmodium falciparum and P. vivax are the most common. Plasmodium falciparum is by far the most deadly type of malaria infection.

Dying from malaria isn't the only problem (although that's certainly inconvenient). The disease has wide-ranging social and economic consequences because of lost productivity and long-term disruptions to normal life. The non-deadly forms of malaria still make a person really sick — fever, headache, chills, vomiting — and once the parasite's in your blood, malaria can recur year after year.

For kids, malaria's symptoms mean a lot of missed school, and the end result may be that a child with malaria never gets a proper education. Likewise, recurrent bouts of malaria mean that adults are regularly unable to work and that further contributes to a family's poverty. In a poor family, an unemployed parent can translate into two missed meals a day. That kind of loss in productivity is enough to send shudders down the spine of an economist. Malaria causes an average loss of 1.3 per cent of economic growth in countries where lots of people are infected. That loss accumulates to keep those tropical countries where malaria is prevalent at a serious economic disadvantage.

Tuberculosis

When Nicole Kidman's character Sabine dies of *consumption* at the end of the film *Moulin Rouge,* it's tuberculosis that consumes her. *Tuberculosis* (TB) is a contagious disease that afflicted many fictional heroines in eras past, but it is also widespread and fatal today. Someone in the world is newly infected with TB every second and one-third of the world's population is currently infected. The good news is that not everyone who's infected with TB actually gets sick from it — only 5–10 per cent, in fact.

Tuberculosis (TB) spreads like a cold. When infectious people cough, sneeze, talk or spit, they propel TB germs, known as bacilli, into the air. (Bacillus is a type of bacteria. Bacilli is the plural. You know the Latin: One octopus, two octopi!) A person needs only to inhale a small number of bacilli to be infected. Luckily, people with TB are only infectious when they are actually sick themselves.

When someone's immune system is weakened, their chances of becoming sick from TB are greater. And there's the downer for billions of poor people. For starters, in order to have a healthy immune system, you need enough nutritious food to eat. That's why one-third of the total TB cases in the world occur in the poverty-stricken countries of South East Asia.

TB's hold on people with a weakened immune system makes HIV and TB a lethal cocktail. The TB epidemic in Africa grew rapidly through the 1990s, mirroring the increase in HIV infections. Now, more people die from TB in Africa than anywhere else in the world. Someone who is HIV-positive and breathes in TB bacilli is many times more likely to become sick than an HIV-negative person. TB is a leading cause of death among people who are HIV-positive.

Cheap, simple nets defeat a killer

Malaria is easy to prevent. A five-year campaign in Kenya to reduce malaria infections and deaths by handing out millions of free insecticide-treated bed nets has had huge success. The program has reduced malaria-related deaths by almost half. Mosquitoes that carry malaria parasites are generally active at night, so bed nets are a cheap and effective way to stop people getting bitten. Insecticide-treated nets repel, disable or kill the mosquitoes.

Want to save a life? Send a net! Join the United Nations Foundation's Nothing but Nets campaign at www.nothingbutnets.net.

Not only is TB spreading through poor countries, some strains of TB are resistant to drugs. Drug-resistant TB develops when a TB patient doesn't complete a cure and the most virulent forms of the bacteria survive in their body, multiply and spread. A cure might be incomplete when

✔ A patient doesn't take all his or her medicine for the required period

✔ Doctors and health workers prescribe the wrong treatment

✔ The drug supply is unreliable

Drug-resistant TB is generally treatable, but it can take up to two years; and the treatment has side effects worse than the disease.

People living in poverty are sicker

The World Health Organization and World Bank have measured the impact of premature death and disability on a population. The measure's called the Disability-Adjusted Life Year or DALY. Figure 12-1 clearly shows that the vast majority of life years lost through illness are lost in the world's poorest countries.

The Disability-Adjusted Life Year (DALY) is a measure of the number of years of life that have been lost through disease. If the life expectancy of a healthy group of people is 75 years but they die at 50, a cost of 25 DALYs is awarded to the disease that killed them. DALYs can be calculated for the average victim of any particular disease or the average person, or, they can be accumulated for an entire population.

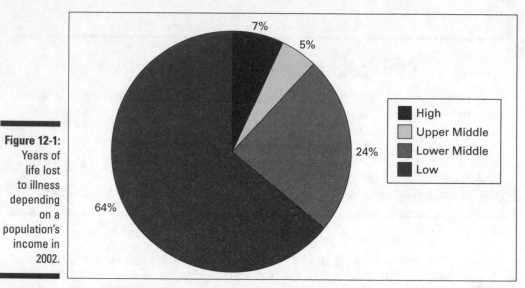

Source: World Health Organization.

Figure 12-1:
Years of
life lost
to illness
depending
on a
population's
income in
2002.

The poorest of the poor are the sickest. For the most part, that means the world's indigenous peoples. Chapter 3 describes in general terms the plight of indigenous people and the overall impact of poverty. Naturally, poverty has direct impacts on the health of indigenous people. Here are some of them:

✔ **Diabetes:** In some regions of Australia, Aboriginal and Torres Strait Islander communities have a diabetes prevalence rate as high as 26 per cent, which is six times higher than in the general population.

✔ **Living conditions:** In Rwandan Twa households, the prevalence of poor sanitation and lack of safe, potable water were respectively seven times and two times higher than for the national population.

✔ **Reproductive health:** For ethnic minorities in Vietnam, more than 60 per cent of childbirths take place without prenatal care compared with 30 per cent for the Kinh population, Vietnam's ethnic majority.

✔ **Suicide:** Among Inuit youth in Canada, suicide rates are among the highest in the world, at eleven times the national average.

✔ **Infant mortality:** Average infant mortality among indigenous children in Panama is over three times higher than that of the overall population (60–85 deaths per 1000 live births versus the national average of 17.6).

Going to the Doctor, Taking Medicine

People living in poverty get sicker and often stay sick for longer. For the most part, this is because poor countries don't have a functioning public health system so access to clinics, health professionals and medicine is limited. Globally, the world spends more than US$4.1 trillion every year on health, which averaged out is about US$639 per person. Of course, that health spending isn't averaged out and the difference between what poor and rich countries spend on their population's health is startling.

Norway's government spends more than any other on its population's health (US$4,508 per person each year), whereas Burundi spends the lowest (US$0.70 per person). The World Health Organization estimates that it takes a minimum of US$35 to US$50 per person per year to provide basic, life-saving services. That makes Burundi's 70 cents look like a heck of an underspend. In fact, there are 64 countries where the total money spent on health — by individuals, government and the private sector — is below the cost of the basic services necessary for survival. The outcome is simple: People die.

Not enough health workers

Health workers are people whose job is to improve other people's health. Doctors, nurses, pharmacists and laboratory technicians make up two-thirds of the world's health workers, working directly with patients. The other third are support workers, such as financial officers, cooks, drivers and cleaners. Worldwide, there are 59.8 million health workers.

Fifty-seven countries, most of them in Africa and Asia, face a severe health workforce crisis. There are fewer than three doctors per 10,000 people in many countries in sub-Saharan Africa, even though one-quarter of the world's sick people live there. It would take another four million health professionals to provide basic services to people across Africa and in rural areas of Asia.

The situation's made worse because of what's known as the *brain drain*. Thousands of doctors, nurses and pharmacists from developing countries have moved to wealthier Western nations in search of better-paid jobs and the chance to give their own children a good education. They leave behind bad pay and working conditions, and possibly an oppressive political climate. They also leave a huge gap in health services for the world's poor. Chapter 16 discusses this phenomenon in more detail.

Sub-Saharan Africa faces the greatest challenges. While it has 11 per cent of the world's population and 24 per cent of the global burden of disease, it has only 3 per cent of the world's health workers. Table 12-2 compares those figures with those for other continents. As the number of health workers declines, survival declines in proportion.

A direct relationship exists between the ratio of health workers to population and survival of women during childbirth and of children in early infancy. (For more information refer to Chapter 2.)

Table 12-2   Share of World Health Resources (America vs Africa)

	The Americas %	*Sub-Saharan Africa %*
Total population	14	11
Burden of disease	10	25
Health workers	42	3
Health expenditure	>50	<1

Source: World Health Organization

Not enough medicine

In many developing countries, sick people don't have access to life-saving medicine. Even simple drugs like pain relief and antibiotics aren't available to the poorest people in the world. Failing health systems are to blame. Drug storage and distribution systems are nonexistent or are poorly managed. The World Bank estimates that for every US$100 spent by African governments on drugs, only US$12 worth of medicines reaches patients.

Health system failures also mean that preventative medications like vaccines don't get to people who need them. Vaccines need to be kept between 2 and 8 degrees Celsius to remain viable. So, unless the required temperature is maintained from the time the vaccine's developed, to the time it gets used — called the *cold chain* — it stops working. Because of this, one of the cheapest and most effective ways to protect the health of the poorest children often doesn't get to those who need it.

International patent rules also affect people's access to drugs. *Patents* provide financial incentives for pharmaceutical companies to discover and develop new medicines. A patent protects the formula from being copied by lots of other companies and ensures that the company that developed the drug profits from it. But it also means that the companies can set the price as high as they want. As a result, sick people in the poorest countries can't afford to buy brand-name medicines because of the price.

Raising a Family

Raising a family is a challenging task that requires a significant investment in resources. The future of a society depends on the health of its children and their mothers, who are guardians of that future. Despite the progress made in the last 20 years, 10.6 million children and 529,000 mothers die each year as a result of poverty.

The death of every child is a tragedy. Imagine the headlines if the Pied Piper of Hamelin stole all the children under the age of five from France, Germany and Italy. Every year, that many children (more than ten million) die before they reach the age of five, most from preventable causes and almost all in poor countries. Six causes account for the death of three-quarters of these children: Pneumonia, neonatal pneumonia or sepsis, diarrhoea, malaria, preterm delivery and asphyxia at birth. All of these conditions respond to basic health care and sanitation.

Nutrition

Good nutrition is the cornerstone of good health. It strengthens the immune system, makes people stronger and helps children learn better. Freedom from hunger and malnutrition is a basic human right and is a fundamental prerequisite for human and national development. The stats explain why: Poor nutrition contributes to one out of two deaths associated with infectious diseases among children aged under five in developing countries.

Nutrition is important at every life stage. More than one in five of childhood deaths occurs during the first week of life, most due to malnutrition in the mother and foetus leading to low birth weights, and made worse by poor antenatal care and lack of skilled birth attendants. Simply feeding mothers properly would directly prevent about one-quarter of these deaths, and would indirectly prevent more than half of them. Combined with a reasonable level of care that included clean water and hygienic conditions, food security for pregnant women and nursing mothers would see infant death rates plummet.

Comparing bony babies

Mothers compare their babies with other babies in their community. Since the judgments they make are comparative, what happens if all the children in a community are malnourished?

A survey in Kerala in southern India showed that there were large discrepancies between the medical assessment of a child's weight and the mother's perception. Nearly half the children in the region were underweight, but almost all of the mothers described their children as normal. This isn't surprising, when those mothers don't have a healthy child to compare their own with.

The tragic aspect of this survey is that good nutrition in the first few years of a baby's life is vital to prevent lifelong physical and mental damage. Until this survey result was published, health workers had not realised that mothers did not understand their children were underweight. It's another reason why education and skilled care for mothers and children are keys to creating health societies.

Preventing disease through immunisation

Immunisation is arguably one the most cost-effective ways to create a healthier society. The initial investment is minimal and it requires no change in behaviour. The benefits are enormous. Not only does it prevent the spread of disease and save lives, but it also saves in health care costs over a long period of time. For example, a study of measles immunisation in Kenya showed that vaccination of 12.8 million children would result in a net saving in health costs of US$12 million over the following ten years; during that time it would prevent nearly four million cases of measles and 125,000 deaths. That's a good investment.

Cheap and effective solutions

The most dangerous threats to children's survival can be fought with relatively simple and inexpensive solutions.

- Breastfeeding provides nutrition and improves immunity to common, often life-threatening illnesses.
- Immunisation prevents measles and other diseases.
- Oral rehydration therapy can save a child from dying of diarrhoea.
- Antibiotics treat newborn sepsis and pneumonia.
- Insecticide-treated mosquito nets help prevent malaria.

Stopping the spots that kill lots

Lots of kids in the developing world die from measles. In these countries, it's the leading cause of death among young children, despite the availability of a safe and effective vaccine for the past 40 years. Measles is one of the most contagious diseases and almost all children who come into contact with the virus catch it if they're not immune. By itself, measles is pretty unpleasant, but it doesn't kill. Measles is more severe if children are malnourished or have weakened immune systems. Children do die from complications from measles. The most serious complications include blindness, brain inflammation, severe diarrhoea, ear infections and pneumonia. Pneumonia is the most common cause of death in children with measles.

Motherhood — a matter of life and death

Childbirth itself is fraught with danger. Every minute, at least one woman dies from complications related to pregnancy or childbirth, and it's the leading cause of death and disability among women of reproductive age in developing countries. The major direct causes of maternal morbidity and mortality include haemorrhage, infection, high blood pressure, unsafe abortion and obstructed labour. The tragedy is that they are easily preventable.

What would it take to save lives? Three simple things:

✔ **Care:** In the developed world, almost all women have somebody skilled to help deliver their baby. In the developing world, more than 50 per cent of women face birth alone, with a family member or with a traditional birth attendant who may or may not be trained. Women in rural areas are most likely to give birth without trained help. For a mother and her newborn, a skilled birth attendant can make the difference between life and death. Skilled care is not only critical for a safe delivery, but also vital during pregnancy and the first month after delivery. For all women to have the safety that this kind of care can provide, the World Health Organization estimates that the number of skilled attendants in developing countries needs to be increased by at least 333,000.

✔ **Nutrition:** Women who are well-nourished are stronger, with fewer complications and healthier babies. One in six infants born in developing countries have a low birth weight as a result of under-nutrition in their mothers. Under-nutrition increases the risk of neonatal deaths, and also causes learning disabilities, mental retardation, poor health, blindness and premature death.

✔ **Contraception:** Modern contraception can help a woman to separate her pregnancies so that she has time to recover physically and financially, and also to allow her to avoid pregnancy if she's unwell, or in danger, or too young or too old.

More school, better health

The better educated you are, the better your health. Statistics demonstrate a direct relationship, particularly with the education of girls. Because mothers are mostly in charge of raising children, the more they know about health and disease, the better.

Diarrhoea is one of the top five child killers in the world. It's also easily preventable and treatable — but only if you know how. The following safeguards are possibly commonsense to you, but are missing pieces of the puzzle that good health seems to be for many poverty-stricken mothers. This is just one of the many ways outlined in Chapter 10 that make education a critical link in alleviating the negative impacts of poverty.

✔ Drinking water from a safe source — or boiling it until it is safe — is a start.

✔ If a child does get sick, then washing hands and disposing of the waste safely is important to stop the spread of the disease.

✔ Getting children to wash their hands before eating reduces cases of the runs by up to 50 per cent.

✔ Treatment of sick children is also cheap and easy. It's the dehydration that kills them, so rehydrating them with a solution of salt and sugar will save their lives.

Living in a Toxic Environment

More than three million children under 5 years old die each year from environment-related causes and conditions. This makes the environment one of the most critical contributors to the global toll of more than ten million child deaths annually — as well as a very important factor in the health and wellbeing of their mothers.

Polluted indoor and outdoor air, contaminated water, lack of adequate sanitation, toxic hazards, disease vectors, ultraviolet radiation and degraded ecosystems are all important environmental risk factors for children and, in most cases, for their mothers. Particularly in developing countries, environmental hazards and pollution are major contributors to childhood deaths, illnesses and disability from acute respiratory disease, diarrhoeal diseases, physical injuries, poisonings, insect-borne diseases and perinatal infections.

In the country and the city, poverty forces people to live and work in environments that make them sick. If people live in poverty, then chances are they live in a hotbed of health hazards including dirty water, no sanitation, bad air inside and outside the home and lots of traffic. People living in poverty are also forced to do dangerous work because they have no other choice. They work long hours with few or no safety regulations and are exposed to all kinds of dangers. No wonder people living in poverty are sick.

Breathing bad air

Bad air makes people sick. Bad air makes it harder to breathe and increases the chances of developing all kinds of diseases. Asthma, chronic bronchitis, and heart and lung diseases are all linked with breathing polluted air.

In rich countries, most people usually have two choices when it comes to the fuel they use to cook food and heat houses. It's gas or electricity. Half the people in the world don't get either of these choices. They rely on dung, wood, crop waste or coal as their fuel. Without proper ventilation — like a chimney — smoking indoors takes on a whole new meaning. Soot and dust pollute the air and make being inside dangerous. Indoor air pollution from smoky fuels kills 1.6 million people — that's one death every 20 seconds — from diseases like pneumonia, chronic respiratory disease and lung cancer.

Women and children suffer the most from smoky fires. They spend up to seven hours a day by the fire, breathing air more than 100 times as smoky as the accepted safety levels. It's no surprise then that the majority of people who die from indoor pollution are women. Children are also vulnerable because they breathe lots of toxic air while their airways are still developing.

A number of attempts to provide clean fuel stoves to people have failed around the world because the stoves were not developed with input from the people intended to use them. Envirofit is an organisation based in the United Kingdom that hopes it has solved that problem by working closely with people, especially nomads who need to carry their stoves with them, to design a stove that works. You can find out more about their project at envirofit.org/clean_cookstoves.html.

Cars as weapons of mass destruction

Forget about nuclear weapons, traffic is one of the worst health hazards facing the urban poor. Road accidents cause about 1.2 million deaths every year, with 90 per cent of them happening in low-income countries, and cars are also major contributors to air pollution. Now that more cars have appeared on the roads, it's also become more dangerous to be a cyclist or pedestrian. In fact, just walking around is a key risk factor. According to the World Health Organization, by 2020 traffic accidents will be the third leading cause of death worldwide.

In the country

The countryside is no rural idyll for agricultural workers in developing countries. They work long hours, doing hard, heavy work, with few safety measures. Even worse, unsafe exposure to farming chemicals can lead to death or serious illness. Are you ready for the list? Chronic pesticide exposure increases the risk of:

✔ Developmental and reproductive disorders

✔ Immune-system disruption

✔ Endocrine disruption

✔ Impaired nervous-system function

✔ Development of certain cancers

In other words, if you get exposed to too many farm chemicals, you're history. Children are at higher risk from exposure than are adults. Pesticides, as well as fertilisers, can also get into water sources — contaminating drinking water and animals that humans rely on for nutrition.

Part IV
Poverty's Outlook

Glenn Lumsden

*'Obviously I'm relying heavily on
their innate sense of the ironic.'*

In this part . . .

Eradicating extreme poverty is an enormous challenge, made more difficult because the problem keeps changing. The world's population is expanding and migrating, creating problems that have not existed until now. Traditional societies are disrupted by change, destroying values that held people together and protected them, yet some of those traditions make it difficult for people to cope with change.

The chapters in this part deal with the complex issues that make poverty worse and are also made worse by poverty. The new challenge of an increasingly chaotic climate compounds the difficulties created by population growth and movement.

Chapter 13

Migration and Human Trafficking

Humanity has always been on the move. Fossil records show people walking across Asia and down the length of the Americas 40,000 years ago. Australia and the neighbouring islands were first populated ten millennia before that. In the last five centuries, large numbers of people have moved from Europe to the New World. Now, Europe's population growth comes mainly from inward migration. People move towards new opportunities and away from adversity such as natural or man-made disasters.

This chapter explores the relationship between migration and poverty. Voluntary migration is often about escaping poverty or, at the least, seeking new opportunities. Unfortunately, not all migration is voluntary. Forced migration and its complement — trafficking — exploit the poor and vulnerable. The trade in human lives is one of the most brutal aspects of poverty and the effort to put an end to it requires international coordination.

People on the Move

Each year, millions of people leave their country of birth to move somewhere else. They relocate for many different reasons: A new and better job, to reunite with family members, for a better life, even for love. According to the United Nations, about 3 per cent of the world's population, or one out of every 33 people, don't live in the country where they were born. About half of these international migrants are women. People migrate over varying distances for different periods of time. They can move for a period of days, weeks or months to suit seasonal or family needs. Their move can also be long-term or permanent. For poor people, migration can and often does offer a rapid route out of poverty, not only for them, but also for the families and communities they leave behind.

People are pulled and pushed into moving by a range of factors:

- *Pull factors* encourage people to leave because of what they believe they will gain: More money, better employment, more opportunities or a better environment.
- *Push factors* encourage individuals to leave behind undesirable things: Corruption, rising sea levels or fewer opportunities.

In any specific case, there will be a combination of these factors. Media mogul Rupert Murdoch, for example, migrated from Australia to the United States to move the head office of his business empire. The more generous tax regime in the United States was a pull factor; restrictions of the Australian regulations a push factor.

Globalisation has radically changed the scale of migration around the world. In richer countries with ageing populations, new migrants satisfy the demand for both skilled labour and cheap and flexible labour. In doing so, migration opens up many opportunities for people from developing countries: More employment opportunities, cheap travel and better communication. It's also easier for women to travel.

Where do migrants move?

An accurate estimate of the size and flows of migration around the world remains a mystery, because many people move within their own country or through unofficial channels. By far the biggest form of migration is within borders from one part of a country to another. For example, in 2001 about 120 million Chinese migrated internally, compared with less than half a million who migrated internationally. The vast increase of people living in urban areas — discussed in Chapter 14 — is a result of this internal migration. Generally, what's at the end of the journey — skills, financial benefits and networks — determines how far people will go.

Many people move to a neighbouring country looking for work. Known as *south–south migration*, this is an important way for people to survive and improve their lives. For the most part, Africans move within Africa and don't go through formal channels to do it. Regional migration across South Asia is also widespread, with many people moving from Bangladesh, Nepal and Pakistan to northern states of India. There's also increasing movement within specific regions of East Asia.

Why countries want migrants

Migration is good for nations when they're growing quickly. The settler nations of the New World were populated by immigrants who fled persecution and economic hardship in Europe. At various stages these nations have had migration policies that range from Australia's 'Populate or Perish' and notorious 'White Australia Policy' to the 'No Welfare for Aliens' policy emerging recently in the United States.

Developed countries such as Australia and Britain have encouraged different types of migrants at different stages over the last 30 years. Australia encouraged the British to leave the cold and wet United Kingdom and migrate to sunny Australia. Restless Britons — known in Australia as Poms — could apply for a subsidised trip to Australia well into the 1970s. They paid £10 for the trip to the other side of the world, and immigration officials housed them and helped them to find employment when they arrived. In Australia these migrants are still referred to as Ten Pound Poms.

At the same time, Britain encouraged many people from newly independent countries that had been under British colonial rule, especially the Caribbean, to leave sunny islands and enter the cold, wet and damp to do the many jobs that were difficult to fill in a booming economy.

Over the last 30 to 40 years there has been a marked change in the direction of migration policies of developing nations. The economic slowdown of the 1970s saw many countries create migration policies to cap the numbers of foreign nationals. Migration policies evolved to encourage skilled migration, complementing the existing labour force and feeding their advanced industries.

The effects of migration

Migration has both risks and benefits. On the positive side, it can help individuals and families

- Increase their income
- Learn new skills
- Improve their social status
- Build up assets
- Improve their quality of life

The home country also benefits. Emigration opens up jobs for people who stay behind, increases trade with overseas countries, and increases the likelihood of tourism and charitable activities. Migrants also facilitate *knowledge transfer* — they take home better technologies, new information and more awareness of health and education issues. Rich countries benefit from a ready supply of unskilled workers. If global trends continue, temporary migration to developed countries could lead to gains of as much as US$300 billion a year in 2025, shared equally between people in developing and developed countries.

By far the biggest benefit is in the form of remittances — money being sent home by migrants. With the increase in migration, remittances have also increased, from US$102 billion in 1995 to US$240 billion in 2007. (This major cash flow is compared with other flows of money around the world in Chapter 17.) Over the past three decades, remittances flows to developing countries have been larger than foreign investment or overseas aid. For example, Ghana received remittances of approximately US$1 billion a year and about the same amount of money in aid.

The potential for poverty reduction through remittances alone is immense. The World Bank has estimated that by 2025, migrants could send home US$356 billion a year — many times more than the historic commitments leaders made to double aid at a meeting of the world's richest nations in Scotland in 2005. That's just the money that's tracked through official channels like the Western Union. It doesn't account for money sent through unofficial channels — money in an envelope.

The picture's not entirely rosy. The lure of wealth earned overseas can be an illusion and many people find themselves in horrendous conditions, far from home and the people they love. This is particularly the case for women, who often face discrimination and limited access to formal employment, social security and health programs.

Migration, of any sort, disrupts family life and puts stress on children. The loss of productive members of society can depress the local economy and make the community poorer. An influx of migrants can lower wages, increase unemployment and lead to social and political tension.

The majority of poor people move within their own country or to the country next door, but skilled migrants go where the bucks are. The top four foreign destinations are the United States (50 per cent), Canada and Australia (20 per cent between them) and the European Union (15 per cent).

The resultant brain drain means that there are fewer educated people left at home. This has a severe impact across all sectors. Chapter 12 discusses how the brain drain affects a country's health system by removing nurses, doctors and other health professionals that the nation needs to take care of the population. (Other consequences of the brain drain are discussed in Chapter 16.)

Forced Migration

When violence or natural disaster strikes, many people are pushed out of their homes, even if they have nowhere else to go. This involuntary migration inevitably causes major upheaval and results in debilitating poverty. It can happen for a variety of reasons and can result in a range of situations, all of them extremely unpleasant.

Homeless in your own country

When people are forced out of their homes and begin searching for a safe place to hide, they generally stay as close to home as possible. This means that most of the people in the world who've lost their homes because of violence or natural disasters are still living in the country where they were born. These people don't appear on the international records as refugees. They're known as *internally displaced people*.

The United Nations High Commission for Refugees (UNHCR) estimates that there were 33 million displaced people in the world at the end of 2006. Almost 15 million of these were still in their country of origin, compared with almost 10 million refugees and 6 million stateless people. About 10 per cent of the internally displaced people were returned to their homes during 2006 but were still being watched by the UNHCR.

Colombia, Iraq and the countries of central Africa are the places with the major populations of internally displaced people. There are smaller numbers in Sri Lanka, the states of the former Yugoslavia and the former Soviet Union. Because these people are managed by their own governments, international authorities don't have accurate methods of accounting for them or monitoring their wellbeing. In some cases, the national governments actively oppose offers of assistance made by the United Nations.

What is a refugee?

Pretty obviously, a *refugee* is someone looking for safety (or refuge). That implies there's some danger threatening them. The actual definition is disputed because people in rich countries are nervous that millions of people will claim to be refugees to get around immigration rules. As a result, different groups interpret the word more or less loosely. Médecins Sans Frontières (Doctors Without Borders) keeps it simple, officially recognising a refugee as 'a person who has been forced to leave his/her home and has crossed an international border'.

The United Nations (UN), as you might expect, prefers more precision: 'A person who is outside his/her country of nationality or habitual residence; has a well-founded fear of persecution because of his/her race, religion, nationality, membership in a particular social group or political opinion; and is unable or unwilling to avail himself/herself of the protection of that country, or to return there, for fear of persecution.'

One characteristic of people fleeing from war and conflict is that they don't have much choice. This often means they escape to a neighbouring country, rather than the other side of the world. During the war in the former Yugoslavia, 3.7 million people fled their homes to the relative safety of the refugee camps in neighbouring states. There are currently more than two million Palestinians living as refugees in huge camps surrounded by Israel and in neighbouring countries. If these victims of conflict don't cross an international border, they aren't refugees and aren't eligible for international assistance.

Most developed countries have tightened their immigration policies to stem the perceived flow of migrants from developing countries. European nations have introduced a range of non-arrival policies, diversion tactics and other restrictive practices.

What's an asylum seeker?

International laws provide that anyone can apply for asylum in another country when they're escaping persecution. People who arrive in a new land without any documentation are *asylum seekers*, despite the attempts of some governments and media agencies to use the emotive term *illegal immigrant* instead. After processing the application for asylum, the asylum seeker becomes a refugee.

There is a perception in some developed countries that people who arrive at the border without official documents are using the confusion in their country as an excuse to bypass proper immigration procedures. The press use emotive terms like *queue jumpers, illegals* and *desperadoes*. In fact, most of these people are simply fleeing. In war-torn countries there's often no diplomatic or UN presence for individuals to apply for migration. In other words, there's no queue to jump, no official procedure to circumvent. In the case of Australia, where the hysteria about refugees from the Middle East reached fever pitch in the 2001 elections, it was simply a case of being one of the few countries in the region that's a signatory to the 1951 Refugee Convention. Those asylum seekers had just kept travelling until they got to a border that would 'process' them.

Jailed for spending six months in a leaky boat

Refugees and people seeking asylum sometimes meet fear and hostility in destination countries. In some cases, the reaction may be wildly out of proportion with the issue. In the early 1990s, Australia introduced mandatory detention for *unauthorised arrivals* — that is, those people seeking asylum who arrived without documentation.

The political heat around this issue rose dramatically in 2001, when a Norwegian ship, the *Tampa*, picked up 438 survivors from a sinking boat in the Indian Ocean. The Australian Government refused to accept the asylum seekers. Eventually New Zealand accepted 150 people, and most of the remainder were moved to the tiny Pacific island of Nauru.

A few months later, the Australian Government won re-election, partly by appeal to anti-immigration sentiment. Campaign material quoted the Prime Minister: 'We will decide who comes to this country, and the circumstances in which they come.'

Until 2007, a conservative Australian Government employed what was known as the 'Pacific Solution'. Asylum seekers caught heading for Australia were moved to detention centres on Christmas Island (an Australian territory in the Indian Ocean), and in Nauru and Papua New Guinea. Being located outside Australia's legal immigration zone reduced their chances of successful legal claims.

About 1,600 individuals — mostly from Iraq, Iran, Afghanistan, Sri Lanka and Myanmar — were detained in this way, and the overwhelming majority were eventually found to be genuine refugees. The total cost to the Australian taxpayers was over $1 billion — more than $500,000 per detainee!

The number of unauthorised arrivals is tiny compared with the 600,000 migrants who arrived in the regular way — on planes with visas — during the same period. It's also much less than the 45,000 or more who arrived with a visa but didn't leave when the visa expired.

The 'Pacific Solution' was formally ended following the election of a new Australian Government at the end of 2007. The last detainee left Nauru in February 2008.

There's also a perception, especially in the mainstream media, that Western nations take a lot of refugees and are being overrun. In fact, the bulk of refugees languish in refugee camps across the developing world. There are eight million refugees in Africa, compared with fewer than half a million in North America and a similar number in Europe. Almost one-third of the total people within the borders of Guinea are refugees! Compare this with Australia where there's one refugee for every 1,600 people. Table 13-1 clearly shows how disengaged the developed nations are from the refugee problem.

Table 13-1	Ratio of Citizens to Refugees	
Nation	*Citizens*	*Refugees*
Equatorial Guinea	7	3
Tanzania	76	1
Canada	443	1
United Kingdom	530	1
United States	578	1
Australia	1,583	1

Checking out permanent refugee camps

Many of the refugees around the world are stuck in limbo. They fled a disaster in their own country and were unable to return. Now they have nowhere to go. Without work, assets or a community to support them, they have almost no opportunity to escape their situation. They're known to the UNHCR as *protracted refugees*.

In almost all cases, protracted refugee situations are caused by a political impasse. Governments refuse to acknowledge the situation, the causes of the refugee crisis or the solutions required to resolve it. In many cases both the home government and the host government deny responsibility for the future care of the refugees. Essentially, everyone simply waits and hopes the situation will go away.

There were 6.2 million people in 38 protracted refugee situations around the world at the end of 2003. This excluded the Palestinian refugees living in Jordan, Syria, Egypt and other countries around the Middle East. Of those 6.2 million, 2.3 million lived in Africa, south of the Sahara. Another

2.7 million long-term refugees live in the Middle East, Asia and North Africa. About half a million live in Europe with a little over half a million in the Americas. The average time since these people fled their homes is 17 years.

Of course, these refugees are poor. Worse, though, is the long-term impact of their semi-permanent homelessness. It's impossible for these displaced people to escape from poverty, and the children born into the refugee camps are condemned to a life of poverty. Both the country that hosts the refugees and the country from which they have fled suffer as a result of their poverty. The home country misses out on their economic and cultural contribution, and the host country contributes resources to maintaining their lives without receiving any economic benefits.

Major protracted refugee situations exist in Pakistan and Iran because of the five million Afghan refugees displaced during 20 years of war. Nepal has been the temporary home for almost 100,000 people from Bhutan for seven years. More than half a million Somali refugees are spread across neighbouring African countries and as far afield as Europe. Armenia, Serbia and Montenegro present similar problems on the European continent.

The UNHCR reports that the problem in each protracted refugee situation is a disagreement between two governments that needs to be handled in a delicate and unique manner. In some cases, most recently in Bhutan and Nepal, it has announced its intention to withdraw from negotiations. The UNHCR fears that its presence may contribute to the stalemate, and it will restrict its involvement to protecting the refugees themselves.

The Terrible Traffic in Humans

Trafficking in humans is a grave human rights abuse. People who are trafficked may end up being sexually exploited, used as labourers or forced into armed conflict (as soldiers, for example). It's a multibillion dollar business.

A formal definition of *trafficking* is the recruitment, transport and transfer of people within countries or across borders, through abduction, deception or force in order to exploit them.

Cheap and rapid air travel, advanced communication technologies and the relaxation of border controls in many countries have made human trafficking easier and more profitable in the last 20 years. Traffickers face relatively few risks because of inadequate international legal frameworks and because their victims are generally powerless.

People are trafficked because there is a market for them. Just as migration is driven by a combination of factors, so trafficking is caused by a combination of push and pull factors. Factors that push people into vulnerable situations include:

- Conflict
- Natural disasters
- Violence in the family
- Unequal status of women
- Uneven economic growth

Among the pull factors that attract criminals to engage in trafficking are:

- Demand for labour, especially in low-paying or dangerous jobs
- Demand for labour in the sex industry

There is little justice for people who have been trafficked. Even if they come to the attention of authorities, rather than being treated as victims of terrible crimes, they are often treated as criminals or unlawful aliens.

The film *The Jammed* shows what happens to young women who are trafficked into prostitution in Australia. Inspired by actual events, it was released in 2007. Project Respect, an organisation that protects the rights of trafficked sex workers, estimates that 1,000 women are trafficked into Australia every year. Go to the film's Web site at www.thejammed.com to find out more.

Child trafficking

Child trafficking is one of the gravest forms of child abuse in the world today. It is a multibillion dollar industry that involves an estimated 1.2 million children every year. The underlying cause of most child trafficking is poverty. Often the children or their families desperately need money, and poverty makes them vulnerable. Factors such as war or natural disasters, family dislocation, lack of laws against trafficking or domestic violence make children more at risk of trafficking. Girls are especially at risk, because in many cultures they often have a lower status than boys.

Children are trafficked because there is a demand for their labour or their bodies. Many are forced to work in the sex industry — for example, in pornography, prostitution or sex tourism. Others end up as labourers in factories or agriculture, as domestic servants or in industries such as mining. Some children are used in armed conflict as soldiers, porters, landmine clearers or sex slaves for soldiers.

Child trafficking happens in every region of the world, but Asian countries including Cambodia and Thailand are recognised as the hubs, particularly for the sex tourism trade. Wealthy countries are often part of the problem, because their citizens provide a demand for trafficked children. For example, citizens of Australia and the United States have been identified as sex tourists in 25 countries. Tourist destinations such as Bali and East Timor are emerging as easy places for child sex exploiters to do business.

Nice rug . . . if you don't know the history

The carpet industry in Uttar Pradesh took off in the 1970s when the Shah of Iran outlawed child labour. The result was a rise in the price of Persian carpets to meet the demand of Western buyers.

The best carpets are made from small knots, and only small fingers are agile enough to tie them. Carpet producers buy kidnapped boys, as young as 5 years old, to work in their factories.

In 1985 the Bonded Liberation Front conducted raids on two carpet factories in Uttar Pradesh. Twenty-five boys from 5- to 12-years-old were released. They told their liberators they'd been lured by the kidnappers on a promise of a trip to the cinema. This was to be kept as a secret from their parents. Once the broker, a local barber, had lured them, he transported them to the carpet factory. He was paid US$7,000 and left the boys to the slaveholder who immediately put them to work.

The boys reported that the slaveholder locked them in a room, branded them with hot irons, beat and starved them so they would work harder. Any mistakes they made resulted in another beating. Work started at 4.00 am with a bucket of cold water poured over them. The boys argued with the slaveholder, demanding they go back to their families. He told the boys they had cost him money and if they repaid him US$1,000 each they would be free to leave.

These boys were lucky to be returned to their families, but they took the brands on their skin and the horrendous memories with them.

Trafficking for cannon fodder

People captured or lured by traffickers are often put to work as labourers in quarries or factories, but in some places around the world, they're forced to become soldiers.

In Burma, men, women and children are abducted from their homes or refugee camps and forced into the military. The women and children take on roles as sex and domestic slaves, as well as combatants. There's documented evidence of large numbers of Burmese children being forced to fight in the army. Children are also used as messengers, domestic support for armies on the move and expendable auxiliaries who advance across minefields in front of the army.

In most developed nations, soldiers have to be 18 years old before they're sent to fight in armed conflict. The United Nations defines a child, for the purposes of soldiering, as under 15. The African Charter on the Rights and Welfare of the Child clearly states the legal age as 18. European nations haven't always been so delicate. Boys as young as 12 joined Napoleon's army, and boys aged 12 and younger were common in Nelson's British navy.

Today, the practice of using children as cannon fodder is most common in countries with ongoing civil conflict. Such societies have a culture of violence and also a very young population with small numbers of fit young men. In some cases that culture extends back for centuries, and a culture of violence overlaps with passionately held beliefs that cause children to volunteer for military service. This issue is explored more in Chapter 6.

Chapter 14

Creating a Planet of Slums

The world's poor are increasingly urban. Urban poverty carries a special set of problems: Overcrowding and poor sanitation endanger the lives and wellbeing of the slum residents.

This chapter looks at the rise of the city as the centre of population growth. The rapid nature of that growth causes many problems for the people who live there. This chapter looks at those problems and the challenges facing the agencies that try to help. We also indulge in a little futurology, predicting the future of cities and trying to identify decisions that governments can make now to avoid the worst excesses of a world dominated by slum dwellers.

On the Move

The greatest population movement in history has been the shift of the majority of people from the country to the cities. Despite being so large, this move is recent; it has mostly taken place over the last century, and it's accelerating.

Migration, of any sort, brings problems associated with change. Traditional cultures and values are uprooted, newcomers are vulnerable to exploitation and governments struggle to keep up with the pace of change. Cities depend on effective organisation to work smoothly. All too often, though, this organisation is put in place only after the problems have got so out of hand they become fully fledged crises.

Poor people migrate to the city to escape the grind of rural poverty. The numbers of rural poor, and the conditions they live in, haven't changed much in 60 years. Chapter 13 talks more about those conditions. The urban poor get so much attention because the number of them has grown so quickly the problems are new and urgent. Because the populations are concentrated, they are also visible and accessible. The whole world can see them and those who want to help can reach many of them at one time.

Ever-growing cities

By 2006, for the first time ever, more than half of all the people on earth lived in cities. A staggering number of people — almost 180,000 across the world — move from the countryside to the city every day.

In poorer, developing countries, the majority of people still live in villages and depend on farming for a living, but this is changing fast. Between now and 2030, the cities of the developing world will account for about 95 per cent of all population growth in the world.

This shift brings other changes. Cities evolve into megacities with more than 20 million people, and millions may live without permanent shelter. Here are some other changes that can make life very tough:

- A rising threat of crime and violence
- Breakdown of traditional values associated with village life
- Degradation of the urban environment, including air and water quality
- Expanding slums and shantytowns
- Psychological pressures in coping with life in a blighted urban setting
- Unreliable water supply and sanitation

Megacities

By 2015 about 20 cities around the world will have populations bigger than 20 million — more than half of these will be in Asia. Of the 20 cities, only two — Tokyo and the greater New York metropolitan area — will be in developed countries. These *megacities* — sometimes called *metroplexes* or *conurbations* — aren't just bigger in scale than the cities you've known; they represent extreme challenges in organising human existence in a small space.

The world's megacities have grown quickly and, in most cases, without being planned. Buildings are often overcrowded and badly constructed. The transport systems in these cities are very poor and roads are often choked with traffic. Trips from one part of the city to another can be long, difficult and dangerous. Electricity and water services are seriously inadequate and so are sanitation and waste disposal services. Air and water supplies are often badly polluted and unsafe.

In these sprawling cities, the gap between rich and poor is dramatic. Shiny shopping centres and skyscrapers sit alongside shacks and shanties. Typically, such cities are both the dynamic hub of a national economy and culture and, at the same time, home to millions living in desperate circumstances.

At the extreme end, Mumbai in India is expected to have about 32 million people by 2015. Despite the speed of India's economic development, the great majority of these people will be poor. There's no precedent for such a concentration of poverty in one place: No-one can predict with certainty what social and environmental consequences will emerge.

On the Margins: Squatters and Slums

For many citizens of very large cities, life is centred on the local, small urban community where they live, rather than the city as a whole. In most cases, the slum — sometimes called a *marginal community* or, even more officially, an *unofficial community* — means more to its residents than the official city. The slum's where they spend most of their time, and where they make their living. Their important social activities happen in their own local community. They belong there and identify themselves with that place.

In different countries and regions, informal settlements have taken on a particular character and have their own local names — from Brazil's *favelas* and Peru's *barriadas* to the *kampungs* of Indonesia and the *shantytowns* of South Africa. The *gecekondu* of Turkey are described in the sidebar 'The sudden suburbs of Istanbul'.

Slums are home to more than a third of the total population in many developing cities. In some African countries — Ethiopia and Tanzania, to name two — more than 90 per cent of city dwellers live in slums. In the case of huge metropolises such as Sao Paulo or Jakarta, this means millions of people.

The sudden suburbs of Istanbul

In Turkey, the squatter settlements are known as *gecekondu* — literally 'it happened overnight'. These settlements appear suddenly, partly because Turkish law protects any home that's occupied at dawn — it can't be torn down unless the person living there has the opportunity to appear before a judge. The law also gives any community of more than 2,000 people the right to register as an independent municipality. These two laws together allow the gecekondu to thrive as squatter settlements that have gained permanency and legitimacy.

The gecekondu of Sultanbeyli is famous for its seven-storied, air-conditioned Town Hall, built by the squatters and occupied by a popularly elected mayor. Sultanbeyli has 300,000 residents, an active shopping centre that includes restaurants, Internet cafés, banks and a post office. It's crowded: 12,500 people squeezing into every square kilometre, compared with 5,000 people for a suburb of most cities in the developed world. One of the major challenges facing the gecekondu as they become official municipalities is that the residents who fled there and built the town from nothing resent being charged rates for municipal services that they feel they've provided for themselves.

Land and legality

Some of these settlements are sanctioned by government, and may even have elected officials and organised services. But others are not, and their buildings can be torn down or their land taken over at any time. That's why the biggest issue for poor communities is establishing their right to remain where they are — legally called their *security of tenure*. Without a legal title to the land where their homes are built, these people face the constant threat of eviction.

Sometimes these evictions are on a huge scale — such as the expulsion of 1.2 million people from the Rainbow Town slum in Port Harcourt, Nigeria, in 2000. The Burmese regime threw about a million people out of Rangoon several years earlier. Similarly, the government of Zimbabwe evicted about 700,000 urban dwellers from Harare in 2005, an action the government code-named Operation Remove Trash.

In other cases, governments have conducted large-scale slum clearances so the land can be used for offices or housing, or even for golf courses and other facilities to serve the middle classes. About 2.5 million people have been evicted from their homes around Shanghai during the past 15 years to make room for new office developments and middle-class housing. Often thousands are moved on to make way for big international events, or just to hide the grim reality of the worst slums from the eyes of international visitors. As many as 400,000 homeless people were shifted out of central Beijing in the lead-up to the 2008 Olympic Games.

Individual slum dwellers and households also face the threat of losing their homes. Many are squatters, living in improvised shelters on land that legally belongs to someone else. Throughout Asia, Africa and Latin America the formal housing sector — both government and private — provides only about half of the shelter required in the cities. The shortfall is made up by housing constructed by the residents themselves, and by people who don't have a permanent sheltered home — for example, the tens of thousands of pavement dwellers in the larger Indian cities.

Settling in: How slums turn into suburbs

Slums are bigger now than ever before, but slums themselves aren't a new phenomenon. In fact, most cities have grown through large, informal, poor and often illegal settlements. London in the eighteenth century, or Paris or New York in the nineteenth, had hundreds of thousands of poor citizens in what were effectively the squatter camps of their day.

In countries as diverse as Brazil, India and Turkey, places that started as informal settlements have developed their own economies, services and even systems for electing local governments. In many countries, squatters and slum dwellers have started associations that promote self-help, initiate urban improvement projects and campaign for squatters' rights.

Life in the City: Urban Ecology

Because people live close together in a city, any gap in the essential services quickly becomes obvious. As people flood into the world's cities from rural areas, the lack of accommodation, clean drinking water and the systems to deal with waste becomes acute. Chapter 11 discusses some of the challenges facing the poor who work in the world's major cities. There are plenty of other challenges as well.

'I still call a cardboard box home'

After food and water, a roof over your head is one of the most basic human needs. Shelter from the weather, security from attack or theft, little privacy, and a place to call home — these are things that almost everyone aspires to.

Homelessness is a fact of life and very visible, even in most cities of the developed world. The Urban Institute estimates 3.5 million Americans experience homelessness at some time every year. In the cities of the poor world, homelessness is an overwhelming reality. Poor people have a tough time finding somewhere they can afford to live and where they can stay for a reasonable length of time. Of course, the quality of shelter is important and so too is personal safety. On top of all that, the shelter has to be close enough to places where they may get a job. It can be better to sleep on a roof or in a doorway close to a potential income than to sleep in affordable quarters that are farther away.

Makeshift shelter is all that's available for most poor people living in the city. Even in the wealthiest countries, the poorer citizens often live in old and rundown buildings, or sprawling, soulless housing projects. But in developing countries, they more typically live in huts or shacks, often made by using improvised building materials such as cardboard and plastic. These buildings may be constructed by residents themselves, sometimes in haphazard or chaotic patterns, or may be a part of a 'slum estate' constructed by a landlord.

Overcrowding is a health and security hazard, contributing further to the pressures on the poor. *Overcrowding*, according to UN-Habitat, means four or more people sharing a room. Few people experience this in developed countries — although it does occur in student dorms, hospitals and accommodation for itinerant workers — but over 400 million people in the developing world share a room with three or more other people.

Inadequate living space is actually a hidden form of homelessness. Overcrowding damages people's wellbeing because it:

- Disrupts children's study patterns
- Disturbs the sleep of both children and adults
- Forces people to retreat to public places for sleep or privacy
- Increases the incidence of domestic violence and abuse
- Makes the spread of infectious disease more likely
- Removes people's privacy and dignity

Sanitation and water

Poor sanitation isn't a nice topic of conversation, but poor cities have a problem that's much worse than the nasty smell it causes. A report released by the United Nations Environment Programme (UNEP) in March 2008 shows that 70 per cent of the world's population aren't connected to sewers and that this causes 1.5 million preventable deaths each year. Sanitation is important wherever you live, and a lack of sanitation that may be an inconvenience in a rural village becomes a crisis in the city.

Concentrated humanity equals a lot of accumulated waste. Most poor cities have little sanitation. At the extreme end, Kinshasa, the capital of the Democratic Republic of Congo, with more than ten million people, is the biggest city in the world to have no water-based sanitation system at all. As a result, dysentery and other waterborne diseases are rife. Table 14-1 shows the top six causes of death in Kinshasa. Three of them, accounting for one-third of total deaths, are partly caused by the lack of sanitation.

Table 14-1	Major Causes of Death in Kinshasa
Cause of Death	*Percentage*
Bacterial infection	17.4
Homicide	16.8
Accidental trauma	8.9
Viral infection	7.2
Waterborne parasite	6.3
Suicide	6.3

Source: American Journal of Tropical Medicine and Hygiene.

Built on the largest river in Africa, in the tropics where the wet season lasts for eight months of the year, Kinshasa is a city where over 150 people drown every time it rains and, because the houses are built on rubbish dumps that leak gases, many people die every night from asphyxiation or explosions.

Almost everywhere in the developing world, effective sewerage systems are restricted to small, wealthy districts within cities. Sometimes this inequality dates back to colonial times. Colonial governments often provided piped water and sanitation only to the homes of the colonial administration. They relied on segregation as the main means of protection against epidemics that killed the local people crowded into the rest of the city. In recent decades, this phenomenon has been repeated in the form of the *gated community* — well-serviced housing estates for the few, protected by keeping out others. Often these suburbs are in the hills, out of the pollution of the city proper.

Urban water supply is critical, but there's actually some good news on this front. From 1990 to the early 2000s, the percentage of people able to access some kind of improved water supply increased. The bad news is that 'improved' doesn't always mean completely safe, and 'access' doesn't always mean being able to get water easily whenever you need it. Some city water supplies may be available only for a few hours a day. Also, the water source — which is sometimes a well, rather than a pipe connected to a tap — may be some distance away. Access aside, water is usually more expensive in poor cities than in the cities of the developed world.

Privatisation of systems in some countries, like South Africa, has seen prices inflate dramatically. Mobile water vendors — whether selling by the bottle or by the tanker load — are the most expensive of all, typically charging ten times the price of public utilities.

Crime and violence

In ancient times, people huddled together for protection from wild animals or bandits. Unfortunately, putting a lot of people in close proximity no longer means safety in numbers. City life is dangerous: Crime, including violent crime, is common.

The United Nations estimated in 2007 that 60 per cent of urban residents in the developing world had experienced crime of some sort during the past five years. While crime rates in North America and Europe have declined since 1980, the opposite is true in Africa and Latin America. Over 25 per cent of criminal incidents involve some violence, and women are twice as likely as men to experience physical intimidation.

Physical factors contribute to the prevalence of crime. Cities bring together large numbers of poor and dispossessed people, who are physically close to wealth but denied access to it. The wealthy need to invest heavily in security — gated communities, alarm systems and security guards — but the majority of the community gets minimal protection. Police resources are usually inadequate and police tend to regard the poor as a threat rather than as potential victims needing protection. Likewise, poor communities often regard police as violent, corrupt and ineffective.

But it's the economy of poor cities that creates the conditions for crime. Competition is fierce for scarce jobs but also for the right to set up a stall on a particular piece of sidewalk or even to beg in a lucrative street. So people find that they have to resort to illegal, or semi-legal, activities just to make a living. (For more information, refer to Chapter 7.)

Although the extent and type of crime varies greatly between and within cities, three factors seem to be especially important:

- ✒ A young population, especially where large numbers of young men are excluded from the formal economy
- ✒ Lack of legitimate economic opportunity
- ✒ Sudden waves of new arrivals from rural areas — sometimes driven by conflict as well as poverty

The link between crime and poverty can be a vicious circle. Businesses find it hard to prosper in a violent environment. Corporations don't want to invest in places where their people are at risk or where their assets can be destroyed. Using gangs or organised crime to provide protection just entrenches the problem, feeding and breeding more violence. Creating a safer environment is actually one of the preconditions for economic progress.

Environmental degradation

Crowded, poor cities suffer from environmental problems. As described earlier in this chapter, water supplies are often tainted by sewage, industrial effluents and garbage, and even the poor-quality water can be difficult to access. Open space in city centres is rare, and the green belts that surround most cities in the developed world have often been eaten away by uncontrolled urban sprawl. This has also meant the loss of valuable farm land. Some other factors create unique environmental hazards.

Battling the elements in badly located cities

For many cities, environmental problems begin with location and geology. Massive cities have grown in places where landslides, floods and other natural hazards pose a constant threat. Jakarta in Indonesia and Manila in the Philippines, for example, are both situated on low coastal plains beneath mountain ranges. Both are in a climate zone where torrential tropical rains lead to massive floods most years, and the cities are right in the path the flood waters take to reach the sea. The slums of Brazil's two giant megacities, Sao Paulo and Rio de Janeiro, are both largely built on unstable hillsides and badly eroded sites.

Rampant growth and unchecked pollution

Uncontrolled industrial pollution is a major problem. Poor regulation of industry and reckless use of chemicals has allowed contamination of the environment to flourish. In some cases, attempts to force industries to reduce effluents have led to active dumping. Heavy metals such as lead and cadmium, pesticides, fertilisers, paints, chemical dyes and other dangerous pollutants can remain in soils and pollute groundwater sources for decades. These pollutants easily enter the food chain.

The consequences of traffic jams

More than any other factor, motor traffic damages urban air quality. The use of automobiles, trucks and motorcycles has burgeoned over the past 30 years. This trend makes getting around cities harder than ever, and has also seen massive diversion of funds to building roads at the expense of public transportation systems. Slow, unreliable and sometimes unsafe bus and train services have encouraged middle-class people to buy a car as quickly as they're able. This adds to congestion and also damages the revenue for the bus services, which then go into further decline.

Mental health and stress

Apart from the demands of the physical environment, life in poor cities can put huge pressure on people's mental health. Moving to the city means many people lose the sense of close connectedness with family and neighbours that was part of traditional village life. Poverty, overcrowding and insecurity, especially when combined with a prevalence of crime and violence, or the experience of war, can promote a sense of pessimism or helplessness.

When people feel helpless they harm their families and themselves. Domestic violence, child abuse, drug use and self-harm are more common in megacities. Mental-health services in the developing world are patchy at best and rarely available to the poorest people. Community building and public-education campaigns have had promising results in a few places but are more often haphazard and have little impact.

The Future of Cities: Hubs or Hellholes?

The challenges faced by the world's largest cities may lead you to conclude that they're just pits of misery. But these cities are real communities, constantly growing and changing, and acting as the hubs for whole regions and countries. In centuries past, New York, London and Paris also appeared as vast encampments of the urban poor.

People living in what are often called slums are part of the process of building new cities. The cities containing these slums can also be

- ✔ Catalysts for new ideas, new industries and new ways of living
- ✔ Centres of government, business, culture and education
- ✔ Places that nurture incredible social and economic developments
- ✔ Transport and communications hubs that connect their countries to the world

Globally, one of the challenges that governments face is reorganising society to reduce the use of resources. Shortages of water, energy and, potentially, food mean that societies at all levels need to be more efficient, waste less and recycle more. These problems will be especially intense in the world's megacities.

Urban farms and local food

Growing, processing and transporting food is one of the major consumers of energy worldwide. Growing food in the cities is potentially a significant part of the solution. Today, most cities are completely dependent on food grown elsewhere and transported over great distances. The contents of the average supermarket trolley in the Western world have travelled many thousands of kilometres to be available on the supermarket shelves. The problem of feeding people in cities with more than 20 million residents is especially severe.

Havana in Cuba was typical of other cities when the collapse of the Soviet Union in 1991 cut off its oil supply. After five years, known to Cubans as the *special period*, local agriculture began to take hold in the city itself. Now the city grows about 60 per cent of its food within the city limits. The story is documented in a film called *The Power of Community*. Chapter 23 lists a range of films dealing with different aspects of global poverty.

Relocalisation

Producing food locally reduces the amount of resources required to feed a city. In the same way, the local generation of energy, the processing of waste and the recycling of water can reduce the cost of providing these utilities.

Implementing projects to reduce the amount of energy consumed in this way is known as *relocalisation*.

Modern society has developed according to a linear model: Resources are extracted from one location, used somewhere else and then disposed of as waste in yet another location. Traditional, organic societies are based on a cyclic model that uses and recycles resources where they're found. Because the new models of settlement are based on these traditional systems, the word *relocalisation* is used rather than the more obvious *localisation*.

Implementing local solutions is an important component of designing cities that can feed and sustain all the people who live in them. These approaches are still experimental, and it remains to be seen if they can be applied to modern society in time to avoid the resource shortages and the other problems that confront the world's megacities.

A number of global movements have emerged to meet these challenges. The Post Carbon Institute, the Relocalization Movement and New Urbanism are some of the formal organisations set up to tackle these problems. Most of them currently operate on a relatively small scale, so it's likely to be some time before these solutions can deal with the problems facing the world's largest cities.

Technological solutions

Artificial food may be the only way that cities of the future can continue to grow and serve the needs of their vast populations. Algae, grown in treated sewage, are emerging as a viable source of food and fuel. Nuclear energy, recycling of human corpses and other technological marvels may sustain life, but seem unappealing at best.

Whether technological solutions solve the problems faced by megacities, or those problems remain unresolved, it's almost certain that the wealthiest people will retreat to relatively natural suburbs outside the most built-up urban areas, while the poorest make do with whatever is left behind.

Chapter 15

Climate Chaos and World Poverty

- -

- -

Yuou can't turn on the TV or open the newspaper without hearing about freak storms, record temperatures, prolonged drought, disastrous floods and other wacky weather. Now, almost all scientists agree: These extreme weather events are related, and they're caused by changes to the earth's climate. What's more, human activity is driving the changes. These changes are called *global warming*, *climate change* or *climate chaos*.

The first people in the firing line as a result of rising sea levels, reduced rainfall and global food shortages are the world's poor. Many of them already live in marginal environments — the flood plains of Bangladesh or the grazing lands that fringe the Sahara Desert, to name two. These places will be directly affected by global warming. However, indirect effects of global warming will include rising food prices, migration and significant economic change. The poor always suffer most from social upheaval.

In this chapter, you discover the basics of climate chaos: What it is, why it's happening and what you can do about it. You gain a better understanding of how climate chaos has come about, and how it's going to affect you, life on earth and people living in poverty. You also look at global responses and the irony that the policies being discussed now hurt the poor, even though they've contributed the least to cause the chaos in the climate.

Climate Chaos: The Unpleasant Truth

The earth's climate is changing. The ice caps are melting, glaciers are receding, rainfall's diminishing. The arguments about whether all this is really happening have died down. The fact that the climate is increasingly unstable stares you in the face every day.

The new instability in the climate is caused in part by increased carbon dioxide, and other greenhouse gases, in the atmosphere. Greenhouse gases in the atmosphere work like a blanket — or a greenhouse roof! — and trap the heat from the sun inside the earth's atmosphere. Carbon dioxide is a by-product of burning coal, gas and oil. It's also a by-product of the chemical reactions that take place in the manufacture and use of concrete and steel.

Because of the increase in greenhouse gases, the earth is getting hotter and sea levels are rising, and it's happening fast. If the current emphasis on economic growth at all costs continues for the next 50 years, the consequences for life on planet earth will be catastrophic.

If those scientists are wrong, and the world is warming for reasons outside our control, it's even more urgent that the world's governments plan for a hotter, drier future because slowing down its arrival will be impossible.

Global warming — what's the gas?

Somebody's pulling the earth's finger, and there's way more gas in the atmosphere than is good for it. That somebody is people. The energy-rich lifestyle you enjoy pumps huge amounts of greenhouse gases into the atmosphere. Here are a few of the culprits:

- **Carbon dioxide:** Mostly generated by fossil fuels used in transportation, building heating and cooling, and the manufacture of cement and other goods. Deforestation releases CO_2 and reduces its uptake by plants.

- **Halocarbon gas concentrations:** Come from refrigeration and other industrial processes.

- **Methane:** Comes from agriculture, natural gas distribution and landfills.

- **Nitrous oxide:** Is released by fertiliser use and fossil fuel burning.

- **Water vapour:** The most abundant greenhouse gas in the atmosphere. However, it amplifies the impact of human activity and remains in the atmosphere for a matter of only days or weeks.

Greenhouse gases alter the climate by changing the amount of solar radiation coming in and the amount of infrared radiation going out. In an ideal state, these are in balance. With more gases in the atmosphere, heat from the earth can't escape and the earth heats up.

Climate change and consumption

A simple relationship exists between the resources that a nation, or a person, consumes and the amount of carbon dioxide they produce. People in the United States and Australia produce more greenhouse gases every year than people anywhere else on the planet. If you live in those countries, you're responsible for about 27 tonnes of carbon dioxide, or its greenhouse equivalent, every year. That's about 80 times the amount of carbon dioxide produced by the average African and 12 times that of the average Chinese.

The United Nations measures the wealth of people in the world by a unit known as *purchasing power parity*. By this measure, people in the United States and Australia are about 60 times richer than the average African and ten times richer than the average Chinese. A person's wealth is not exactly equal to their impact on global warming, but it's not a bad indicator.

What's in that burger?

Meat is an enormous source of greenhouse gases. Modern, feedlot farming is very energy intensive, but even traditional grazing animals release a lot of methane in their manure or the gaseous emissions from under their tails. Methane is a powerful greenhouse gas, about three times as strong as carbon dioxide.

A Swedish report, *Energy Use in the Food Sector*, released in 2000, identified the amount of energy consumed in every stage of the food production process. Using these figures a number of consultants, including Jamais Cascio at Open the Future, have analysed the carbon emissions associated with the production of common foodstuffs. Cascio's estimate that the average 130-gram cheeseburger involves the emission of between 3 and 5 kilograms of carbon dioxide is consistent with many other assessments. A sizable chunk of those emissions are from the methane emitted by the cow during its lifetime.

The average cheeseburger's carbon dioxide is about the same amount of greenhouse gas involved in driving the family car for five minutes or growing one kilogram of tomatoes in a market garden in the developed world. The average Chinese person emits a total of three kilograms of carbon dioxide in five days. That includes all their consumption put together.

The reason given by the United States delegate at the conference in Bali in December 2007 for naming China, India and Brazil as a stumbling block in the discussion about enforceable emission targets is that their economic growth will result in major emission increases. China's emissions passed those of the United States in early 2008. It's expected that the emissions from the entire developing world will pass those of the developed world by 2018.

Figure 15-1 shows the global greenhouse emissions for 2008 and those estimated for 2020. (The gas is measured for the equivalent of a billion tonnes of carbon dioxide — CO_2e. The e stands for equivalent.) This assumes that current population projections and economic growth will be maintained, and that developing countries will achieve the 20 per cent cut in emissions that most governments have committed to. The argument put to the conference in Bali by the United States delegate is based on the convenient fact that Chinese, Indian and Brazilian emissions seem to be responsible for the entire growth in global emissions.

The fact that has been conveniently forgotten is that there are more than five times as many people in the developing world as there are in the developed world. Individuals in the United States currently produce 12 times the amount of greenhouse gas as people in China. In 2020 it is expected that they will still produce four times the amount. Right now, the developed world as a whole has one-fifth of the population but uses four-fifths of the resources. In 2020 the developed world is projected to have about one-tenth of the population but to still consume one-third of the resources.

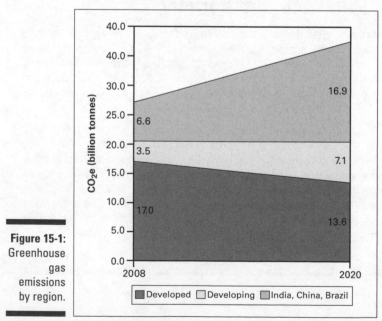

Figure 15-1: Greenhouse gas emissions by region.

Source: United Nations.

Figure 15-2 shows the more meaningful picture, in terms of how well off people are, of the per capita emissions for the same parts of the world using the same estimates. The developed world is still many times better off than the developing world.

Clearly, the campaign to reverse global warming faces the same challenges as eradicating extreme poverty: Wealthy countries take more than their fair share of resources and use every opportunity to maintain that imbalance. It is almost obscene, in the face of the broad picture painted by Figures 15-1 and 15-2, to argue that Chinese and Indian economic growth should be limited to protect the economic interests of the developed world. To counter this, you need to lobby your government representatives to vote in international forums and give the developing world a fair go, even if it means slowing down economic growth at home.

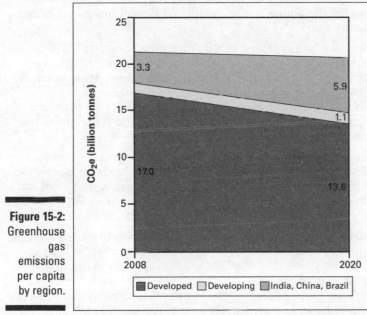

Figure 15-2:
Greenhouse gas emissions per capita by region.

Source: United Nations.

Going, going, gone: The vanishing planet

Many parts of the planet are radically affected by global warming. Although they may appear to have little to do with you, some of them will have a powerful impact on food supplies, or global weather systems that will come knocking on your door. The list that follows describes the most dramatic of these effects.

- **Islands:** Some Pacific island states have been referred to as the canary in the coalmine for climate change. The analogy dates from the nineteenth century when canaries were taken into the coalmines where they died if dangerous gases were present, warning humans to get out ... fast.

  The small island states in the Pacific Ocean are the first nations to go under when sea levels rise. In Tuvalu, a couple of king tides have already covered the whole island, destroying agriculture and drinking water for many years.

- **Coral reefs:** Have you dreamed of a holiday on a coral reef? Well don't wait too much longer. The world's coral reefs are on the way out. Global warming is making the oceans more acidic. Also, an effect known as *global bleaching* is caused by warmer water that drives out the polyps that keep the coral alive. Up to 10 per cent of coral reefs were destroyed in a warming event in 2001, and one-third of the remainder are in danger.

- **Land:** Ocean views? Within the next 50 years, the view may have eaten your house as sea levels rise, along with your neighbours for kilometres inland. Bye-bye to the coastline as you know it. It's not just the coast that's going to disappear. Arable land — that is, land that humans can grow food on — will disappear as well.

- **Ice and snow:** The glaciers and ice shelves of the world may not seem to have a direct impact on you — unless you get your water from high mountain catchments — but as they disappear because of global warming a number of changes are taking place. That ice reflected lots of heat into space — a process known as the *albedo effect*. Now heat is being absorbed by the rocks, accelerating global warming.

Dominion Over Nature

For thousands of years, humans have assumed that it's their God-given role to use the resources of the earth to improve their own life. However, rising temperatures or sea levels, or shrinking glaciers, or fish stocks, or arable land or water supplies, all indicate that the earth may now be in climate chaos. *Climate chaos* is a symptom of the stresses that have been placed on natural systems by human society.

The following sections list a range of these stresses. Some stresses will be amplified by changes in climate. All of them impact on human society and, because they're most vulnerable, disproportionately affect the poor.

Disappearing forests

The forests that get all the press are the rainforests — the lush, fecund, tropical forests of the Amazon, equatorial Africa and South East Asia. Rainforests are home to over two-thirds of all species on the planet. But there are many different kinds of forests, including temperate forests, cloud forests, pine forests and alpine forests. They all help regulate the earth's temperature and are home to more plant and animal species than any other ecosystem.

All types of forest are threatened. About 45 per cent of the earth's original forests are gone, mostly cleared during the past century. People cut them down for timber or to clear land for farming. Invasive species damage the health of forests, and drier conditions associated with global warming and the resultant fires damage them beyond repair. The destruction of these forests releases immense stores of carbon into the atmosphere — every hectare of forest stores about 500 tonnes of carbon, which the forest would normally convert to oxygen. The indigenous people in those forests join the world's poor at the back of the queue of people seeking protection from climate chaos unleashed by cutting down their forests.

Advancing deserts

The green parts of the planet disappear at the same time that desert regions increase, creating an environmental crisis of global proportions. Advancing deserts directly affect between 100 and 200 million people. If action isn't taken, experts think that 50 million people may be forced from their homes within the next ten years. If that happens it'll create all kinds of global instability.

Desertification is one factor, along with the scramble for scarce resources. This fuels conflicts like the one in Sudan that has killed as many as 200,000 people and driven 2.5 million from their homes in four brutal years.

The salt of the earth

Many different salts are stored in the crust of the earth. They come from the weathering of rocks over many thousands of years or from sea salt stored in the soil millions of years ago when the land was underwater, or from salt carried onto the land in the rain and wind. While the salt remains underground, it's okay. But humans have removed the vegetation that stabilised the soil chemistry and watertable, and then poured irrigation water onto the exposed soil. As a result, salt that's been stored safely underground for millennia has come to the surface and is left there as the water evaporates. The excess salt in the soil means that nothing can grow in it. Rising sea levels also cause salinity, as salty water comes inland during king tides and pollutes the ground and soaks into freshwater aquifers.

The gradual loss of farm and grazing land to rising salt is a massive problem. Dry areas with major irrigation programs — Australia, India, Northern Africa, Eurasia and midwest North America — have all lost significant areas of farmland because of salination. Some areas will take generations to recover. One proposed method of recovery is to plant 80 per cent of the land with native vegetation and leave it for a century to re-establish the watertable. This has massive implications for the area of land available to grow food.

Biodiversity and global resilience

The World Conservation Union documents the plant and animal species that are threatened with extinction. The 2004 Red List contains 15,589 threatened species and accounts for 12 per cent of birds, 23 per cent of mammals, and 32 per cent of amphibians on the planet — and the researchers say that they're underestimating the numbers. Use the Web site www.iucnredlist.org to look up the 2008 Red List when it becomes available.

The loss of habitat to human activity is the most pervasive threat to animals globally. Over 86 per cent of threatened birds, mammals and amphibians live in regions where the human population is rapidly expanding.

These extinctions threaten humans because a diverse range of species make the world's ecosystems flexible. When geological or astronomical events suddenly change the world's climate (or other environmental conditions), the wide variety of plants and animals allows the earth to quickly adjust to the new conditions. In the same way that a farm growing one crop is very vulnerable to a single pest or hard frost, so a planet with a handful of species is much more vulnerable to changes in climate or other conditions.

New world dodos

The dodo is infamous for having had the bad manners to become extinct during recorded human history. Even more impolite, it was the first recorded extinction to be caused directly by humans. The dodo may have been the first recorded example, but the woolly mammoth, sabre-toothed tiger and other megafauna on all continents disappeared within a few thousand years of humans appearing on their scene. Nor was the dodo the last. Species are now disappearing at 50 to 100 times the natural rate, and this number is predicted to rise dramatically. If this continues, about 34,000 plant and 5,200 animal species — including one in eight of the world's bird species — face extinction. Human beings have caused the greatest extinction crisis since the natural disaster that wiped out the dinosaurs 65 million years ago.

This loss of biological diversity — or *biodiversity* — destabilises ecosystems and makes them less productive. The reduction in biodiversity also weakens an ecosystem's ability to deal with natural disasters such as floods, droughts and hurricanes, and other stresses like pollution. With the frequency and severity of disasters increasing as a result of global warming, extinctions will increase. Extinctions are irreversible and — given the world's dependence on food crops, medicines and other biological resources — pose a direct threat to humanity.

Dying rivers

Human civilisation was born on a river bank. Over millennia, river basins have provided food, water, irrigation, transport, incomes and livelihood for billions of people. But the world's rivers are in a bad state. In recent decades, more than 20 per cent of the world's 10,000 freshwater species have become extinct, threatened or endangered. Rivers suffer from reduced flow because dams and irrigation divert water to farms and cities. They die as invasive species crowd river banks and drive out their native fishes, and choke the flow of water along their courses. Agricultural, domestic and industrial pollution fouls their waters and renders them undrinkable.

Even the greatest of the world's rivers — including the Indus, the Nile, the Murray-Darling and the Colorado — struggle to reach the ocean. The Yellow River, the cradle of Chinese civilisation, flowed uninterrupted for millennia. Then, for the first time, it dried up in 1972. Since 1985 it's dried up every year. In 1998, it was dry for nearly eight months.

Overfished, acidic oceans

Oceans cover 70 per cent of the earth's surface and are home to an amazing variety of life. One-fifth of the animal protein consumed on the planet comes out of the sea. One-tenth of the food consumed in Japan is seaweed, and globally more than 100 million tonnes of seaweed are consumed each year. The microscopic organisms floating on the surface traditionally produced more than 25 per cent of the oxygen pumped into the atmosphere each year.

Life in the oceans is now in serious decline. One of the biggest threats is overfishing and the destructive fishing practices that come with large-scale commercial fishing operations. About 158 million tonnes of fish were harvested worldwide in 2005 — a sevenfold increase since 1950. Almost 76 per cent of the world's fish stocks are fully exploited or overexploited, and many species have been severely depleted, largely because of our growing appetite for seafood.

In the North Pacific Ocean an enormous concentration of plastic over 200 kilometres in diameter has formed. It's in the North Pacific Gyre, pictured in Figure 15-3. The North Pacific Gyre is the place where the currents from the west coast of America, Asia, the Arctic and the Equator converge in a giant spiral. At the centre of that spiral, millions of tonnes of rubbish float in the middle of the ocean, gradually breaking down into smaller and smaller pieces. In its early stages, it creates a deadly trap for seabirds, turtles and other marine life that get caught up in it. The plastic looks like multicoloured, floating sand, and ends up in the digestive systems of jellyfish, turtles and myriad sea birds. The toxins accumulated in this plastic contribute to the disruption of natural hormones in a wide variety of animals, including humans.

Figure 15-3: The North Pacific Gyre collects plastic and other rubbish from a vast area, creating a poisonous desert at sea.

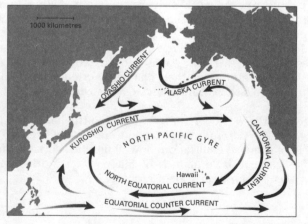

Deforestation, urbanisation and agriculture are degrading the quality of the water that makes it to ocean. Fertiliser and other chemicals from households and commercial agriculture, and even oil and other pollutants from our city streets, all end up in our oceans. Every eight months, 40 million litres of oil (nearly 11 million gallons) — the amount that came from the *Exxon Valdez* spill — washes off our streets and driveways and ends up in the ocean.

The increasing concentration of carbon dioxide in the atmosphere not only causes global warming, it also results in more carbon dioxide being absorbed by the ocean. That extra carbon dioxide changes the chemistry of the ocean so it's more acidic. The higher acidity threatens marine life, including corals and shellfish, whose shells dissolve in acidic water. These creatures may become extinct later this century from the chemical effects of carbon dioxide, even if the planet warms less than expected.

People: A Plague Like Never Before

The stresses and strains on the planet, of which global warming is one symptom, have become significant because there are so many people.

The cities of the world consume a huge volume of resources from the surrounding countryside, and produce enormous quantities of waste. Imagine what you would think if your body contained cells that multiplied many times faster than the cells of your skin, bones and other organs. If those cells formed large, unproductive clusters that robbed the neighbouring tissue of nutrients and water, medical experts would diagnose it as a malignant growth and would take radical measures to eliminate it.

If you view the earth as an organism, as many scientists do, the metaphor of the world's cities as tumours, or humans as an infection, will not surprise you. Even if you don't find that thinking about the earth as an organism is helpful, the fact that humankind has killed so many other species and is now threatening the ice caps, ocean currents and global rainfall patterns defines the human species as a disruptive influence on the planet.

Exploding population

The world's population is growing, and many people are worried that it's out of control. The United Nations, the World Health Organization and many other international organisations expect it to settle down, though — at a little under ten billion people. The reason is that people have fewer children as they get more affluent.

Table 15-1 looks at five of the world's poorest and richest countries and the birth rate in each of them. It's clear — the richer you are, the fewer children you have. Most European nations have negative population growth. The birth rate in these countries is lower than the death rate. It is only through immigration that their populations will continue to grow.

Table 15-1	Number of children per woman, by nation		
Poor Country	*Children/Woman*	*Rich Country*	*Children/Woman*
Burkina Faso	6	Canada	1.53
Sierra Leone	6.47	Australia	1.79
Mali	6.52	Norway	1.85
Guinea-Bissau	7.07	Ireland	1.96
Niger	7.19	Iceland	2.04

Source: United Nations Human Development Report.

Why do the poor add to their problems by giving themselves more mouths to feed? The simplistic answer? It's a retirement policy. There may not be a contract and there may not be a cash payout when you reach your golden years, but the idea is that your children will keep you through your twilight days. The more children you have, the better care you can expect. The challenge for organisations attempting to address overpopulation is reversing this age-old belief.

Increasing afflience and education will eventually stabilise world population. That stabilisation of the world's population won't come about without concerted effort. This leads directly to the decreased birth rate needed to stabilise world population. Even if the world population settles at 9.5 billion, that's more than enough people to put huge pressure on the world's resources. A stable population, though, allows governments to manage resources by adjusting consumption and emission levels without having to take population growth into account.

Oil depletion and a post-carbon world

If you look at the earth by night from a satellite, the most extraordinary feature is the brilliance of the millions of electric lights in the world's cities. This is dramatic evidence of the technological wizardry that has driven the growth of human civilisation over the last century, and it's also striking evidence that the planet is out of balance.

That light has been created by burning the energy captured over billions of years from sunlight by plants and then stored as fossil fuels. The sunlight was converted as it hit the earth by plants into complex carbon molecules. Those plants died and became part of the peat bogs, rainforests and swamps covering the earth. These rich sources of carbon were buried and transformed into oil, coal and natural gas.

Half of the world's known oil reserves have been burned in the 150 years since they were discovered. The US Department of Energy and the Organization of Petroleum Exporting Countries officially estimate that the oil will run out in the next 40 years. While the supply of oil slows down, the price will rise, because demand will continue to increase. At the time of writing, oil prices had broken through the psychological barrier of US$100 per barrel. This was quadruple the price of ten years ago and shows no signs of coming down. Even though the United States believes it has secured the vast Iraqi oil reserves through legislation presented to the Iraqi parliament in December 2005, the oil hasn't started to flow yet, and will only last for about one decade.

Oil is different from other resources, such as iron or wheat, because it drives all other industry. The global economy is transported by oil-fuelled ships, trucks and planes; manufacturing depends on oil-based machinery; agriculture uses oil- and gas-based pesticides, fertilisers and equipment. Cheap energy has driven recent global economic growth. Without cheap oil, many facets of the economy you have grown up with won't be possible.

Of course, it's possible to create transport fuels using coal or sunlight or algae or other crops like palm oil. The cost of extracting that fuel, though, is considerably higher than the cost of drilling a hole in the ground and letting the oil gush out under its own pressure. It is possible that the world will never again enjoy the rapid growth you've enjoyed for most of your life. Currently, most people in developed nations live as comfortably as someone in classical times who owned 40 slaves. If you own a car, you move around in comfort that was once only available to kings, and at ten times the speed. It is cheap energy that has made this possible. When energy prices rise, your current lifestyle might become the preserve of the very rich.

Polluting and poisoning

Some people, especially those in responsible positions in government and corporations, take the view that pollution is an unfortunate and undesirable side effect of progress, but that economic development is more important than maintaining clean water and air.

With a global population set to stabilise at a little under ten billion people, it doesn't take much pollution from each individual to create a hazardous world that no-one can live in. Globally, climate chaos is the latest symptom of atmospheric pollution. The ozone hole over the Antarctic has been another major pollution event of recent times.

Local pollution problems are generally caused by small particles and the photochemical smog that comes from automobile traffic and industry. At each end of the nineteeth century, England and the United States were forced to address the problem of air pollution to avoid widespread sickness in those countries. Now China faces similar problems.

In addition to the ongoing problems with air pollution, China has suffered a number of catastrophic events in which major rivers have been poisoned.

- ✔ A petrochemical explosion in northern China polluted the Songhua River with benzene and caused towns along the Russia–China border to truck in water for a number of weeks.

- ✔ In February 2006, 20,000 people in a village on a tributary of the Yangtze River were without water for days after a spill involving fluorine, amine nitrate and phenol.

- ✔ In February 2008, 200,000 people in Hubei resorted to emergency water supplies for a week because of a spill of permanganate and ammonia. It was the second time in four months that the province had been affected.

- ✔ Chinese officials admitted that 60 per cent of Chinese rivers are dangerously polluted and that underground water in 90 per cent of Chinese cities is too contaminated to drink.

Although China may represent the most visible and severe pollution threat on the planet today, rivers in Europe, America and across the world are the source of intense negotiations between nations and states that have to share the water. The section about fighting over water in Chapter 16 lists some of these negotiations.

Medicine for Mother Nature

Governments currently argue over the terms of international agreements to determine which countries will make what commitments to reduce the amount of greenhouse gases they produce. While they horse-trade, it's easy to despair about the prospects for human life on planet earth.

You can help by reducing your *ecological footprint* — the amount of land area required to support your consumption of natural resources. It's hard to know just how much difference you can actually make. The good news is that you can make a significant difference in a number of ways:

- ✔ **Investing wisely:** Make sure you put your investment or retirement money where it will do good, not harm, to the developing world.

- ✔ **Lobbying newspapers and politicians:** You get to vote only once an election cycle. Keep the pressure up between elections.

- ✔ **Providing support:** Action and lobby groups are doing these things all the time. Getting involved with them will make the most of your efforts.

- ✔ **Setting an example:** Your friends, neighbours and colleagues care as much as you do. It simply might not have occurred to them that it is quite simple to make a real difference.

- ✔ **Spending wisely:** By considering the ethics of the companies you buy from you send a message to companies that ripping off the world's poor will hurt their sales in the developed world.

- ✔ **Voting:** By demanding that your political representatives protect the world's poorest people you exercise your democratic right.

The limits to growth

One of the biggest challenges in protecting the future is the central role that growth has in everybody's way of life. When that growth comes at the cost of future lives, it's not worth having. People argue about whether growth is necessarily linked to future shortages, but current growth is causing the problems identified in this chapter.

China is constantly identified as the biggest challenge to the world economy, to reversing climate change or to reducing demand for oil. Don't forget, though, the Chinese economic miracle depends on people in rich countries buying the products made in their factories. If you watch what you buy, and concentrate on buying things that last a long time and can be repaired, you can make sure that your consumption does not fuel unwanted growth.

Renewable energy

The greenhouse gases that cause climate chaos come from transport, electricity generation and construction. If you use public transport, cycle and walk as often as you can instead of driving the car, and send goods by rail and ship instead of by truck and air, you can reduce the contribution you make to transport-related emissions. It only takes a concerted effort by a large number of individuals to make a major difference to the way transport companies organise themselves.

In the same vein, if you purchase electricity from renewable sources and get behind programs to generate electricity in your community, the electricity industry in your area will quickly get the message and begin investing in renewables at the expense of fossil fuels.

Building for the long term

Steel and concrete are massive producers of greenhouse gases. Not only do they require large amounts of energy to manufacture, the chemical processes involved produce carbon dioxide as a by-product. Because of the large volumes of greenhouse gases involved, it's important to build things that will last a long time. A century ago, buildings were constructed to last at least 50 years. As energy prices have dropped in the last century, building companies have pressured governments to relax building codes. Now, buildings are made to last only 15 to 50 years.

By investing only in buildings that are built to last, you can make a significant contribution to the awareness that building for the short term is a major waste of resources and a cause of climate chaos.

Solving the problem technically

Some people think that it's possible to re-engineer society to maintain the lifestyle of the richest countries and still reduce the amount of greenhouse gas they emit. Amory Lovins is famous for this view, and you can find out more about his ideas at www.rmi.org, the Web site of his think-tank, the Rocky Mountain Institute. For example, he points out that cars are ten times heavier than the passengers they carry, so ten-elevenths of the fuel burned is used to move the car, not the people. By enacting regulations to cut the weight of cars in half, governments could halve fuel consumption and emissions in a decade without doing anything else.

The relationship between wealth and impact on climate chaos varies because some activities emit more greenhouse gases than others. Manufacturing and using concrete, for example, emit large amounts of greenhouse gases. On the other hand, sailing wooden yachts emits almost none. As countries work to develop economic activity that emits less greenhouse gas, it may be possible to increase wealth without increasing greenhouse emissions.

Sustainable development

The distances between your home, work and the place your food is grown are a major cause of global warming. Over thousands of years on all five inhabited continents, small villages surrounded by food have grown up within a day's walk of each other and the nearest town. Major civilisations built transport networks that brought those towns within a day's travel of the nearest city. Many cities contained the original villages with remnants of countryside between them. It is only in the last fifty years that urban sprawl has overridden this model and significantly increased the distances that food and workers travel.

If you work where you live and eat food that has not been transported or processed, you will be healthier and have less impact on the environment. If you buy things made locally and pay local people to provide services, instead of buying machines, or outsourcing those services to the other side of the world, you can help reverse the excesses of the global economy, including extreme poverty.

It's good fun being green

The impact that you make in your home every day is affected by the things you buy and the actions you take. The advice given in books such as *Sustainable Living for Dummies* by Michael Grosvenor (Wiley Publishing Australia, 2007) makes it easy to reduce your impact on the planet. By replacing appliances with low energy equivalents, doing more things by hand and doing as many local activities as possible, you can significantly decrease your negative impact on the environment.

Learning to Live With the Thermostat Up

Global temperatures will increase for two decades, regardless of whether the scientists are right that industrial pollution has caused global warming, and regardless of whether politicians can negotiate an international solution that will reduce emissions over the next 20 years.

Adapting to a changed world poses a serious challenge to governments in developing countries. These countries lack the capacity and resources to assess climate risks and to make the necessary changes. Prevention is better than the cure, so helping poor countries adapt to climate change before it causes disaster can save lives and resources. Every US$1 invested in pre-disaster risk management in developing countries can prevent losses of US$7. You can read more about effectively preparing for disasters in Chapter 6.

Here are some things that will change as the globe gets hotter:

- **Travelling bugs — mosquitoes on the move:** The kinds of mosquitoes that carry deadly diseases such as malaria and dengue fever are tropical beasties. They live in swampy regions in hot climates. As more regions of the earth get hotter, the mosquito will move to places where it never used to live. One of the biggest killers of children under five in the developing world is coming to a town near you.

- **Developing drought and fire management plans:** You've already seen some of the wild weather that's associated with climate change. Most temperate countries have recently experienced the worst drought in centuries. Fire seasons are more extreme and megafires that burn for months are common, causing long-term damage to the forests.

- **New approaches to water management:** When rivers dry up and rainfall decreases, the twentieth-century approach of building bigger dams will no longer work. New solutions that rely on local collection and recycling of water will become increasingly important.

- **Migration and resettlement:** Governments that plan for the long term will start moving major population centres as well as agricultural activity. Settlement on low-lying coastal areas and investment in infrastructure near sea level is probably unsustainable.

Regardless of the detailed response to global warming, it is those countries with the most resources that will be able to act fastest after they get these plans in place. The poorest countries in the world will struggle to do any more than they have always done, surviving each day as it comes and dealing with the disasters as they emerge.

Part V
Economics and the Levers of Change

Glenn Lumsden

'He says he'd be keen to trade . . . places with you.'

In this part . . .

The world is changing, and this affects where and how people live, and how they experience poverty. We begin this part by outlining who's got what and show you which regions are most affected by the global scramble for resources. We then look at how this mad scramble is displacing populations and driving people from rural to urban areas, only to end up slum-dwellers or to move from one country to another. Many are getting caught up in human trafficking in what's become the modern slave trade. It's people who live in extreme poverty who are the most likely victims.

This part also examines the political factors affecting poor nations and the power that Western money has over these countries — and the poor who live in them. We look in detail at the impact of aid on struggling populations, how trade and world markets affect the poor, and the debt trap that affects poor nations lurching from crisis to crisis.

Chapter 16

Scrambling for Global Resources

. . . .

In This Chapter

▶ Understanding the impact of agricultural agreements and water shortages

▶ Identifying the wealth found underground

▶ Examining the value in manufacturing

▶ Defining the infrastructure that benefit populations

▶ Comparing brain versus brawn

. . . .

1 n the nineteenth century, European nations claimed most of the world's landmass as colonial possessions. In the twentieth century, global commerce interwove those same lands into the global economy. The twenty-first century has opened with a scramble for increasingly scarce resources:

   ✔ The sea-floors of the Arctic and Southern oceans are being claimed by many different countries.

   ✔ The oil reserves of the Middle East are the focus of an intense war that Dick Cheney promised 'will not end in our lifetimes'.

   ✔ The African continent is subject to posturing and investment from China and the United States that reminds many diplomats of the cold war.

This chapter surveys the global landscape to see where the most important resources are located. Perhaps even more important than where they are is the question, 'Who controls them?'

Securing Land and Water for Food

Food is essential. It's simple: If you don't eat, you die! Until the world becomes a B-grade, sci-fi TV show where you can beam up a lamb roast, food comes only from crops and animals — as it has for millennia. In short, food requires two resources that are increasingly scarce — land and water.

Living off the land

You may be surprised to know that despite the importance of agriculture in people's lives, agricultural products account for less than 5 per cent of the current value of global production. Also surprising: Three out of four of the world's hungriest people live in rural areas. For these people, rural life doesn't mean lush green pastures. It means living on the land that no-one else wants.

Access to arable land, though, doesn't guarantee enough to eat. Every Indian, for example, has about four times as much land available for growing food as every Japanese person. Japan has 337 people per square kilometre and only 13 per cent of its land is suitable for farming. India, on the other hand has 328 people per square kilometre and about 54 per cent of its land is arable, which means that it's able to be used for agriculture.

One reason that poor countries earn less from their land is that wealthy countries economically protect their farmers. The sections highlighting the causes of hunger in Chapter 9 detail the facts. One-quarter of a trillion US dollars are handed out to farmers in wealthy countries every year. Subsidised crops and foodstuffs are dumped on the world market for much less than their production cost. As a result, unsubsidised countries can import food products at less cost rather than grow their own. This may seem good for the buyer — who doesn't love a bargain? — but local farmers can't compete and so don't grow food, and that means the loss of export dollars, jobs and livelihoods. Farmers on both sides of the globe become welfare recipients thanks to the subsidies.

In a global economy farmers are tempted to grow the crops that bring the highest return. Chapter 9 discusses the impact of growing cash crops to earn export dollars. Wealthy corporations can have more influence on whether a nation can feed its people than the availability of natural resources.

Take the Amazon rainforest, for example. Between 2000 and 2006, Brazil lost an area of rainforest about the size of Greece! This land was cleared to grow crops used to make processed food sold in the northern hemisphere. This short-term exploitation of that fragile landscape damages the environment and exacerbates poverty in Brazil. Because the landscape takes generations to recover, the source of livelihood for local farmers is lost forever. In the meantime, wealth is transferred from the local economy to the shareholders of international corporations.

Instead of grabbing land with soldiers and flags, twentieth-century corporations do it legally through bank loans and contracts. Other examples of recent changes in land use that benefit foreign shareholders rather than local owners include

- ✔ Clearing of rainforest in Borneo to grow palm oil for energy production

- ✔ Use of the North American Free Trade Agreement to force Mexican farmers to grow corn for ethanol production in the United States

- ✔ Planting of jotropha (a desert shrub) and other biofuel crops in marginal land in North Africa for the European fuel industry

- ✔ The threat to traditional landowners in northern Australia from proposals for large-scale tropical agriculture

Chapter 17 looks in detail at the way that international capital influences the agricultural sector of the economies of many poor countries.

Fighting over water

Mark Twain famously observed that 'Whiskey is for drinking, water is for fighting over'. Many places in the world have proved his point: A shortage of water has led to many serious disputes between states and nations:

- ✔ Across China and India, watertables are falling as cheap electric pumps allow medium-sized farms to irrigate their crops.

- ✔ The Three Gorges project on the Yellow River diverts water from the Brahmaputra River that feeds Bangladesh and Burma into China.

- ✔ Eleven nations along the Danube have signed the Danube River Protection Convention to manage and share the limited water on which they all depend.

- ✔ The states of Colorado, California and Nevada and neighbouring Mexico have recently renegotiated access to the water of the Colorado River, which no longer reaches the sea.

- ✔ Australia's Murray–Darling River System is the source of water for 70 per cent of the nation's fresh vegetables. However, by 2007 it was so dry the government began buying back farmers' water rights, effectively a one-off payment to stop growing food.

Imagine a planet where nuclear-powered desalination plants ring the world's oceans; corporate nanotechnology cleans up sewage water so private utilities can sell it back to consumers in plastic bottles at huge profit; and the poor who lack access to clean water die in increased numbers. This sounds like a science fiction dystopia, but Maude Barlow, in her recently released book *Blue Covenant: The Global Water Crisis and the Coming Battle for the Right to Water*, describes it as the most likely future. The proceedings of the Asia-Pacific Water Summit held in Beppu, Japan, in December 2007 — available at `www.apwf.org` — indicate that she's not too far off the mark.

You may take water for granted. If you live in the United States, you splash around close to 400 litres of the stuff, on average, every day. So, while you lounge around your hotel pool in the middle of the Las Vegas desert, spare a thought for the billion people who get by on five litres a day — that's barely enough to wash your socks in, and only a quarter of what some toilets use every time you flush them. Oh yeah, and spare a second thought for the millions of girls and women who are so busy walking for hours each day to collect that water that they can't go to school or do paid work.

Maintaining fish stocks

Some people fish for fun — for the thrill of the catch and the story about the one that got away — but most people fish for food. Fish is a valuable source of protein, family income and export dollars. More than one-fifth of the animal protein eaten on the planet comes from the ocean.

The oceans have seemed to supply a boundless quantity of food but recently one fish species after another has gone into serious decline. In December 2007 it was reported that over 60 per cent of the tuna caught in the Eastern Pacific was considered juvenile. That indicates that the population isn't breeding as fast as it's being eaten, so fewer adults exist every year. The inevitable result is a rapid decline in numbers.

Scientists have warned about danger to big eye tuna numbers since the populations of Southern bluefin and Atlantic tuna collapsed in the 1990s.

A meeting of the UN Food and Agriculture Organization (FAO) in Rome in 2007 heard that international agreements are necessary to save the 50 per cent of commercially fished species that are now considered endangered. The outline of the agreement proposed by the FAO is as follows:

- ✔ Countries need to stop arguing over who has the right to fish how much, of what, from where, and learn to work together.

- ✔ Illegal fishing has to be stopped. That's easier said than done — ever tried locating a boat at sea when you're not sure where it is?

- ✔ Fishing restrictions will only work with appropriate compensation. There's no point telling a poor fisherman using his meagre catch to support an extended family that he can no longer fish, without offering him some other way to earn a living.

Grabbing as much ocean as possible

During 2007 a number of countries, including Russia and the United Kingdom, made claims over vast areas of both the Southern and Arctic oceans. Some claims were made on the grounds that sovereign waters should extend 350 nautical miles from the coast rather than the current 200 miles. Others were made on the basis of obscure explorations carried out over a century ago.

Some of these claims appear to be driven by the possibility of exploring for oil on the sea floor of these polar regions after the ice melts owing to global warming. However, these areas are also heavily contested fisheries. Some of the disputed areas are currently in international waters; others are administered by nations without sufficient resources to protect them.

There may be confusion about the reasons for these claims, but there's no doubt that a new scramble for resources is taking place in out-of-the-way corners of the ocean.

Underground Wealth

Oil, minerals, metals, diamonds: The wealth beneath your feet goes a lot deeper than the earth and earthworms. Mining has been a source of great wealth since classical times and drives the economies of some of today's richest countries, such as Australia. Mining also provides a significant contribution for many other developed economies, especially Canada and the United States.

Underground resources are in great demand by modern economies. For nations that have an abundance of them, there's the potential to greatly increase their revenue. So it seems crazy that about half of the world's most mineral-rich states and six of the world's most oil-rich nations are also some of the poorest countries.

The phenomenon that mineral wealth and economic wealth don't always go hand in hand is widely discussed. Groups such as Mining, Minerals and Sustainable Development, the International Institute for Environment and Development, and the Economic Commission for Africa — as well as many universities around the world — have all released papers on the topic.

Discovering who's got what

If you understand where in the world the major resources are located, it's much easier to identify where the resources appear to be exploited at the expense, rather than for the benefit, of the locals.

Some notable owners of underground resources include

- ✔ **Oil:** The nations of the Middle East hold 57 per cent of the world's known oil reserves. While some of those oil states have become very wealthy, there's relatively little investment in broadening their economic base. Oil-rich developing countries include some of the poorest countries in the world, notably Nigeria and Kazakhstan (about 3 per cent). Russia (9 per cent) and Venezuela (6 per cent), on the other hand, also have major oil reserves and use the wealth generated by those sources to diversify their economies. The United States still has a significant (2 per cent) share of the world's reserves but it peaked in 1970 and US consumption now far outstrips its production capacity.

- ✔ **Coal:** Many nations in the world have substantial coal reserves including China, the United States, India, Russia and Australia. Among the few rich countries without natural access to coal, Japan stands out as a resource-poor nation with significant wealth. Europe is largely self-sufficient in coal, with major deposits in Germany and the United Kingdom.

- ✔ **Iron ore:** The basis of the world's manufacturing industry, iron ore is predominantly found in Australia, China, Russia, the Ukraine and Brazil. Of these nations, only Russia and China have globally significant steel industries. The other nations export the raw ore for processing elsewhere. The bulk of Australia's iron ore goes to Japan.

- ✔ **Bauxite, aluminium:** Australia, Guinea and Russia are the three major centres of this thoroughly modern mineral. It has been exploited only since the discovery of electricity because extracting aluminium from the ore, bauxite, uses vast quantities of electrical energy. The United States and Russia own the vast majority of the world's aluminium operations, although China invested heavily in processing in early 2008.

Keeping development aboveboard

Natural resources don't have to be a curse. To make sure these underground resources make, rather than break, nations, their development needs to be aboveboard. Systems and regulations need to be in place that

✔ Make it easy to track where the resource money is going, helping to stop corruption

✔ Publicly reveal any concessions granted to the companies exploiting the resource

✔ Protect the workers and people who live near the resource, offering them similar protections to those in the developed world

✔ Keep the earnings and relevant tax revenue in the nation where the resources are being mined

✔ Prevent mining companies from polluting the environment

Drilling for the black stuff

Across the globe, about 84 million barrels are consumed each day. The contents are black and sticky and have an unmistakable smell. You can't talk about the global economy without talking about oil.

Oil prices change more often than you change your underwear. Because prices are dramatically higher now than ever before, those countries that control the world's oil supplies have a pretty powerful lever over the rest of the world economy. Oil is used to make pesticides and plastics, to transport goods, and to power industry and agriculture and build the infrastructure on which the economy runs.

Oil, like other resources that produce enormous wealth, doesn't always deliver the wealth to the country where the resource is found. In fact, some observers have coined the phrase *resource curse* to explain the negative impact that the discovery of resources has had in some countries. Professional diplomats and politicians call the resource curse the *paradox of plenty* because they find it overly simplistic to say that rich countries rip off poor ones. To be fair, the economics of the process is quite complex. For more information on this topic, see the related sidebar 'Grasping the resource curse'.

A powerful example of a country suffering from the resource curse is Nigeria. Over the past 30 years the African nation has received more than $350 billion in oil money! Yet during this time the number of Nigerians living in poverty has more than doubled from 30 to 70 per cent. Instead of using the billions to invest in stuff that would benefit the whole country — such as schools, health care or roads — the money has been used by corrupt officials and their cronies to line their pockets and buy up weapons that have plunged the nation into ongoing conflict.

Pipeline to East Timor

When East Timor gained independence in 2002 after a 24-year Indonesian occupation, a maritime border with Australia in the Timor Sea didn't exist. International law puts the border midway between the two countries but Australia withdrew from the treaty governing border disputes shortly before East Timor's independence.

Why did it do that? Well, one possible reason is billions of dollars of oil and gas. Australia pointed out that it had agreed to give East Timor 90 per cent of the tax and royalties flowing from the drilling of the oil and gas in a raw state. Sounds generous, doesn't it?

In part, it was. Investment in a brand-new nation is a risk. Partnering with Australia reassured investors, and it meant that the resource could be developed so that money would start flowing in.

What the Australian government didn't mention, though, is that the really big bucks in oil and gas are made in the refining, or downstream, revenues. Australia wants those revenues to help develop its Northern Territory. East Timor wants them to help lift the vast majority of its population out of abject poverty.

Timor is pushing for a pipeline to be built to its south coast where it plans to construct a refining plant. The bean counters reckon it could create up to 10,000 jobs as well as many spin-off industries and training and education opportunities.

Taking the underground aboveboard

When you sit in the hair salon, you may not give much thought to the source of energy that's blow-waving your hair. In recent years most of the energy has originated from below ground — coal, oil, uranium. But unlike a bad haircut, once oil and minerals have been mined they don't grow back — not in your lifetime, anyway!

Luckily there's an almost inexhaustible source of energy just 150 million kilometres (93 million miles) away, at the centre of the solar system. A gigantic fusion reactor, the sun, beams down almost one kilowatt of energy on every square metre of the planet — in the temperate regions anyway. (It's hotter at the equator and cooler at the poles.) It's this energy that fuels the wind, the evaporation of water and the growth of plants. Even oil and natural gas are simply the result of solar energy captured by plants over billions of years.

There's another source of renewable energy. The sun and the moon exert a gravitational force on the world's oceans and deliver large amounts of energy through the tides. Gravity also makes water run downhill. Running water can be harnessed to power hydroelectric projects using large dams or underwater turbines.

Grasping the resource curse

When a significant resource is found in a poor country, international corporations rub their hands with glee because it means it can be exploited at low cost with little hindrance. The effect on the nation that owns the resource is very destructive. How does this happen?

✔ The most fundamental problem is that the mining or extracting corporations can bring enormous pressure to bear on elected officials. By threatening to build ports, processing facilities and support offices elsewhere — or simply by bribing officials — they can negotiate extremely generous terms for the resources they exploit. This works in developed as well as developing countries but has a much greater impact when a country is poor.

✔ A more subtle effect, known as the *Dutch disease,* is the impact that a highly priced resource has on a nation's currency. When demand is high, the value of the currency rises and so the agriculture and manufacturing sectors become less competitive. As the price of the rice grown in that country, or the plastic buckets manufactured there, rises compared with prices elsewhere in the world, the country sells less of those goods on the international market. The country becomes more dependent on the new, highly priced resource and less able to feed and clothe itself.

✔ If one sector of a national economy booms, local investment tends to move to that sector away from other industries. With that investment goes the development of skills and knowledge. When the resource dries up or demand for it drops there is a shortage of skills in other industries.

✔ The prices of natural resources, known as commodities, tend to go up and down with supply and demand, making it difficult to predict income.

✔ The riches earned from a new resource can exacerbate wars about access to those resources or fund wars fought for other reasons, such as ideology.

Renewable energy is generated by the sun, wind and tides and by burning or processing plant matter. Renewable energy has received a lot of attention recently because fossilised energy sources pump carbon dioxide into the atmosphere. Those fossilised resources are also finite and will run out one day. Wind power now provides more than 3 per cent of Texas wind electricity and over 20 per cent of Denmark's. Renewable energy is predicted to grow by a factor of 15 over the next 20 years. The United States invested over US$10 billion in renewable energy in 2007.

From Thing to Bling: Manufacturing

Manufacturing is the production of finished goods from raw materials. That's when oil becomes petrol and plastic garden furniture; iron becomes steel and washing machines; and gold becomes jewellery. It's a more reliable way of making money than digging things out of the ground. This process involves significant investment and requires cooperation between the investor and a wide range of stakeholders, including the government of the nation where the operation takes place.

Unskilled, labour-intensive manufacturing directly benefits the poor because it creates a lot of jobs and spreads the wealth generated from the manufacturing process through the local economy. It also builds up the skills and infrastructure in that economy. More sophisticated manufacturing industries can be developed on that base of better skills and infrastructure.

More industry clearly leads to more wealth: The 48 poorest countries produce less than half a per cent of global exports. One of the keys to eradicating poverty is to diversify the sources of income. If you have a diversified economy and a broad manufacturing base you're much better able to ride the peaks and troughs of world prices and plan for the future.

Accounting for the factory factor

From classical times, poor countries have tended to ship their raw materials to rich ones. The resources are then processed, turned into their end product and sold. For example, during the nineteenth century, cotton grown in India and Virginia was shipped to Manchester in the United Kingdom and turned into clothing, then sold around the world, returning a generous profit to the English factory owners.

The owner of the factory has traditionally been the person controlling the profits generated by the process. The grower, or miner, makes much less money than the person converting those raw materials into processed goods. The economic principle at work is that the profit should accrue to the person who takes the risk. What tends to happen, though, is that those with the capital minimise their risk any way they can. The use of military force to protect the empire's commercial interests is as old as the concept of empire.

Since the 1970s the traditional relationship between capital and manufacturing has begun to shift. Manufacturing is no longer the exclusive realm of the richest countries. Asian countries have been getting in on the game and China is now the world's manufacturing powerhouse. Marketing and retailing, however, has remained in the hands of the West.

Barbie: A global ambassador

Lots of little girls love the politically incorrect, busty blonde known as Barbie. She's not only lovable, she's also a neat illustration of the world economy at work. Here's what goes into getting the latest Barbie into the hands of excited little girls around the world:

✔ She needs a body and she needs some hair. Typically, Japan and Taiwan have been responsible for getting the materials together to tick this box.

✔ Places like China or Indonesia pull it all together. Their cheap labour costs make them a good bet for this type of work.

✔ Barbie's moulds — the thing that gets the pouty lips and anatomically question-able bust just right — are produced in the United States, as are the paints that give her that glow.

✔ Barbie wouldn't be Barbie without those cute little outfits that turn her into *Space Station Barbie* or *Safari Barbie*, and let her be sold over and over to the same kid. Once again, China steps in with the cloth.

✔ When Barbie's ready, she's boxed and shipped to the customer out of Hong Kong, destined for stores like K-Mart, Target and Wal-Mart and eventually some happy kid's loving hands.

This explains where Barbie comes from but where does Daddy's cash go? Well, based on decade-old figures, when Barbie leaves China, she's worth about 2 bucks; 35 cents goes to the Chinese factory workers, and 65 cents covers the cost of the materials. The other dollar goes on transportation costs, overheads and profits for Chinese factory owners.

When she disembarks in the United States, Barbie will retail for around $10. About $7 goes on marketing, United States transport costs and retailing. That leaves another buck for Mattel (Barbie's parent company) to call profit.

Meeting the new manufacturers

There's no shortage of manufacturing success stories in formerly poor countries: South Korea, Thailand and Taiwan are famous examples. Other countries — like Brazil, India, Mexico and Argentina — have also made significant progress.

Brazil was once tagged by France's former president General de Gaulle as 'not a serious country'. Now it's the tenth biggest economy in the world with a broad industrial base. Brazil's problems, however, stem from the huge divide between rich and poor: Nearly 25 million Brazilians don't earn enough to feed themselves properly. This pattern is visible in many other newly industrialised countries as well.

Mexico is now the 13th largest economy in the world and, like Brazil, it has a large export-oriented manufacturing base. Free trade agreements with the United States, the European Union and other countries have opened its economy to trade — with mixed results: It still has a large number of very poor people. Despite this, modern Mexico is a far cry from the stereotypical Hollywood image of a Mexican peasant sleeping under a huge sombrero!

China is now the second biggest economy in the world. The country had such strong growth because of its ability to corner the market in cheap labour, and in doing so it has dramatically reduced its overall level of poverty. Manufacturing jobs that used to go to countries like Indonesia or Malaysia now go to China. And the Great Red Dragon doesn't just make dodgy kids' toys that are guaranteed to break a few days after Christmas. Like Japan 40 years ago, China has invested the profits from low-cost manufacturing in sophisticated industries making high-quality goods.

Watching jobs disappear

America's electronic engineers are nervous that China and India will take over the design of computer chips as industries in Asia become more sophisticated. However, some analysts argue that there's nothing to worry about because chip design is less profitable than research and development, which will stay in the United States. In the same way that the production of raw materials was assigned to the colonies in the nineteenth century, and manufacturing outsourced to the third world in the twentieth, the optimists argue, so basic services will shift to the developing world in the twenty-first century. The pessimists question how much industrial activity you can let go before you lose control of the lot.

In Finland a pattern of sending lower paid jobs overseas supports the idea that productive work can be outsourced without damaging profits. In the 1980s the Finnish economy shifted to high-tech manufacturing and research and development. Nokia, Finland's largest corporation, produces a mobile phone every nine seconds. Most of the manufacturing has since left Finland, but research and development is still firmly based there.

The recent history of Japan gives weight to the argument that the nations that control the manufacturing gain significant economic power. You may be old enough to remember that over 50 years ago Japan was considered a developing country that wasn't expected ever to make anything good enough to compete with Western goods. People referred to incontinence as having a Japanese bladder (i.e. a weak bladder). Now Japanese electronic goods, cameras and manufacturing equipment are considered world class and Japanese corporations own many worldwide brand names including Metro Goldwyn Mayer, Columbia and RCA Records.

The future of global poverty doesn't depend on whether the head offices of global companies remain in New York and Amsterdam or shift to Shanghai and Mumbai. For economic growth to play a part in eliminating extreme poverty, it's essential that the control of the profits moves out of the hands of an elite few in the richest nations of the world and is shared among all nations. Unless profits are shared globally, the global economy is simply extending the colonialism discussed in Chapter 5. The unfair division of profits ensures that poor countries will stay poor forever.

Falling for free trade zones

More than a hundred developing countries now have *free trade zones* that employ about 43 million people. Poor countries establish them to create jobs, and big multinational companies set up factories there to take advantage of the tax benefits. These free trade zones generally have no (or very few) taxes or import or export duties, and they're renowned for their very, very cheap labour. Sri Lanka offers incentives such as a 20-year tax-free holiday and 100 per cent repatriation of profits. This allows companies to import raw materials to the free trade zone, get local workers to transform them into saleable items like t-shirts and sneakers, then export them to sell in the West without paying a cent in tax.

The poor countries that set up free trade zones are desperate to create jobs: So desperate, in fact, that they often turn a blind eye to obvious violations of human rights. Workers in the Sri Lankan free trade zone work 12 hours a day, seven days a week for about US$70 per month. In the Shanghai free trade zone, workers get only US$0.21 per hour despite the poverty line in China being estimated as US$0.87 per hour. These workers become poorer the longer they work. Chapter 11 contains a section on the new slavery that discusses the long-term implications for the global economy.

Roads to Success: Infrastructure

Life moves pretty fast these days. No matter how hard you try, there's never enough time to do everything you want. How much harder would it be if you didn't have the modern services and organisations to support you? Take the simple example of making a cup of coffee. This can be done in about a minute — the time it takes to boil the kettle or heat up the coffee machine. But imagine, for a moment, that you must walk two kilometres along a dirt track to lug home your daily supply of water, scrounge the hills for firewood, then grind the coffee beans it has taken several months to harvest, shell, dry and roast. It's enough to make a caffeine addict go cold turkey.

The collective name for all the services that make modern life possible — did you say bearable? — is infrastructure. *Infrastructure* includes roads, rail, pipes, wires and satellites that deliver the components of your daily needs.

Benefiting the whole population

Good infrastructure makes life easier and reduces the effort required to do things. For an isolated rural community cut off from the rest of the nation during the rainy season, one bridge that provides access to important services like schools and health clinics can radically alter their wellbeing.

Infrastructure has an economic impact as well. The cost to farmers and manufacturers of getting goods to market is directly related to the quality of infrastructure. India has such a lousy transport system that up to 40 per cent of farm produce rots before it gets to market. Some countries lose the majority of their water through leaky pipes.

Traditionally, infrastructure has been provided by governments on behalf of the whole population. Now, many governments hand this responsibility over to private corporations. Whether you think this is a good thing or not largely depends on your political views.

Poor governments are unable to dictate terms to large companies about the provision of infrastructure and are at a negotiating disadvantage. For example, poor electricity and water supply in India meant that Intel recently chose to build a chip assembly plant in Vietnam instead. Also, widespread protests have taken place in India because water supplies sold by the government to Coca-Cola are actually needed by the local community. Those protestors feel the government ruled in the interests of big business instead of local people.

Following the great road of China

China is heralded as a great economic success. A big part of that success has been built on bitumen, known in some countries as asphalt, macadam or tar. Studies in China have shown that road building has been the area of government investment that has reduced poverty most.

When Chinese policy reform began in the late 1970s, the country's transport infrastructure was pretty poor. During the 1980s, trade and investment boomed and roads became clogged with traffic. New roads were needed where roads had never run before.

The Chinese made a national priority of developing their road network in the mid 1980s. Highways and freeways were built between major cities and to link remote agricultural areas with urban centres. Travel times and transport costs declined as food and manufactured products reached markets and ports more easily. The growth of the Chinese economy in the last decade is possible only because of that investment in infrastructure.

Spanning the digital divide

Not all infrastructure is built with tar, steel and concrete. The Internet, for example, has revolutionised the way everyone does business. Twenty years ago no-one would've guessed you could fall in love online, deposit your money in banks on the other side of the world or complete university degrees in another continent from the comfort of your home.

A divide has opened between people who have access to the Internet and know how to use it, and those who don't. The rich, healthy and well-educated people who have access to information technology get richer, healthier and better educated, while the have-nots miss out on global opportunities. One country that's been quick to get in on the act is India. Many of the big-name computer and software companies conduct their research and development in India. This has brought great opportunities and wealth to the country. At the same time, it has opened the digital divide within India.

Poor nations can participate fully in the global economy only if they invest in modern communications infrastructure as well as roads, rail and plumbing.

Valuing Brains Versus Brawn

As economies develop, demand for luxuries and services grows. The richer a country is, the larger its service industry tends to be.

Compare a tribal village with modern Manhattan. Aside from the local priest and possibly the chief, most people in a tribal village do real work. On the other hand, sophisticated societies generally have a middle class that does the paperwork and organises everyone else. Manhattan, for example, is almost completely dependent on the rest of the world for food and goods.

The institutions that drive the global economy are all service industries. The stock exchanges, financial institutions and media organisations generate higher returns on investment than the ownership of factories and control of raw materials.

Education (covered in Chapter 10) is essential to create this value. Educated people are better farmers, have better health, contribute to a stable democratic society, earn higher wages and help grow their country's economy. The sections that follow deal with the relationship between education levels and the global economy.

Read this . . . to take the prize

Chapter 10 makes it clear that most illiterate people live in developing countries. To escape poverty, you need to know more than how to read and write. If you want your country to have a modern and open economy, most of the population has to finish secondary school, at least, and a fair few need to go on to tertiary and technical education.

The following facts should convince you that this is true:

- Nearly 120 million kids around the world have no access to any education at all.
- Nearly 860 million adults can't sign their names or read a book. More than two-thirds of them are women.
- Africa is at the centre of the global education crisis with 40 per cent of its children not going to school at all. Those who do, get an average grand total of only 3.5 years of schooling.
- All the countries that have achieved continuous economic growth have done so with a literacy rate of at least 40 per cent.
- Everyone in the world could have a basic education if governments spent US$6 billion a year more than they currently spend on education. (The United States spends about US$8 billion a year on cosmetics, and Europeans US$11 billion a year on ice-cream!)

Graduating with a world-class degree

The world's economy is now largely dependent on high-tech industries and information and communications technology. Because of this, a country's economy will perform well only if the workforce is highly educated. As a result, developing countries with limited numbers of educated people fall further behind as the global economy grows.

Countries like Taiwan and South Korea invest heavily in tertiary education. Their university systems once catered to a small elite and have now been transformed into a mass education system. They lead the world in the percentage of young people who attend college. In Taiwan, there has been a 163-fold increase in student numbers in the last 50 years!

The United States has some of the best universities in the world — 17 of the top 20 to be exact — but the quality falls off pretty quickly after that. You don't have to look far to see this pattern of inequality in education repeated in economics. America is a rich country, the richest in the whole world, so the following facts may come as a surprise:

- The top 5 per cent of the population own more than half the wealth in that nation.
- One in eight Americans is poor; one in six American kids is poor.
- According to the International Literacy Survey, 50 per cent of Americans have low literacy skills.

The inequality in the US education system means that its workforce is less educated than comparable industrialised countries like Germany or France. This ultimately affects America's economic performance, leading it to look abroad for its skilled workers.

Poaching and the brain drain

Most of the good universities in the world are in the West, as well as most of the cutting-edge research and innovation. This means that the top students in the developing world choose to study away from home.

Developed countries entice foreign students with attractive educational scholarships, and then offer permanent residency to the best students among them. Not only students are poached. The United States, United Kingdom, Canada and Australia also actively recruit foreign medical workers, especially from African countries. The effects are explained in Chapter 12.

These factors contribute to a massive brain drain from the developing world to the West. The poorer countries invest in education to lift themselves out of poverty but that investment is effectively diverted to prop up the economies of rich Western nations. The migrating professionals take that investment with them when they leave. No wonder progress in reducing poverty is so slow; it's like struggling two steps forward and then being pushed one step back.

Hello, India calling

India has been able to revitalise its economy through a knowledge and information revolution. This path is quite a different one from China's focus on labour intensive manufacturing. India has a better education system than many of its competitors and has many English speakers. One of the positive benefits of India's colonial past, these language skills mean that India can offer niche services to the global economy.

India's investment in information technology (IT) services and education is now paying off. Information technology exports currently exceed US$10 billion and grow at 30 per cent each year. Indian software companies used to send their employees overseas to work, offering their services at knock-down rates. Now super high-speed satellite links allow them to work for global companies from India. For example, because of the time difference between India and its biggest markets, Indian programmers can fix IT problems overnight ready for their clients first thing in the morning.

At the moment India's service industries employ only 1.6 million people. That number is just a drop in the ocean of India's huge population. To create jobs for the ten million young people entering the Indian workforce every year, India needs labour-intensive manufacturing as well as a vibrant IT sector. Unfortunately, India has chronically under-invested in infrastructure. You can't transport goods if there aren't enough roads, railways or bridges.

Chapter 17

Harnessing the Might of Money

- -

In This Chapter

▶ Understanding wealth distribution

▶ Following money around the world

▶ Getting a grip on globalisation

▶ Looking at the upsides and downsides of a global economy

▶ Taking the bull by the horns

- -

You can buy your car from Germany, your coffee from Ethiopia, your clothes from China and your entertainment from the United States. You can shop on the other side of the world without leaving home, thanks to the Internet. You live in a global economy that engages almost everyone on the planet in some way.

This chapter is specifically concerned with the central role of money. If the economy is a river, then money is the water. This chapter looks at where the money is, how cash flows from one nation to another, how the global economy hangs together and the impact of the global economy on world poverty.

Checking the Balance

Cash flows where money grows. People who have money invest it where it will make them more money. The wealthy have always had an influence on political affairs, and a lot of politics is about controlling the flow of wealth. The sentiment can be summed up in the cynic's version of the golden rule, 'The person who has the gold, rules'.

Because of the might of money, it's important to remember just how much money is held by the developed countries. The world's poorest people are starving and dying, while the world's richest people live like ancient kings. Extreme poverty can be eradicated simply by reducing the size of the gap between rich and poor. Almost no-one expects that gap to be eliminated, but almost everyone agrees that it's wrong for a billion people to be hungry and dying.

You can begin to understand the scale of the problem by looking at the figures from the World Institute for Development Economics Research for the year 2000. The organisation compared the wealth of each region around the world with how many people lived there. Table 17-1 compares the percentage of the world's people and wealth in each region. You can see how wealthy the average person is in that region, compared with the average worldwide, using the wealth ratio column of the table.

Table 17-1	Global Wealth Distribution in 2000		
Region	Percentage of Global Population	Percentage of Global Wealth	Wealth Ratio
North America	6.1	34.3	5.6
Asia: High Income	4.5	22.9	5.1
Europe	14.9	29.5	2.0
Oceania	0.6	1.2	2.0
Latin America and Caribbean	8.2	4.4	0.5
Asia: Other	17.4	3.1	0.2
Asia: India	15.4	0.9	0.2
Asia: China	22.8	2.6	0.1
Africa	10.2	1.1	0.1

This table shows that the smaller number of people in wealthy countries have a much bigger pile of wealth. By dividing the percentage of the world's wealth in a particular region, by the percentage of the world's population, you get a ratio of wealth per person. The global average would be one — 100 per cent of the wealth, divided by 100 per cent of the people. North Americans, then, are 5.6 times wealthier than the world average and Africans have less than one-tenth of the world average. The shocking implication of those figures is that North Americans are, on average, 56 times richer than Africans.

In Table 17-1 China and India are shown separately because of the size of their populations and the amount of media attention their economies get at the moment. If you add the figures in the table for North America, Europe and Asia: High Income (Japan, Taiwan, Singapore and South Korea) together, it turns out that only 25 per cent of the world's population have 87 per cent of the wealth!

The distribution of wealth is often talked about in quintiles, or fifths, of the total population. If the wealth were evenly spread, then each fifth of the population would have one-fifth of the wealth. In reality, the poorest quintile — mostly living in Asia and Africa — has less than one-twentieth of the wealth. The richest quintile has more than 85 per cent.

This is an example of what is known as the eighty–twenty rule: The richest fifth (20 per cent) of the population controls four-fifths (80 per cent) of the wealth. The significant fact is that the richest quintile is more than 16 times wealthier than the poorest quintile.

Observing Cash Flows

If money makes the world go round, what's driving the money? Obviously, people put their money to work where it earns them the biggest return. The decisions about where money will be invested are a major influence on the global economy, individual nations and, hence, global poverty. The owners of capital and the governments that regulate the flow of capital are the two main protagonists in the great game that's the global economy.

The following sections outline the international channels through which these vast rivers of money flow. The purpose of mapping this high finance is to understand its impact on the world's poor.

What's all this money doing?

When you add all the numbers up, about US$5 trillion is legally traded in the international arena each year. Most of that is involved in trading between the developed nations. Some of the other amounts of money that changes hands are listed here:

- $25 billion is spent by tourists in the developing world
- $100 billion is given in aid by rich countries

✔ $100 billion is paid in tariffs that disadvantage developing countries

✔ $130 billion is paid in interest by developing countries

✔ $200 billion is sent home by migrant workers

✔ $240 billion is spent on farm subsidies in rich countries

✔ $500 billion is estimated to be spent in the international drugs trade

✔ $700 billion is spent by tourists worldwide

✔ $1,000 billion is officially spent on military hardware

✔ At least $1,000 billion changes hands in the form of bribes

✔ Up to $3,000 billion changes hands in money-laundering schemes

These numbers make the national economies of poor African countries look pretty pathetic. Equatorial Guinea, for example, has a gross domestic product (GDP) of about US$25 billion. International aid is also a very small fraction of the amount of money going around the world. Chapter 18 contains a section that breaks down the international spending on aid.

Investment: The golden goose

Banks, corporations and individuals send money from one side of the world to the other in the hope of making a few bucks. It's called investment. Investment is a powerful force for growth, and the right type of growth can reduce poverty. Chances are that you're involved in investments overseas. You may not be the rich tycoon who's buying up factories abroad, but your retirement funds are likely hard at work building a road somewhere, extracting resources or financing a factory.

Specifically, what we're talking about here is *foreign direct investment* (FDI) — money invested in another country. FDI is the heart of the global economy but it's only good for the lives of poor people if the conditions are right. Investment influences national economies through loans, aid and shareholdings. Major financial institutions actively use investment to generate wealth for themselves. It's a major international challenge to design financial systems that allow investors to profit while also helping the poor.

You're not powerless when it comes to investment. In most Western countries investment is literally compulsory in the form of retirement plans, pension funds or superannuation funds. Employer contributions to superannuation have been compulsory in Australia since 1992. The US Congress has been encouraging defined contributions to retirement plans since 1980 but the practice remains more common in government organisations. Contributory pension schemes in the United Kingdom play a similar role.

Take some time to investigate any pension funds that you or your employer have contributed to and find out what your retirement money's doing while you're working. Check out the types of investments your fund offers and compare them with others that might be available. Are the funds happy to support child labour if it turns a profit? Or do they have some ethics? Send a message to the companies you invest in by putting your cash to good work in an ethical investment fund.

Unless you're an active and engaged investor closely involved in managing your own retirement fund, your money is almost certainly invested in a *managed fund*. Managed funds offer a mixture of investments that keep your money safe while offering a reasonable return on investment. The fund allows you some choice about what that mixture is.

Different investment products have a different mixture of investment types. Most funds vary the proportion of money invested in real estate, equities and bonds, for example. Ethical funds, on the other hand, usually allow you to dictate that the money is invested in companies, or projects, that follow particular principles. This gives you the opportunity to influence the effect of your investments on the world's poor.

Trade: Looking for the win–win

Trading is the exchanging of goods — I'll trade a Team Rocket set of Pokémon cards for a holographic Japanese Omastar, for example. Most people in the world use money as a neat way of valuing the exchange. Trading is generally a better way to build a decent nest-egg than simply hoarding whatever spare change you can get your hands on. It's not the misers of the world who have money to burn.

Asia offers an example of international trade working to the advantage of poor countries. Countries across Asia were rife with poverty just a few decades ago. Trade has undeniably helped spur them on to become the great industrial powerhouses that they are today. That's not to say that Asia has eradicated poverty, but parts of Asia have certainly come a long, long way.

It's a mantra of global economists that developing countries can improve their economic position by engaging in the global economy. The problem for the world's poor is that trade doesn't always follow that principle. In fact, a good deal of trade is simply a rip-off.

Global trade is many times greater than it has ever been, even when you take into account the size of the human population. The flow of trillions of dollars around the world makes many people better off. The challenge is to make everyone better off. Chapter 19 deals in detail with the nitty-gritty of international trade and how it can entrap poor nations.

Licensing: Paying for brainpower

Trading ideas, or intellectual property, as well as things is commonplace today. Whether you're talking about trademarks, copyright or patents, licences protect the investment made by creators and innovators. The trade in ideas helps support artists, writers and inventors.

The problem is that large companies sometimes use their clout to control the availability of life-saving drugs to poor countries, or bend the rules to the disadvantage of people going about their daily business. The damage this abuse of intellectual property laws does to poor countries is discussed in the section of Chapter 12 about medicine.

Debt: Holding nations to ransom

Anyone who has borrowed more than they can afford to repay knows how hard it is to get out of the debt spiral. The amount of money owed to rich banks by poor countries is mind-boggling. In some cases, countries will never be able to pay back the loans they have accumulated, unless they're given some form of debt relief.

Debt has long had a bad reputation as a home wrecker. From Roman times until the Industrial Revolution it was illegal for Christians to earn interest by lending people money. Muslim law continues to oppose charging interest on loans because it violates the principle of kindness and takes advantage of the needy.

Chapter 20 looks in detail at the *debt trap* and how it is responsible for a large part of the global poverty that confronts the world today.

Aid: More please

The flow of money from rich countries in the form of aid designed to alleviate poverty is in the order of US$100 billion a year. This is a lot of money, but it's less than the US government has spent on the war in Iraq every year since 2004. It's also less than one month's global expenditure on oil.

The aim of international aid agencies is to use aid dollars to create long-term benefits for poor nations rather than simply alleviate a temporary shortage of cash. Chapter 18 discusses the role of aid in alleviating poverty and the success and status of various approaches.

Tourism: Spreading affluenza

The twentieth century bred a new species. They travelled in swarms, rode on air-conditioned buses and snapped photos of their grinning faces everywhere they went. They're called tourists.

Most tourism is confined to rich countries, but the right kind of tourism can reduce poverty. Each year some US$25 billion is transferred to poor countries through tourism. That's a lot of potential for helping the poor.

The wrong type of tourism can make things worse. It can deepen inequalities, cause environmental problems and redirect much-needed money into making tourists comfortable instead of going into public services. South East Asian countries have been especially troubled by the foreign *sex tourist* who fuels a sex industry that exploits and trafficks men, women and, sadly, children.

In 2004 more than 750 million people headed to foreign lands as tourists. They dropped more than US$700 billion as they flitted about the globe. This amount has increased almost every year for the last ten years but is expected to drop slightly as air fares rise in line with oil prices. Topping the list of most-visited nations were France, Spain, the United States, China and Italy.

Remittances: Sending cash home

When the going gets tough, the tough get going. Millions take that sentiment quite literally and head to 'greener' pastures in foreign lands. Many of these migrants send their earnings back home as *remittances*.

We're not just talking about a few nickels and dimes, either. In 2005 the World Bank estimated that nearly 200 million migrants sent home more than US$230 billion. That's more than double the amount of international aid given by rich countries each year. And that's counting only *official* remittances tracked by the financial institutions. An unknown number of informal transfers take place on the black market, and in people's luggage.

India, China and Mexico are the big recipients of this flow of money, each earning about US$20 billion in the last decade. Not every country can take advantage of the potential of remittances. Countries with rich neighbours that have open-door immigration policies are best placed to reap the rewards.

Unlike some cash flows, remittances make a direct and immediate difference to the poor. Money sent home tends to be spent on basic family welfare such as food, clothing and education. Remittances keep millions of people around the world above the poverty line.

Illicit flows: The black market and beyond

Not all flows go through official channels. Up to US$1 trillion (that's 12 zeros!) is paid in bribes each year; hardly an insignificant cash flow. And the knock-on effects are equally huge. Turn to Chapter 7 for a blow-by-blow description of how these under-the-table deals prevent the poor getting what they need.

Millions of people are also involved in producing illicit drugs and trafficking or selling them. Illegal drugs make up as much as 14 per cent of the world's agricultural produce. The United Nations Office on Drugs and Crime estimates this trade generates up to US$400 billion a year. That's about 1 per cent of the world's GDP or about 8 per cent of world trade!

Hiding all these ill-gotten gains is big business too. *Money laundering* is the job of making dirty money look legitimate. Some countries count money laundering as their main industry. Belarus makes up nearly a third of its GDP in this way. Globally, money laundering accounts for between 2 and 5 per cent of global GDP, according to Dow Jones. That's between US$1 and $3 trillion!

While pondering these vast flows of illegal funds, don't forget about your bog-standard, run-of-the-mill, old-fashioned crime. The dividends of a morally questionable lifestyle immersed in the dark underbelly of society can be considerable. In 1999 international crime syndicates cleared about US$1.5 trillion.

When cash doesn't cover it

Measuring the value of illegal trade is almost impossible, because criminals don't complete tax forms. Also, not all of the profit from black market deals is converted directly to cash. One of the ways that global criminals circumvent the watchful eyes of the world's customs agents is to keep exchanging things from one place to another place where the rules are different. Drugs manufactured in Afghanistan might be exchanged for undeclared diamonds in Nigeria and then converted to US dollars in Singapore.

Recognising Globalisation

You know you live in a global economy because you see television pictures from all over the world and, through the Internet, can read a newspaper from anywhere in the world. You can buy gourmet food from Europe, textiles from Cambodia, plastic goods from China and books printed in India more cheaply than you can buy their locally made equivalent. You can probably afford to travel anywhere in the world at least once in your life. In global terms, you're rich.

These are all benefits of globalisation that you enjoy. *Globalisation* is the process of linking the world's economies more closely. The official language is *increasing interdependence*. The danger for the world's poor is that your benefits might be paid for by their poverty.

Shrinking the world

If you spend much time travelling, you know that countries are growing more similar. You can buy a lot of the same food wherever you are in the world. Cars are pretty much the same the world over, and many countries watch the same television shows. Economically, politically, socially and culturally, countries are connected and getting closer. That's globalisation at work.

If you want political examples, just look at the European Union. Decisions are made at a level above the nation-state. Trade and labour flow freely between members. The United Nations and its agencies are another example. Countries voluntarily sign up to these organisations on the understanding that they will lose some independence. The result is that many decisions are taken on a truly international level.

One way to picture globalisation is to imagine the world as getting smaller every day. London, for all intents and purposes, is no longer as far from Beijing as it used to be. Sure, the distance in kilometres is no different, but it takes less time to travel between the two cities than ever before. The ease with which communication flows is at an all-time high; and both products and people move between the two places as never before.

New name, old game?

Globalisation makes countries more closely integrated economically, politically and culturally, but it's hardly the first time this has happened. You've heard of the Roman Empire, right? In the time of the Romans, trade spanned the known world. Enormous exchanges of people and technology took place.

Other historical periods have also seen something like globalisation: Genghis Khan's Mongol Empire of the thirteenth century established overland trade routes, and the colonial imperialism of the nineteenth century set up overseas ones. So what's up with this globalisation thing? What's so new and important about it this century?

Part of the answer is that this time round the globe is completely circumnavigated. You've seen the pictures from space; you know that this time it really is a global empire. By contrast, the Mongol or Roman civilisations hadn't even mapped the entire world. If entire continents are left out, it can't really be called globalisation now, can it?

Perhaps more significantly, local culture and politics have been particularly affected as well this time round. Cheap energy and global communication networks bring individual citizens close together. Messages fly around the world in seconds and people move around in days. The impact of modern globalisation on individual citizens is many times greater than anything the subjects of Roman or Mongolian rulers ever experienced. For more on this topic, see 'Cultural Imperialism' later in this chapter.

Checking the Fine Print

Advantages and disadvantages lurk behind every aspect of the global economy. It's difficult to analyse the implications of each news story on the global economy as it blips across your screen. To give a little context, here's a bird's-eye view of the good and not-so-good aspects of the global economy.

Realising the benefits

Better communication leads to greater understanding, and the power of a network is multiplied by every additional person added to it. The scale of the modern world is leading to completely new opportunities for humanity.

Efficiency

Large businesses have a number of advantages. Size brings efficiencies, fundamentally because management costs do not expand with the volume of money a business turns over. The amount of influence that a company has on governments, the media and its customers also increases with size. Large companies have large marketing budgets. They can span several continents and get access to raw materials at the best possible prices. They can move production or services to wherever the labour force is cheapest.

On the other hand, global communication networks and cheap, rapid transport allow small organisations to play in the global marketplace. A two-person business operating from a garage can trade globally and, if it knows its stuff and provides great service, can compete with the largest players.

Globalisation breeds efficient corporations through economies of scale and outsourcing of tasks best done by small organisations with specialist skills.

Choice

There's nothing quite like choice. Going to the supermarket and choosing what you feel like for dinner. Picking out your new car, the colour, the best features from anywhere in the world. The global economy gives you choice. Well, if you have the money, anyway.

You may even have choice in terms of who you work for, how long you work, or even where you work. Hundreds of millions of people move to other countries for work. It might be personal preference or it might be based on where you can earn the most.

Stability

No-one goes to war unless they think it's in their interest. And when two countries are getting rich by doing business together, war is not in either of their interests. Economic integration is one of the most powerful ways of ensuring that two countries don't come to blows. It breeds stability.

Globalisation encourages the tackling of problems at the global level. Tackling environmental issues or cross-border criminal activity is virtually impossible for one country alone. But with cooperation and international organisations, these problems can be addressed.

Better legal coverage

Even laws are subject to the forces of globalisation. Countries such as Australia have put in place new legislation allowing them to prosecute their own citizens for crimes committed abroad. This means that a sex tourist who engages in underage sex overseas can actually be convicted and do time in his or her home country — up to 17 years for a single offence.

International laws have also been established to ensure that governments treat other nations with dignity. The tribunals that have investigated the behaviour of tyrants like Slobodan Milosevic and Saddam Hussein have received widespread support. Despite success prosecuting its enemies, the United States has repudiated the International Criminal Court. This significantly undermines the development of international law.

Counting the costs

Being part of the global economic system isn't all good, especially if you're on the losing end of a deal involving a sum with 12 zeroes in it!

Exploitation

People who work on the ground in poor countries see first-hand the downside of a market-driven, global economy. Money seeks profit, so concern for the environment, human rights and the long-term interests of any particular nation come well down the list. All of these problems hit the poor hardest.

Labour standards are thrown out the window as poor countries compete for business by offering lower standards and wages than their neighbour. This sparks a 'race to the bottom'. Governments trade the wellbeing of their people for a short-term injection of cash.

Trade agreements can have a less than beneficent outcome. The North America Free Trade Agreement (NAFTA), for example, has been used 16 times by US-based companies to override Mexican and Canadian laws banning pollution.

Hidden inefficiencies

Corporate accountants consider environmental and social costs of doing business as 'external'. That's an accounting term meaning that they're somebody else's problem. The rule is, if you can make someone else pay, you should. When a government offers cheap electricity to an aluminium manufacturer, the company shareholders are justifiably pleased. The local people who have to pay more for their electricity, though, may not be so happy. You can hardly blame the aluminium company for seeking the best deal; it's simply the way that money works.

The role of governments is to regulate business activity in the interests of the people they represent. The problem for the world's poor is that most governments are not looking out for their interests. International organisations striving to eradicate poverty face this uncomfortable fact every day.

Instability

An integrated world economy generally brings political and economic stability. In specific locations, however, the impact of the global economy may be quite destabilising. Examples include the Asian financial crisis of the 1990s and the bursting of the dotcom bubble in 2000. Either way, the thrashings of the global economy have global implications.

As poor countries open up their local economies to the global system, economic pressures can change the status quo. What was previously a productive and efficient sector may collapse. Production may turn to new goods or services. With these shifts comes unemployment. The poor bear the brunt of these changes, and the impact can be long lasting.

Cultural imperialism

The downside of a global consumer culture that probably gets most attention in the Western press is the damage to local cultures. National identities disappear under the overwhelming force of global cultures. People give up the languages and customs of their grandparents to participate in the world economy.

By definition, this homogenisation of culture means the loss of diversity. It also spreads global problems like cigarettes and alcohol. Local cultures and traditional values provide a contrast to the global culture that might offer relief or give people alternatives. As that diversity disappears, so do those options.

Not everyone gets to enjoy the dubious benefits of immersion in the dominant culture. The world's poor are involved in other ways: Growing the beans that pad out Starbucks' coffers, sewing the clothes that adorn the fashion-conscious, manufacturing the components that make up the iPod, or pressing the CDs that carry the tunes of pop music's latest diva. Have a look at Chapter 11 find out about the roles played by the poor in the global economy.

Steering the Global Juggernaut

Globalisation and the world economy are amoral. Technological change and economic systems are tools in the hands of people. There have been many technical advances that appeared to have a negative impact at the time they were introduced. All change has consequences and some of those consequences aren't good.

When the printing press appeared, illustrators of manuscripts and travelling storytellers were upset by their diminished role in society. Similarly, mental arithmetic is not as widely practised and taught today as it was 40 years ago before calculators became available.

Whether change is welcome or not depends on how it's steered and who's doing the steering. The final outcome of a particular cultural or technological change may not be clear for decades or centuries. Sometimes governments with the best intentions put regulations in place or support development that turns out to have a negative impact.

You can make a difference by getting involved. Interact with the global economy. Marshal your spending power, influence your friends and lobby your government to address the challenges facing the world's poor. The global economy is steered by decisions made by the millions of individuals who buy the goods it produces. In a global world, you can make a difference by making your own decisions and standing by them. Others will follow your lead.

Controlling the cash

Trade, investment and loans aren't just random, uncontrolled flows. There are plenty of institutions that try to keep some checks and balances in place:

- ✔ **Banks:** Money is power. And you can't talk about changing the world without looking at the guys holding all the money. Banks make decisions about who gets what and at what price (interest rates). The decisions made by the suits in Zurich or Manhattan have huge implications even for the beggars on the streets of Nairobi or Kinshasa.

- ✔ **The Bank and the Fund:** The World Bank and the International Monetary Fund were set up to govern financial relations between states. They now focus almost exclusively on lending to developing countries. The trouble is, they're not very good at it. Both institutions have a rather poor track record when it comes to helping the world's poor. Chapter 19 describes the role these two institutions have played in exacerbating world poverty.

- ✔ **Trade:** The Global Agreement on Tariffs and Trade (GATT) was born shortly after World War II. But it didn't grow into a fully fledged organisation until 1998 when it became the World Trade Organization (WTO). The WTO is designed to encourage and regulate the global trading system to ensure it's free and fair. Unfortunately, right now it's neither of these things. Chapter 19 explains why.

- ✔ **Development banks:** It may sound like an oxymoron, but so-called development banks have sprung up around the world with the objective of making profit while alleviating poverty. They promote economic and social development within their regions but are, generally, more concerned with high-level politics than with what is good for the people on the ground. Consequently, they've had major wins and losses.

Tracking the corporation

If being the keepers of money gives power to the banks, then the guys making all the money must have power too. In fact, they are interlinked. The financial institutions that own the world's biggest corporations are also shareholders in the world's biggest banks.

Today's largest multinational corporations have budgets greater than those of many countries. Of the world's top 200 economic players in 2001, only 56 were countries — 144 were corporations. General Motors, Wal-Mart, ExxonMobil and DaimlerChrysler all have revenues greater than the GDP of the 48 least developed countries. That's big bucks. So it's no wonder that multinational corporations can wield enormous influence over international relations. Here are some examples of how companies have a major effect on the wellbeing of many people:

- Large international companies often have the ear of politicians. The oil industry in the United States has direct influence on both foreign and domestic policy. Business interests have played a large part in slowing down action to address global warming. Businesses have political power.

- At least 15,000 Indians died in an industrial disaster at a Union Carbide pesticide plant in 1984. Up to 120,000 people in the area continue to suffer severe health problems as a result of the disaster. Local worker groups blamed cost-cutting and inadequate safety regulations for the catastrophe. Union Carbide claimed sabotage was the cause.

- Cocoa growers in Africa's Côte d'Ivoire supply close to half the world's chocolate. They're heavily involved in both child labour and slavery, but the major chocolate producers continue to buy their beans; and customers, like you, continue to buy their chocolate. The companies are more interested in profit than justice, and customers don't make the connection between their chocolate and enslaved children.

- The pharmaceutical industry is never one to shy away from a fight. From South Africa to the Philippines to India, pharmaceutical companies have taken on entire countries in their quest for greater profits. Check out Chapter 19 for more on Big Pharma.

FLOODLIGHT

Good for body, soul and business

How many international high-street cosmetics retailers can you name? Only one comes to mind for co-author Adam — that may be because he's a guy, or it may be because he works there — and that's The Body Shop. The Body Shop is a very visible campaigner for fair trade. And its actions speak louder than its words.

The Body Shop began selling homemade cosmetics in the United Kingdom in the 1970s. Its founder, Anita Roddick, knew that a successful business needs a unique selling point. And she had just that. Her niche was social and environmental activism. It turned out that people were willing to pay higher prices for products with environmentally sustainable natural ingredients.

The Body Shop doesn't just preach its activist messages, it lives them. The cosmetics company refuses to test its products on animals (something its founder claims makes them ineligible to sell to the Chinese market),

it promotes fair labour practices and safe working environments, and campaigns for *Trade Not Aid* — 'creating trade to help people in the Third World utilise their resources to meet their own needs'.

It has to be said that The Body Shop hasn't escaped criticism. Shareholders have taken issue with the extent of the social activism within the company. Critics have even claimed it uses its social values as selling points without doing enough to back them up with action. And of course, The Body Shop has recently been purchased by L'Oréal, a French cosmetics group with a less sparkly corporate social responsibility record than Anita Roddick's.

Whatever the future of The Body Shop, its success clearly demonstrates that people will pay for social responsibility. It also shows how you, the customer, can make a difference simply by spending your cash in the right places.

Getting a conscience

Companies increasingly recognise their responsibility as corporate citizens to the rest of society. This responsibility goes beyond simply complying with the law and means not discounting the lives of people affected by the company's commercial activity. The buzzword is *corporate social responsibility* and it requires companies to account for the long-term effects on the environment and the people they work with.

Corporate social responsibility is good for business. Here's why:

- ✔ **Investing in people:** If individuals working for you care about the morality of how you do business, then you should too. If you want to keep a happy and productive workforce, being a good and conscientious employer is a great way to do it.

- ✔ **An insurance policy:** After news broke of Nestlé cashing in on African mothers by peddling powdered milk to them, they had a rather slow year. It can take decades to build a brand, but minutes to destroy it. Nestlé is still recovering from the black mark. Taking social responsibility seriously helps corporations ward off these risks.

- ✔ **Keeping a shiny reputation:** Economics tells us that price and quality are all that matter to the customer. But reality tells us that a company's reputation and practices have impacts too. Prospective customers get a warm fuzzy feeling when they know that a company is being a good citizen. That means more cash for the company.

Corporate awareness of the need for social responsibility may not be the answer to all the world's woes, but it certainly is a tool that helps you coordinate your purchasing decisions. In fact, a corporation's only legal imperative is to maximise the value for its shareholders. Keeping customers and staff happy is the only reason a company needs to be socially responsible. By organising, customers and staff can make companies care.

Organised individuals are the most powerful force in the world. By coordinating your purchasing decisions and sharing them with your friends, colleagues and anyone else who'll listen, you actually can change the world. By the way, every corporation is only a large organisation of individuals. So you're in good company.

Chapter 18

Delivering Aid That Works

id is help given by wealthy countries to poor countries to deal with an emergency or to undertake long-term development. Aid is generally provided in the form of money, goods or services. Increasingly these days, funds are lent rather than given (officially, that's not aid).

Aid by itself isn't enough to eradicate poverty, but it can play a vital role in greatly accelerating development through initiatives such as the following:

✔ Improving transport, electricity and telecommunications infrastructure

✔ Restoring and developing health and education systems

✔ Reducing mortality and malnutrition rates among children under five

✔ Providing clean water and sanitation

✔ Reducing the incidence of HIV/AIDS, tuberculosis, malaria and other diseases

✔ Reforming the civil service, police, military, judiciary and legal system

Aid accelerates the development of a country, or helps it overcome a set-back to its development. However the money is given, the intention of providing aid is to help countries stand on their own feet, not to bail them out temporarily. The mantra for aid agencies is, 'Give a man a fish and you feed him for a day, but teach him how to fish and you feed him for a life time.' If poor countries had to rely completely on economic growth alone, many of them would be stuck forever; many more would take decades to make changes that are urgently needed now.

This chapter outlines how international aid has evolved, what challenges aid agencies face and how you can help to ensure that aid does what it's supposed to — alleviate the effects of global poverty.

Who's Who in the Aid Zoo

There are three main types of aid:

- **Bilateral aid:** Aid from the government of one country directly to another. This money is dispensed through the government's aid agency such as AusAID in Australia, USAID in the United States or DFID in the United Kingdom.

- **Multilateral aid:** Aid from the government of a country to an international agency, such as the United Nations, the World Bank or the International Monetary Fund, or to regional development banks.

- **Individual aid:** From individuals through non-government organisations (NGOs) such as World Vision or Oxfam. Very rich philanthropists like Bill Gates and Warren Buffett set up their own agencies, such as the Gates Foundation.

Bilateral aid

Government aid is important because governments have the resources to meet the challenge of development and relief. The downside of government aid is that it's also political and it often comes with strings attached.

The United States supports aid programs that encourage economic growth, agriculture and trade, global health, democracy, conflict prevention and humanitarian assistance. It works in four regions of the world:

- Sub-Saharan Africa

- Asia and the Near East

- Latin America and the Caribbean

- Europe and Eurasia

European nations tend to focus on Africa, the eastern part of Europe and the countries west of China.

Australia's aid program is focused on its neighbours in the Asia–Pacific, where two-thirds of the world's poor live. Australia also sends some aid to Africa and the Middle East. AusAID is the Australian government department that distributes funds, contracts aid work to Australian and international companies and monitors the government's overseas aid program. Its programs support a variety of approaches, from small grass-roots projects by local non-government organisations through to huge infrastructure or government reform programs directed by the World Bank.

Multilateral aid

Multilateral agencies — international organisations with countries as members — can bypass national politics when it comes to aid. Pooling funds from many donors means there's a lot more to go round and a lot more can be accomplished as a result.

Multilateral agencies such as the World Food Programme (WFP) implement a lot of their programs through partnership with NGOs. This means that they take cash from governments and other donors, use it to buy food and store it until a crisis arises, but then pass the food on to NGOs to actually get it to the people. The WFP realises that its strength lies in fundraising and high-level strategy and that other agencies are better at ensuring that the food actually saves lives.

Unfortunately, multilateral institutions can be as susceptible to global politics as national ones. When deliberation in the United Nations Security Council ends in deadlock, the organisation can grind to a halt. Nothing gets done. And when countries like Russia, China and the United States who sit on the Security Council all have the right to veto and decision, inaction is often the order of the day.

Individual aid

Unless you're Bill Gates, individual generosity doesn't generate the resources to eliminate poverty on a global scale, even though the programs that individual aid funds do make a dramatic difference to many poor communities. For example, globally, individuals give about US$8.8 billion through organisations such as Oxfam, World Vision and BandAid. This is only 13 per cent of the amount of aid paid by the world's richest countries in 2002 — approximately US$58.3 billion.

These aid agencies are known as *non-government organisations (NGOs)* because they're independent of any government. Not all NGOs collect individual donations and distribute them internationally, though. There are non-government organisations with all types of funding models, doing all types of work. Most NGOs were set up simply to get things done without having to wait for the wheels of government to turn. Many of the NGOs today grew out of war and conflict.

- ✔ The Oxford Committee for Famine Relief was formed in 1942 in response to famine in Greece, objecting to the use of starvation as a weapon of war. Oxfam (Oxford Famine, Oxfam, get it?) has grown into a confederation working in more than 100 countries with an annual budget of over $300 million.

- ✔ Save the Children began as a response by concerned Britons at widespread hunger in Germany after World War I.

- ✔ World Vision cut its teeth saving the orphans of the Korean war in the 1950s. It now employs nearly 25,000 staff members in 90 countries with an annual budget of over $2 billion. The World Vision partnership works with about 100 million people across the world and has more than five million supporters and volunteers.

- ✔ CARE — originally the Cooperative for American Remittances to Europe — was originally set up to provide relief to the survivors of World War II. It used to send CARE packages to Europe before it evolved into the Cooperative for Assistance and Relief Everywhere.

- ✔ Amnesty International can trace its inspiration back to the Spanish Civil War; and Médecins Sans Frontières harks back to civil war in Nigeria.

Ever since the 1970s, NGOs have multiplied like bunnies. Today there are somewhere between 10,000 and 40,000 . . . and that's just the international ones. When you include local NGOs it gets pretty hard to count. The United States and India are estimated to have nearly two million each! There are no limits when it comes to defining NGOs. They can be big or small, religious or secular. They can focus on helping communities develop or on providing relief after emergencies. They can be national or international, and they can focus on particular areas or cover everything under the sun.

NGOs can be all about doing or they can be about talking — and both have their place. They get their funding from different places: Some NGOs rely entirely on grants from governments and institutions; others sell goods like Fairtrade products or goods produced in the communities in which they work. There are some that rely wholly or in part on private donations. NGOs are a rather eclectic bunch.

Figuring Out If Aid Works

If you decide to tackle your waistline by a rigorous combination of diet and exercise, you'll find yourself a few kilos lighter and feeling mentally and physically better about yourself in no time at all. Great stuff, but you may not know which worked best — the diet or the exercise?

A similar dilemma exists when measuring the impact of international aid. People's lives may improve or get worse because of changes in the economy, or in the political climate, or in the terms of trade. Because so many variables exist, in the end, you're left unsure whether aid works. The flab-fighting analogy has another similarity: Battling poverty is much easier when aid is available as part of the solution. You can't prove the exact outcome it has, but you can show that it does help.

The prime minister of the United Kingdom, Gordon Brown, wrote in the *Guardian,* 'A century ago people talked of what we could do *to* Africa. Last century, it was what can we do *for* Africa. Now, in 2006, we must ask what the developing world, empowered, can do for itself.' When you talk about solutions to poverty it's easy to forget that the people who make the biggest difference are the poor themselves. They just need help.

As Brown says, the role of those in richer countries is to help support those in poor countries — to empower the poor.

Making a difference

Aid *is* working. Over the past four decades, the total number of deaths of children under 5 years old has fallen by about half. That's about ten million living humans who might otherwise be dead, every single year. It's still not enough — the other half are still dying — but it proves that aid can make a difference.

When aid is done well, lives can be saved and lives can be changed. Aid improves life in the following areas:

- ✔ **Diseases follow the dodo:** Take smallpox. In the late 1960s the disease was killing two million people a year. Today, thanks to concerted international efforts, no-one is dying from it. And cases of polio are down from 350,000 in 1988 to fewer than 2,000 in 2005. Hopefully within our lifetimes polio will also go the way of the dodo.

- ✔ **Reducing disaster's impacts:** The Indian Ocean tsunami in 2004 could have led to millions of people dying from disease, infection and exposure. Often, more people die after a disaster from these causes than during the disaster itself. Thanks to the efforts of NGOs, multilateral agencies and governments around the world, the deaths were largely limited to those caused by the wave itself. Emergency relief is saving lives all round the world.

- ✔ **Needles for all:** In the 1970s just 5 per cent of the world's population were being protected by vaccinations. It's now up above 70 per cent and rising. Millions of lives are being saved each year thanks to a few jabs.

✔ **Clean water:** Thanks to aid projects that have improved water quality and helped many to live more hygienic lives, millions of children are no longer at risk of diarrhoea. In 1980, 4.6 million kids died from the infection. By the year 2000, this number was down to 1.5 million.

✔ **Primary school attendance:** More children than ever before are completing a basic education today. And the knock-on effects for their health, their children's health and the health of their country's economy are immeasurable.

✔ **More skilled health personnel attending births than ever before:** Every region in the world gives both mother and child a better chance of emerging healthy from the difficult process of childbirth.

Aid has also been making a huge difference by bringing peace, economic opportunities, new skills and education; improving the health of the environment; building up infrastructures; helping to foster democracy; and empowering communities to take control of their lives.

Stretching your dollars

Just because your country's stuffed and paying through the nose to cover the interest on its debt, it doesn't mean you have to miss out on financial support. Community development banks have proved incredibly successful in helping the poor to access funds that can set them up for life. *Community development banks* typically provide small loans to help poor people kick-start their own business. If you're poor, chances are no conventional bank is going to look at you twice. That doesn't stop you having a great idea or untapped skills that could turn a profit. Often, the loans aren't to individuals but to groups of people working together in a new business or a cartel.

These banks quickly discovered that women are a good bet. They're less likely to drink or gamble a loan away, and they tend to be diligent about making repayments. So women have become frequent borrowers from these institutions. The Grameen Bank (introduced in Chapter 1) is a great example of this mechanism at work.

Many organisations operating independently of governments have seen the positive effects of community development banks and decided to get in on the action. They've provided these small loans (calling them *microfinance, micro-credit* or *micro-enterprise development*) to the communities in which they work.

One of the downsides of microfinance is that it tends to help the moderately poor. But the very poorest are often without the skills needed to make use of such loans or even access them in the first place. Despite this small caveat, community development banks and microfinance show how a little money in the right place can go a long way. They also demonstrate that it's not handouts the poor need, but the freedom and power to change their own lives.

Working to the Millennium Development Goals

A concerted effort to eradicate extreme poverty was declared by 192 countries in the year 2000. Known as the United Nations Millennium Declaration, the statement sets out the top priorities for international efforts. The experience of the last century has taught people in the aid sector many lessons. One of the toughest lessons learned is that you need to know what you want to achieve, and you also need to specify targets and ways of measuring progress toward these targets.

The official Millennium Development Goals, together with the targets that have been set for making progress towards those goals, are covered in the following sections. The indicators used to measure progress towards those targets and the current progress that has been made on each of those indicators are available at www.un.org/millenniumgoals, on the official United Nations Web site.

The Millennium Development Goals are a touchstone in the aid sector. International diplomats, government agencies and most aid workers use the goals, targets, indicators and the terms used to express them as a reference point for programs to eradicate world poverty. If you want to get involved in this sector, study up on the goals, so you're talking the same language as everyone else.

Goal 1: Eradicate extreme poverty and hunger

The primary focus of the goals is to eliminate extreme poverty. Note that the emphasis is on extreme poverty, rather than poverty generally. Also, the targets set for measuring progress are to halve extreme poverty by 2015 rather than eliminate it altogether. The formal targets are to

- Reduce by half the proportion of people living on less than a dollar a day
- Reduce by half the proportion of people who suffer from hunger

Goal 2: Achieve universal primary education

Education is critical to helping a population climb out of poverty. The importance is outlined in detail in Chapter 10, along with the reasons why special emphasis is given to educating girls. The target for 2015 is to ensure that all boys and girls complete a full course of primary schooling.

Goal 3: Promote gender equality and empower women

Feeding, educating and empowering women improves the health of everyone in a society and gives children a much better chance in life. The role of women in helping their families escape poverty is the subject of Chapter 8.

The target set in the Millennium Development Goals focuses on the young. The aim is to eliminate gender disparity in primary and secondary education by 2005, and at all levels by 2015.

Goal 4: Reduce child mortality

The death of newborn babies and very young children saps the resources of a society. Aside from the grief and suffering caused by infant death, it means that women are pregnant or nursing more often, which impacts on their health and their productivity. Chapters 8 and 12 discuss child mortality in some detail. The aim is to reduce by two-thirds the mortality rate among children under five by 2015.

Goal 5: Improve maternal health

Next to looking after babies, looking after mothers before and after they give birth is the most powerful way to improve the overall health of a population. You can read more about maternal health in Chapters 8 and 12. The measure of success for this Millennium Development Goal is to reduce by three-quarters the maternal mortality ratio.

Goal 6: Combat HIV/AIDS, malaria and other diseases

Diseases inflict great hardship on their victims and indirectly on the whole society. When a disease is rampant — as AIDS is in many African countries — it has a major social and economic impact, as described in Chapter 12. The targets set to measure success towards this Millennium Development Goal are to

✔ Halt and begin to reverse the spread of HIV/AIDS

✔ Halt and begin to reverse the incidence of malaria and other major diseases

Goal 7: Ensure environmental sustainability

The long-term survival of any country is dependent on preserving its ability to feed itself. Some of the environmental challenges facing the poor are related to climate change and are dealt with in Chapter 15. Other environmental issues are dealt with as part of the discussion around health in Chapter 12 and living in slums in Chapter 14. Whatever the specific impact of a particular problem, as a general rule it's fatal to extract resources in such a way that following generations have no future. The targets set under this Millennium Development Goal intend to

✔ Integrate the principles of sustainable development into country policies and programs, and reverse loss of environmental resources

✔ Reduce by half the proportion of people without sustainable access to safe drinking water by 2015

✔ Achieve significant improvement in lives of at least 100 million slum dwellers by 2020

Goal 8: Develop a global partnership for development

All developing nations, and all agencies working to help the poor, recognise that unfair trading rules impoverish poor countries. To eliminate extreme poverty, the poorest countries in the world have to be given a chance to get ahead economically. To measure progress towards this goal, seven separate targets have been set:

✔ Develop further an open trading and financial system that's rule-based, predictable and non-discriminatory, and includes a commitment to good governance, development and poverty reduction — nationally and internationally.

✔ Address the least developed countries' special needs. This includes tariff- and quota-free access for their exports; enhanced debt relief for heavily indebted poor countries; cancellation of official bilateral debt; and more generous official development assistance for countries committed to poverty reduction.

✔ Address the special needs of landlocked and small island developing states.

✔ Deal comprehensively with developing countries' debt problems through national and international measures to make debt sustainable in the long term.

✔ In cooperation with the developing countries, develop decent and productive work for youth.

✔ In cooperation with pharmaceutical companies, provide access to affordable essential drugs in developing countries.

✔ In cooperation with the private sector, make available the benefits of new technologies — especially information and communications technologies.

Seeing into the future

Aid can work. But it could be bigger and it should be better. The following list outlines the reasons why the thinking about aid needs to be shaken up.

✔ Aid workers have a responsibility to make sure the quality of projects keeps getting better and that lives are improved as much as possible. They need to work well with other agencies to maximise impact.

✔ Governments must live up to their obligations to provide more aid. They should meet their commitment of 0.7 per cent of their incomes to aid. And governments in developing countries must offer greater support and not obstruct aid projects. It's up to you to make sure that your government isn't getting away with anything untoward.

✔ Too much aid is caught up in politics. It should be given on the basis of need, not political strategy. Aid should have a poverty-reduction focus. But development and relief projects must also seek greater involvement from the targeted communities at all stages — from conception to completion.

✔ Aid should work alongside other processes to eradicate poverty. Aid, trade and debt should work hand in hand to end the vicious cycle of poverty.

✔ Aid shouldn't be seen as a means to redistribute the wealth of the rich to those less fortunate. It should be targeted at wealth creation and long-term improvements in the quality of life of the communities in which it is spent.

Putting Aid In Perspective

When the international community sets its sights on something, things can change suddenly. If you're reading this in Nyala in Sudan's troubled region of Darfur or in East Timor's capital, Dili, you won't be able to throw an aid worker without hitting a shiny white Toyota LandCruiser. These global hot spots are awash with international funds.

In the early 1990s, Mozambique was struggling after decades of civil war. In an effort to rebuild, Mozambique became one of the most aid-dependent countries in the world — about 40 per cent of its annual income in 2000. Uganda's international aid was still very high at half that percentage. But these countries were the exceptions. Very few countries ever feel that level of impact from aid money.

The high tide for aid budgets was 2005. For the very first time, total aid flows passed US$100 billion. That's certainly nothing to be scoffed at, but the flow in global aid pales in comparison to the other ways that the world has to blow a large bucket of money. Chapter 17 lists some of the amounts of money that flow between countries. The US$1,000 billion that governments officially spend on military hardware and the US$200 billion that poor migrant workers send home are two figures that put the aid budget in perspective.

Promises, pledges and procrastination

Since 1960 rich countries have given US$2.2 trillion dollars in aid. That may sound like a rather impressive figure, but it's not close to what they promised.

In 1970 members of the Organisation for Economic Co-operation and Development (OECD) — the global rich boys' club — pledged 0.7 per cent of their incomes to overseas aid. But sadly, more than 35 years on, only a few countries come anywhere near this figure. The average amount of aid given by these countries is 0.33 per cent of their national income. This is a shortfall of more than US$100 billion a year that is not getting to the poor.

But a few countries — most notably those Scandinavians — deserve a pat on the back. Table 18-1 lists the guys who were at the top of the class, ranked by the percentage of national income spent on aid in 2006.

Table 18-1	Top Ten Aid-Giving Nations	
Rank	**Nation**	**Percentage of GDP on Aid**
1.	Sweden	1.02
2.	Norway	0.89
3.	Luxembourg	0.89
4.	Netherlands	0.81
5.	Denmark	0.80
6.	Ireland	0.54
7.	United Kingdom	0.51
8.	Belgium	0.50
9.	Austria	0.47
10.	France	0.47

Source: Organisation for Economic Co-operation and Development (OECD).

Setting standards

For decades, aid agencies have gone to work without anyone looking over their shoulders: No-one to make sure they're doing their job properly and professionally. By contrast, water utilities, energy suppliers and transport authorities usually have government-run bodies to keep them in check. Lives depend on these businesses doing their job right. The same is true of NGOs and aid agencies. Yet there's no-one to police their work.

To address this, NGOs have taken matters into their own hands. One fruit of their collective labour is *Sphere*. This is a comprehensive set of guidelines that has taken seven years of discussion and research to develop. These guidelines are designed to help relief agencies become accountable and professional. They're perhaps not as comprehensive as they could be. They may not be applicable everywhere, under all conditions — after all, every disaster's different — but they do form an excellent basis for setting minimum standards that all agencies should adhere to.

Sphere sets out standards in areas like shelter, supplies, water, sanitation, hygiene, food, nutrition and health. Things like the minimum amount of water that's needed per person per day for drinking, cooking and personal hygiene — it's 15 litres by the way. It also says that no household should be more than 500 metres from a water point, and it indicates that survivors of a disaster should be provided with a minimum of 2,100 kilocalories' worth of food each day.

Sphere is a work-in-progress, but it's a significant contribution to the professionalisation of the aid world.

Bringing up the rear of the pack are the United States and Australia. The Aussies came in at a rather pitiful eighteenth on a list of 22 at 0.25 per cent, but the United States trailed at nineteenth on the list with 0.21 per cent — the third worst performer of the entire class of rich countries. Greece is at the bottom of the table, giving just 0.17 per cent.

Rich countries in the European Union have renewed the pledge of the 1970s to increase their aid spending. By 2010, overseas development aid should be at 0.56 per cent of national incomes, and by 2015 it should be up to the promised 0.7 per cent. It's up to you to hold your government to these promises. Shout it from the rooftops. Write to your politicians. Let them know you have heard their promises and expect results!

Motivating governments to give

For better or for worse, overseas aid is now seen by most donor governments as delivering a benefit to the donor country as well. It might be as simple as playing well to the nightly news for political advantage at home, but all too often the aid offered by governments is part of a regional strategy that is far from altruistic. When aid stops being about caring and sharing and starts being about control and leverage, things inevitably go wrong for the recipients.

Political agendas are rarely designed to benefit the poor. Aid should focus on improving the lives of the poorest, but the reality today is that overseas aid doesn't come anywhere near this. Governments are after as many of the following items as they can get:

- **Brownie points:** Aid is an issue that is becoming increasingly important to voters with the rise of social movements like Make Poverty History and the ONE campaign. Giving aid can earn a government brownie points with their constituents.

- **Neighbourly love:** Wars don't respect political boundaries, so you really want the guy next to you to be strong and stable. For example, today's conflict in Sudan regularly spills across the border into Chad. The Democratic Republic of the Congo is experiencing the world's worst humanitarian crisis, and the fighting associated with that has huge implications for neighbouring countries. Rich countries pour billions of dollars into their poorer neighbours to prevent them becoming political hot spots. Australia backs the South Pacific Islands, whereas the United States looks after the Caribbean and keeps an eye on Central America. The United Kingdom and other European countries are increasingly focused on Africa.

- **The aid boomerang — right back at ya:** What's better than spending money on something worthwhile? Not spending the money, but still getting the credit. Aid is often given under very strict conditions. A lot of overseas aid comes back to the donor country as consultant salaries or is spent on their own companies. It's a great way to get the credit without the costs. And it might look good on paper, but developing countries don't get anywhere near the benefits that the donors claim.

- **A political foot in the door:** It's the old Mafia way of doing business: Let me help you with your problems today, and some day I will call upon you to return the favour. Aid can be about gaining political leverage and getting your way.

- **Interest on aid:** If you've ever given money to an aid agency or charity you probably didn't expect them to pay it back. It wouldn't be much of a gift that way, would it? But sometimes governments claim to be giving 'aid' but demand interest and repayment. The debilitating effect this debt has on poor countries is detailed in Chapter 20.

- **Markets for arms sales:** You probably think of aid as involving vaccines, education and training. But some cunning bureaucrats think instead of tanks, military advisers and fighter planes. The US aid budget includes debt relief (which it shouldn't) as well as security for US embassies and personnel. Broadening the definition of aid means you can spend your budget on whatever you like, call it aid and get brownie points for it. Bonus!

- **Picking favourites who'll scratch your back:** Commonsense indicates that aid should be delivered to the most needy first. But over the past five decades sub-Saharan Africa — the poorest region on earth — has received less than 20 per cent of international overseas aid. Too often, aid serves the strategic and economic interests of the donor government with little thought given to the needs of the poor.

Most professionals involved in working to eliminate poverty encourage governments to pay attention to the plight of the international poor but believe that, often, governments are too selfish to deliver what's required. There's an emerging consensus among aid workers that independent agencies, totally focused on real outcomes for the poor, are better placed to distribute aid donated by national governments. Oddly enough, most governments of rich countries are not too enthusiastic about that idea.

Where the aid goes

When the world's aid budget finally topped US$100 billion in 2005, it wasn't because your government suddenly became more generous. The lion's share of today's aid budgets can be explained by politics and pragmatism, not generosity.

The Organisation for Economic Co-operation and Development (OECD) list of the top recipients of international aid from 2003 to 2004 is shown in Table 18-2. You can see from this list that aid isn't given because of need. With the exception of the Democratic Republic of the Congo these countries are of strategic importance in the eyes of the West. Iraq alone accounted for some US$21 billion of 2005's total overseas aid. Countries send aid to where they have political interests — such as fighting terrorism.

Table 18-2	Top Ten Aid-Receiving Nations
Rank	*Nation*
1.	Iraq
2.	Democratic Republic of Congo
3.	China
4.	India
5.	Indonesia
6.	Afghanistan
7.	Egypt
8.	Pakistan
9.	Ghana
10.	Vietnam

Source: Organisation for Economic Co-operation and Development (OECD).

Do you have any idea which country has received the most aid from the United States? We'll give you a hint. It's not renowned for its levels of poverty. Life expectancy in this country is 79 years at birth and average incomes per person are US$26,000. It's Israel. Until 2005, Israel received far more money from the United States than any other country. Aid to Israel isn't aimed at overcoming poverty. It's because Israel is seen as a key ally in the Middle East.

The breakdown of aid spending makes depressing reading. In 2005, less than US$10 billion went on humanitarian aid, yet more than US$20 billion was spent on debt relief — US$14 billion of this was for Iraq alone! But debt relief was not supposed to be part of the promised 0.7 per cent of GDP given in aid. In most cases, it just wipes out debt already paid many times over.

When you put all these facts together, the landmark figure of US$100 billion global aid given in 2005 was only reached because of the special cases of Iraq and Afghanistan, along with the growing movement to provide debt relief.

Compare this slow progress with the speed of reaction to the Boxing Day tsunami of 2004 — one of the deadliest disasters in modern history. Approximately 230,000 people lost their lives across five countries. By the end of January 2005 — five weeks later — US$7 billion had been pledged by individual citizens to help the affected regions.

Action Aid, one of the United Kingdom's largest charities, estimates that as much as half of all global aid is what they call *phantom aid*. That means it goes up in smoke, eaten up by some of the following:

- Corruption
- Bureaucracies
- Consultants from rich countries
- Military spending
- Debt relief

The spike in aid during 2005 was an anomaly. Aid dropped 5.1 per cent from US$106.8 billion in 2005 — a record high — to US$103.9 billion in 2006. Overseas aid for the next couple of years is likely to fall well below 2005 levels and if the figures from 2006 are any indication, it's a pessimistic outlook, at least in the short term.

Chapter 19

The Lie of the Level Playing Field: World Trade

In This Chapter

▶ Examining the recent history of trade agreements

▶ Understanding the trade imbalance

▶ Looking at new ways of trading

What could be fairer than an economic system in which everyone is free and equal? In theory, every nation is free to do business with any other nation, without unfair tariffs or other trade barriers. It certainly sounds fair, right?

The advantage of trade is that it allows people to specialise and swap scarce skills and resources to mutual advantage. In a world where one group has food, another water and a third tools, all three parties are better off if they trade than if they hang onto what they've got. You can't eat tools! That theory is known to the boffins as the *principle of comparative advantage*.

The problem is that the global trading system on display today is neither free nor fair. Despite the rhetoric about free markets and fair trading systems, the playing field is far from level. And guess who benefits most from that imbalance? Certainly not the world's poor.

This chapter outlines the development of today's global trading system, and why it's rigged to keep poor countries in their place. Finally, we follow the adage that it's no use complaining unless you have a suggestion. The chapter finishes with an outline of some things that can help world trade flow in ways that ensure a decent feed for the poorest billion people in the world.

Binding Trade: A Century of Regulation

Trade has always been an important path to riches. This chapter describes global trading patterns and points out that wealth generally accrues to a small number of people. Governments regulate trade in an attempt to prevent too much power accumulating in a small number of hands.

The regulation of trade is an important part of the effort to eradicate extreme poverty. Oxfam estimates that 128 million people could escape poverty simply if the share of world exports coming from Africa, Asia and Latin America were lifted by 1 per cent. It's not a bad start!

Twentieth-century chaos

Trade is largely responsible for the expansion of civilisation, but the other side of the coin is what happens when it goes wrong. The economic rollercoaster of the Great Depression in the late 1920s provides a stark example of how much economics can hurt. The crisis saw unemployment in some countries hit nearly 30 per cent. Across the world, entire industries were devastated. In some towns in the north of England unemployment peaked at closer to 70 per cent. Millions of families were left destitute. A British government report calculated that one in four Britons in the 1930s lived on a subsistence diet. Those figures seem unbelievable today.

Trade tariffs and barriers erected in response to the Great Depression made it even worse. After World War II, economists felt that rules were needed to keep international trade free and open so there was no repeat performance of the Great Depression. Those rules became the post-war economic order.

A system for governing international trade was intended to be part of the Bretton Woods system, described in the sidebar 'A small town in America decides the fate of the World'. That agreement created the organisations that regulated international trade for the last half of the twentieth century. The International Monetary Fund (IMF), the World Bank and the International Trade Organization (ITO) were the three pillars of the global financial system set up at Bretton Woods. Because the money came from the IMF and the World Bank, they're often referred to as *the Bank* and *the Fund*. As for the ITO, it never got off the ground.

After the war, the United States needed markets for its exports. Europe was near ruin, and there were no obvious takers for US products. In 1947, the

United States implemented the *Marshall Plan* and pumped nearly $13 billion in grants — equivalent to 10 times that today — into redeveloping Europe. The combination of American cash and the stability in international currency trading institutionalised in the Bretton Woods system brought decades of wild growth in North America and Western Europe.

By the 1970s, the Bretton Woods system began to crumble. The dollar was over-valued and the political power of the United States declined. In February 1973 the Bretton Woods currency exchange closed and was replaced by the floating currency regime that the world knows today.

Organising world trade agreements

And so it was that the GATT took centre stage. The General Agreement on Tariffs and Trade (GATT) attempted to reduce international trade barriers by agreement. From 1947 onwards, round after round of high-level negotiations tackled tariffs and subsidies. Some progress was made in freeing up world trade, but the oil and debt crises of the 1970s sent many countries back to the drawing board. The GATT had buildings and employees but was just a draft agreement, never fully ratified, and had no authority. It was replaced by the World Trade Organization (WTO) in 1995.

A small town in America decides the fate of the world

Bretton Woods is a sleepy little town in New Hampshire in the northeast of the United States. It has a couple of golf courses, a ski resort and a rather grand old hotel. Oh, and it's where rules of international trade were decided.

A conference held in the town in 1944 gave birth to what became known as the Bretton Woods system. It was a set of institutions designed to revitalise the global economy that had been decimated by World War II. For nearly 30 years those rules governed commercial and financial relations between nations.

In the wake of World War II, everyone seemed to be predicting mass unemployment and recession. No-one wanted a repeat of the Great Depression of the 1930s. Financial integration was believed to encourage peaceful relations between states. The Bretton Woods system was designed to stabilise these interactions and promote international economic growth.

The system gave enormous advantages to the rich countries that controlled it. The British delegate to the conference, John Maynard Keynes, officially summed up the conference as a remarkable success, observing 'if we can continue in a larger task as we have begun in this limited task, there is hope for the world'. He privately observed that the stability came at considerable cost. 'It puts the United States in control of the world economy,' he said.

Unilateral consensus: Washington calls the shots

During the 1980s, the fans of free trade really got their act together. Favoured states in Latin America and Asia started receiving enormous development loans. But these loans had conditions. They required countries to put in place a standard set of economic policies before the cash would flow. These policy and loan deals were known as *structural adjustment packages.*

Structural adjustment packages insisted that borrowing governments lifted import and export restrictions and eased subsidies. The packages promoted certain economic activities, specifically resource extraction (mining and drilling for oil), foreign investment, balanced budgets and privatisation. The thinking behind these loans became known as the *Washington Consensus* because the principal peddlers (the Bank and the Fund) were headquartered in Washington, DC.

The United Nations Conference on Trade and Development (UNCTAD) is the agency of the United Nations that's responsible for promoting development-friendly trade. It reports that the World Bank's push to liberalise Africa had some rather unpleasant side effects. Among them:

- ✔ Erosion of the middle class
- ✔ 'User pays' health and education services
- ✔ Wage inequalities
- ✔ Widening trade imbalances

In short, the policies of the World Bank didn't help Africa or its poor. The bank failed because it didn't take adequate account of the impact of its policies on poverty or equality.

Pushing loan addiction

Structural adjustment is a bit of a dirty word nowadays, probably because it was one of the most destructive set of economic policies ever to have been inflicted upon developing countries.

Not everyone suffered. Some leaders managed to skim hundreds of millions off the loans to feed their own bank accounts. Some private individuals fared rather well too. After being squeezed, some South American farmers turned, in desperation, to growing coca for a living. They discovered that the international narcotics trade paid rather well.

For everyone aside from the corrupt politicians and drug-growing farmers, these adjustment packages were disastrous. They pushed entire countries into greater poverty. Here are three examples of the problems that emerged.

- ✔ Mexico saw its income inequality grow markedly during the adjustment years. The rich got richer and the poor got poorer.

- ✔ Argentina teetered on the brink of economic collapse for years before finally succumbing to turmoil.

- ✔ In the late 1990s the so-called *Asian tigers* — Taiwan, Korea and Malaysia — skirted an economic abyss brought about by inequities in the external investment that drove their rapid growth.

Structural adjustment has been particularly brutal in Africa. The promised growth didn't take place. Health and education systems remain chronically underfunded. To top it all off, most African countries have a huge debt to repay. Chapter 20 details the impact of debt on Africa and other developing countries.

To be fair to the big-wigs in Washington, structural adjustment packages have been undergoing a bit of an overhaul lately. In 2002 they began to allow for greater ownership by the recipient country, giving them more control over the direction the reforms would take. The packages are now supposed to align with the Millennium Development Goals (MDGs) detailed in Chapter 18. Will this refurbishment bring about positive change for the world's poor? Only time will tell.

Loading the Dice: Trade Imbalance

Rich countries, including the United States and the European Union, use tariffs, quotas and subsidies to protect their own primary producers and manufacturers against competition. (Find out what tariffs, quotas and subsidies are in Chapter 2). At the same time, trade negotiators from these countries strut the world stage, demanding free trade agreements.

For farmers in poor countries, it's a lose–lose situation. Many are among the world's most efficient producers, but they can't sell their produce on world markets as cheaply as subsidised farmers in rich countries, who often sell their goods below the cost of production. If they stop farming, they join the urban poor. If they grow cash crops for large companies, they're paid the minimum possible price for their crops.

Tariff barriers make exporting goods more expensive for poor countries. It's estimated that tariffs cost developing countries US$100 billion a year — as much as they receive in aid. While wealthy countries agreed in principle to reduce barriers like subsidies at the meeting of the World Trade Organization in Uruguay in 1986, 21 years later total farm support from rich countries remained at almost exactly the same level — approximately US$240 billion per annum.

One consequence of high tariffs is that many developing countries depend on just a handful of commodities — such as coffee, sugar or cotton — as their major exports. This makes them vulnerable to market price fluctuations and leads to a wide variation in how much countries earn for what they export compared with what they pay for imports. This is known as having 'volatile terms of trade'. Imagine if your household budget varied wildly from month to month. That's what budget management is like for many developing countries who depend on commodities as their main export.

What a country exports has direct consequences for the poor people living in that country. The export of higher proportions of agricultural raw materials is associated with worse levels of female life expectancy and malnutrition in children under 5.

'Here, sign this' — trade agreements

Unfortunately, rich countries have been using trade agreements to gain better access to markets in poorer countries at the expense of the poor. This happens because of the imbalance in bargaining power. Rich countries have it, poor ones don't. As a result, developing countries are susceptible to bullying. The current, unfair trade agreements are still going strong, but Europe and the United States have other trade tricks up their sleeves. They can dip into this extra bag of tricks whenever they're forced to drop unfair subsidies and tariffs because of international pressure.

International agreements

The General Agreement on Trades and Tariffs (GATT), the World Trade Organization (WTO), and the World Bank and the International Monetary Fund (the Bank and the Fund) are described in the section 'Twentieth-century chaos' earlier in this chapter.

GATT was focused on liberalising manufactured goods (giving an advantage to the developed world) rather than raw materials, textiles or agriculture (which would provide an advantage to the developing world). The Bank and the Fund used structural adjustment packages to help developed countries force their way into developing markets and left many countries debt-ridden.

Failing the fairness test at Doha

The Doha round of WTO trade negotiations started at Doha, Qatar, in November 2001 to make the international trade rules fairer for all countries. But rich countries don't want to give up the source of their wealth, and the Doha round has become an ongoing saga of poor countries trying to wrest some of the world's trade from rich countries.

In 2003, trade delegates met in Cancun, Mexico. It looked like developing countries might actually get some wins when they banded together to create the G20+, a bloc of developing nations accounting for 60 per cent of the world's population, 70 per cent of its farmers and 26 per cent of its agricultural exports. The intention of the G20+ is to negotiate as one voice against some of the bigger players. But the talks stalled, and no progress was made at subsequent meetings in Hong Kong, Geneva and Paris. The latest meeting was in Potsdam, Germany, in June 2007. And yep, you guessed it, it ended in an impasse.

Trade negotiations

Today, the World Trade Organization (WTO) is the preferred mechanism of developed countries to remove impediments to trade. The WTO functions under a rule of law: Countries that suffer a violation of trade rules are entitled to impose subsidies against the offender. Although this can and has been effective, it's an asymmetrical relationship. The rich and powerful members of the WTO have more weight and influence than the smaller ones.

Even when the WTO declares something illegitimate, it can be a lengthy process before the offending policy is reversed. This reinforces the imbalance of power: Rich countries find it easier to enforce rulings than poor ones.

The negotiations under the auspices of the World Trade Organization have been stalled since the Doha round in 2001. The related sidebar details the history of stalled talks this decade.

Regional agreements

A regional trade agreement is an alternative to the international agreements brokered by the World Trade Organization and then given force of law. The United States and members of the European Union have been signing regional trade agreements left, right and centre for a couple of years now. On the surface, trade agreements seem like a good idea: A few countries sit down together and work out what's a fair trading relationship.

You don't have to look any further than the pioneer of trade agreements to see what can go wrong. The North American Free Trade Agreement (NAFTA) governs trade relations between Canada, Mexico and the United States. Since it was signed in 1994 there have been very few complaints from the United States. But Oxfam reports that Mexico saw 15 million small-scale farmers and their families devastated by the flood of rice and wheat from the United States. Sure, average Mexican incomes are up slightly on what they were in 1994, but nothing compared to the rise in food prices. Corn prices in Mexico, for example, have risen more than ten times. As well, US companies have used the trade agreement to overturn local regulations that control pollution and labour laws, so they can do business more cheaply in Mexico.

License this!

Another group of laws that have crossed national boundaries are the intellectual property laws. Rich countries regularly use them to control the flow of goods from poor countries. When cheap Taiwanese computers and entertainment systems began flooding the North American market in the 1990s, the United States cited intellectual property breaches to remove the island nation's status as a most favoured trading partner.

Intellectual property (IP) rights are important to encourage innovation and creative endeavour. A *patent* gives a legal right to the owner to control the use of an innovation. You can patent anything from a pharmaceutical drug to a car design. It gives the owner sole rights to use it or the right to give someone else permission to build it, sell it, or whatever. That's called *licensing*. Patent holders usually charge for a licence.

Intellectual property laws protect the investment that companies or individuals put into research and development. The following example may help you imagine the commercial reality of business with no legal right over innovations:

1. A car company puts millions of dollars and years of research into a new fuel-efficient engine design.

2. The company prices the cars with this new engine to cover those development costs.

3. A rival company looks under the hood and copies the results of their hard work.

4. The copy-cat car sells for a lot less because the price doesn't include any research and development costs.

5. Millions of people buy the copy-cat car and the company that invented the engine goes broke.

In fact, without the protection offered by intellectual property laws, the original car company probably wouldn't have invested in the new engine. So intellectual property law helps companies to innovate. Where's the problem? The answer is that companies use the laws set up to protect them to extract the maximum price for their goods. In poor countries this is often enough to prevent them having access to important goods, such as life-saving drugs.

Pushing drugs and TRIPping up the poor

Drugs are big business — even legal ones. Drug sellers stretch the rules. Some activities undertaken to protect drug companies' profits raise questions about who has more of a social conscience — the drug cartels of South America or the big pharmaceuticals, collectively labelled *Big Pharma*, of North America and Europe. Fourteen million people die from preventable diseases every year, but Big Pharma, and the governments that represent them, withhold essential drugs in the quest for greater profits. Overall, 30 per cent of the world's population lacks access to essential medicines that could be provided if pharmaceutical companies were prepared to forgo some profit.

Morocco's Marrakech was home to the signing of the 1994 Trade-related Aspects of Intellectual Property Rights (TRIPs) agreement. Signatories agreed to recognise United States patent law as applying within their jurisdiction. Trade agreements are usually about liberalising trade, but TRIPs restricted trade flows. TRIPs was pushed by the European Union and the US government, with the major pharmaceuticals whispering sweet nothings in their ears. Its primary function is to protect the interests of Western pharmaceutical companies in poor countries.

Some journalists commented that the effort didn't make commercial sense. The average person on the street in Luanda or Kinshasa can't afford drugs churned out in Switzerland. Africa makes up less than 2 per cent of pharmaceutical revenues. The answer lies in the future. Drug sales in emerging markets in 2005 soared by close to 25 per cent. Today's poor are tomorrow's customers, and Big Pharma doesn't want to let them go.

Some companies donate their drugs to developing countries but these donations aren't adequate to reach everyone who needs them. Nor is corporate gifting a long-term solution. Governments need to act to take the decisions about who can access drugs and when out of the hands of these Western companies.

Following a public outcry over the unfair TRIPs agreement in 2001, the World Trade Organization changed tack and brokered an agreement protecting the public health of the poor over profits for the rich. Generic versions of vital drugs can now be manufactured legally in poor countries. An Oxfam study shows that the first round of anti-retroviral drugs (ARVs) cost about US$10,000 per patient per year. Now, generic drugs have helped slash that to approximately US$130 a year. But this isn't the end of the story:

✔ **Make but don't sell:** US delegates have repeatedly argued that countries manufacturing generic versions of drugs aren't allowed to sell the drugs to other nations. India, Brazil and South Africa are large and efficient producers of these drugs and have a large enough market to make manufacturing worthwhile. Poorer and smaller nations, though, simply can't access the drugs they need.

✔ **Back for more — TRIPs plus:** With Big Pharma enthusiastically egging them on, US negotiators have been frantically signing poor countries up to regional trade agreements that include similar conditions, known as *TRIPs plus*. These new rules go even further in removing public health safeguards for the poor.

Avast! Biopiracy afoot

Vast sums are poured into research each year by multinational companies but some cunning corporations have found shortcuts to profit. Why do the research yourself when others have already done it for you? The practice of pinching traditional, indigenous knowledge and slapping a patent on it has been dubbed *biopiracy*. It has flourished under the TRIPs agreement described in the previous section.

For decades, pharmaceutical companies have been 'rediscovering' traditional knowledge. In 1995 the University of Mississippi Medical Center decided that it had found a great new wonder-drug in the spice turmeric. They promptly patented it. The trouble is that the spice, used in Asian cooking for hundreds of years, was well known and widely used for its healing properties. Two years later, the patent was dismissed, but only after lengthy litigation.

Even basmati rice was patented by a multinational based in the United States. Indians have eaten basmati rice for thousands of years but in 2000 the company RiceTec, from Texas, was granted a patent over the popular grain by the United States Patent and Trademark Office. Luckily, India had the resources to fight back and quash the claim.

Look mum, I invented coffee!

Nothing is quite like the smell of fresh coffee. The drink has become so popular that it's now the world's second most traded commodity, after oil. Over US$80 billion-worth is traded each year, giving it the name *black gold*. But not everyone's getting rich from it. The story of your grande low-fat soy latte is a classic tale of globalisation, greedy corporations and exploitation of impoverished Third World farmers.

The trouble is, the growers aren't seeing the profits. In an attempt to increase their take, Ethiopia decided to trademark three of its most popular brands: Harar, Yirgacheffe and Sidamo.

Thirty countries have already approved the trademark application. But in the United States it was found that the coffee company Starbucks already had a trademark that conflicted with Ethiopia's application. The $8 billion-a-year multinational was using these names to sell coffee all over the globe. Harar and Sidamo coffee sells in Starbucks for about US$55 a kilogram. But Oxfam reveals that Ethiopian farmers see only between one and two dollars of this.

Nevertheless, in 2006 a royalty-free licence was offered to the multinational in exchange for giving Ethiopia ownership of the names. But Starbucks rejected the offer.

You may well wonder what right Starbucks has to trademark the names of regions in Ethiopia that have been growing coffee for more than a thousand years. Perhaps you should direct your questions to the United States Patent and Trademark Office.

Of course, some multinationals have done the right thing. A Swiss-based drug company discovered that the Chinese had been using a particular tree to make a malaria treatment. Novartis developed the drug to sell around the world, but provides it at cost or even free to developing countries.

Innovating without martyrs

Patent laws were developed to protect innovators but they're not the only way to help bring about innovative research and development. Here are some potential solutions to the drug dilemma:

  ✔ **Cover the costs:** Poor countries aren't where the profits are. So let drug companies recoup their research investment in rich countries, but provide drugs to the poor at cost. Slum-dwellers in Africa aren't able to buy drugs at the same price as the bankers of Switzerland.

- **Compulsory licensing:** When cheap drugs can save lives, poor countries should be allowed to enact *compulsory licensing* and produce generic versions of patented drugs without paying huge licence fees.

- **Encourage research:** Drug companies aren't the only ones who can do research. Universities and institutes can be encouraged through grants and awards to invent and develop new drugs. Most importantly, freed of the profit-making incentives of Big Pharma, they may actually research drugs that help the poor of the world, rather than more profitable anti-ageing creams and weight-loss pills.

- **Copyright-free software:** For years Microsoft enjoyed a near-total monopoly in Internet browsing by bundling Internet Explorer with its operating system. In just a few years, a free alternative, Firefox, broke Explorer's dominant market share. Firefox is not the only open-source software challenging commercial software. Pharmaceuticals developed in universities can be shared freely with manufacturers under similar arrangements, radically reducing the cost of pharmaceuticals.

Developing New Terms of Trade

Economists are renowned for the assumptions on which they base their predictions. Here's a joke to illustrate the point: An engineer, a geologist and an economist stranded on a desert island find a can of food. Ravenously hungry, the engineer proposes to smash it open with a rock. The geologist calmly suggests that natural forces will eventually do the job. Enthusiastically offering to break the deadlock, the economist pipes up, 'Let's assume we have a can opener . . .'

Okay, it's not so funny but it does make the point that flawed assumptions lead to flawed decisions. The fact that millions of people are dying each year is evidence there is something wrong with the assumptions behind the world's trading regime. The following sections examine the assumptions and offer some alternatives that may lead to a better outcome.

Assumptions that backfire

For decades the International Monetary Fund and the World Bank have prescribed economic liberalisation and free trade as the answer to the troubles of the world's poor. But the assumptions about the impact of trade are not reflected by reality. Conditions in the poorest countries differ from the ideal world in which those assumptions were made. Here are some wrong assumptions about the way trade and economic liberalisation work:

✔ **Growth generates jobs:** The theory goes that economic liberalisation will cost some people their traditional jobs but economic growth will deliver new ones. In many poor countries this simply isn't happening. The poor lost their jobs and have stayed unemployed.

✔ **A safety net exists:** Okay, so a few people get screwed over by liberalisation, but they'll be taken care of. Unemployment benefits, free health care, retraining — the state will look after them, right? Does this sound like the way it really works in any poor country you've read about in this book? Even rich countries struggle with welfare and health-care systems. How can the poor ones do it any better?

✔ **Trade's all you need:** The Washington Consensus assumes that if a poor country removes tariffs, reduces taxation and balances the budget it will pull out of poverty. But wait a second, where's the income? Import tariffs account for as much as 20 per cent of government revenue in some countries. Cutting income reduces public spending. At the very least, a transition strategy is called for.

✔ **Trade's fair:** All the assumptions are based on the principle of comparative advantage, introduced at the beginning of this chapter. If you reduce tariffs and subsidies, but no-one else is playing by the rules, you are at a distinct disadvantage. Poor countries often find themselves trading the wrong way on a one-way street.

✔ **Wealth trickles down:** The guys who push structural adjustment packages say that economic growth makes everyone better off. In many countries economic growth does help the poor to get a bit richer. But it's rarely at the same rate as the rich. The end result is massive inequality. Sometimes it results in virtual slavery, as described in Chapter 11.

Of course, these problems may be with the way trade is implemented, or because the rules aren't properly applied. They may even be transitional or short-term problems. In the meantime, though, the poor are dying by the millions because of these problems. They're the least able to bear the added costs and risks that comes with liberalising trade.

Looking behind the assumptions

World Bank studies link trade with economic growth and the statistics are widely promoted and quoted. The same studies show that growth leads to increased average incomes. But the facts are not so straightforward:

✔ **Chicken or egg:** Okay, so trade and income generally grow together. That doesn't mean trade causes growth. In some cases it's more plausible to suggest the relationship is the other way round: Economic growth leads to increased trade. The sidebar 'China: Trading up or growing up?' illustrates that possibility.

✔ **Hidden causes:** Other factors may be responsible for increasing levels of both trade and economic growth. A factor could be a technological advance, a shift in the price of a particular commodity or a change in internal political stability.

✔ **The danger of averages:** The claim that increased average incomes make the poor better off also has to be questioned. Extreme poverty exists in relatively wealthy South American countries.

The evidence as to whether increased trade leads to economic growth is mixed. Some examples suggest that economic growth through trade liberalisation does help the poor. Other examples show that the poor can suffer from liberalisation. The fate of the poor seems more dependent on the decisions made by the national government than on the nation's global trade figures.

China: Trading up or growing up?

China doesn't do things by halves. When the country experienced a Cultural Revolution, 38 million died from famine. When China decided the population was growing too fast, the one-child policy was introduced. And when building a dam, China spent over US$100 billion to flood a 600 kilometre-long reservoir that displaced 1.9 million Chinese and reduced the flow of major rivers across southern Asia.

So when China put its weight behind economic growth and development, the country saw the fastest sustained growth of any country during that period. It averaged 10 per cent per year.

The effect on poverty was enormous. World Bank figures show that in 1978 nearly 30 per cent of the Chinese population lived in poverty. By 1998, levels of poverty had fallen to below 10 per cent.

During the last quarter century, China has become a key player in the global economy.

In fact, Chinese trade has grown so fast that its exports grew from half the amount of the United States in 2000 to surpass it in 2006. It's now the biggest exporter in the world.

Free-trade advocates point to China as an example that proves the value of free trade. But critics suggest otherwise. The country's growth began in the 1970s, and the 1980s saw limited imports into China but a rapid growth in exports. It was not until the 1990s that China truly began to liberalise its economy. Even now, China keeps a tight control on the value of its currency and the export of profits from companies based in China. Far from demonstrating how free trade causes growth, China's growth suggests that protectionist policies are necessary to start and nurture economic growth, even though free trade may be the best way to accelerate it after it gets up and running.

Rethinking trade

Free trade on its own doesn't make countries richer; having an external market is a larger factor. China's economic growth has come from Japanese and American consumers. Exporting goods makes a country richer.

The development potential of trade is real, and governments in developing countries see it. So far the potential has gone largely unrealised for the poor. There are some things rich countries can do to help out:

- **Help improve the capacity in developing countries.** Invest in infrastructure so goods can reach markets quickly and cheaply. Make sure roads, rail, power and communications are capable of supporting domestic growth and export demands.

- **Help poor countries to reform their bureaucracy and tackle corruption.** Offer advice on streamlined policies to help with the creation of new businesses. Help them to build strong institutions and policies.

- **Accept that one size doesn't fit all when it comes to trade.** Allow different policies for the poor, for the rich and for those in between. Accept that in the short term developing countries may need to protect some of their industries. New businesses may need help to grow before competing internationally.

- **Dismantle unfair subsidies.** Rich countries should lower trade barriers and play fair. Let the poor in on the game.

Cleaning house

We've criticised the legalities and trade barriers that rich countries impose on the poor. But developing countries can't escape at least some of the blame. Many poor countries have obscenely complex laws and trade barriers that get in the way of trade with their neighbours. It can take a month to get goods out of Ethiopia, whereas goods can leave the European Union in under a day. That has to cause trade problems!

Similarly in sub-Saharan Africa, it takes on average more than two months to start a new business and requires 200 per cent of annual per-capita income to register. By comparison, in Australia it takes only two days and 2 per cent. Rich countries have a lot to answer for in terms of the inequalities of world trade. But poor countries can themselves do more to level the playing field.

Taking corporate responsibility

Companies are regularly brought to task in the media for their impact on the environment or their workers. Chapter 4 outlines a number of consumer-led campaigns that have resulted in companies brushing up their act rather than lose their reputation as good corporate citizens.

It is not only consumers who can keep an eye on what companies are doing and whether they are using their economic power for the benefit or detriment of people with very little power. Governments and multilateral organisations have a number of tools for keeping watch on what large companies do. One of these tools is *triple bottom line reporting*. As well as the bottom line that shows profit in dollars, there are two more showing the environmental and social balance for the company's activities.

Ratified by the United Nations and many other groups, the triple bottom line is increasingly being used to determine which companies are good corporate citizens. Also known as Profit, Planet, People or *sustainability reporting*, this approach keeps track of the environmental and social balance sheet of a company's activities as well as of its bank balance. It's related to *green accounting* and *full cost accounting*.

The approach has been fleshed out by many public utilities around the world, and many Australian government agencies, for example, have detailed documentation on presenting triple bottom line reports when submitting proposals to government.

To judge the impact that a company has on the world's poor you would examine the social balance sheet. When a company sells valued products at a low margin to poor countries — that is, products that the countries could not get any other way — its social capital increases. If it uses its resources to undercut poor farmers, however, its social capital decreases.

By regulating the activities of companies based on the social costs of doing business, governments can potentially curb the worst excesses of global capital on extreme poverty.

Chapter 20

Escaping the Vortex of Debt

*O*nly the outrageously optimistic, or the greediest financiers and world leaders, still believe that developing country debt is repayable. Yet most poor countries remain enslaved by the burden of debt. Developing countries owe their creditors US$2.6 trillion: More than one trillion of that money is accrued interest on loans! But who's actually to blame for this debt crisis?

- ✔ **Borrowers:** Normally those who borrow money are responsible for paying it back. The responsibility is harder to pinpoint when you're talking about debts that have been racked up over decades. Governments change, regimes fall and people die. Who really owes it? Naturally, some responsibility must lie with the borrower country — which actually means the people who live there.

- ✔ **Lenders:** Most institutions handing out cash are pretty tight with it. Unfortunately, they weren't playing it safe during the oil crisis of the 1970s. The moneylenders and financial institutions neglected their shareholders and threw money at the poor — regardless of their ability to repay it — and must also bear some of the blame.

- ✔ **Institutional backers:** The World Bank, the IMF and governments in Europe and the United States all pressured indebted countries to keep up their repayments, even at the cost of failing health and education systems. And when it got too hard, these guys were the first in line to push developing countries to take out more loans to keep up their interest payments, pushing them deeper into debt.

Why try to blame anyone at all? Well, this one's easy — it's the only way to work out who should pay. And in this particular blame game, it's about time for the lenders (multilateral institutions and Western governments) to pony up and take some responsibility.

Setting the Debt Trap

International tensions over finances are hardly new. History is punctuated with debt crises where borrower countries have been unable to pay foreign demands. Classical Rome taxed Asia Minor (Turkey) and Syria to breaking point. The nineteenth and early twentieth century had similar periods, including the reparations exacted from Germany after World War I. Sadly, no-one in the 1970s seemed to remember those earlier crises, or say anything that could make a difference, anyway.

If you rack up too much on your credit card or don't meet your loan repayments, some spotty clerk in some faraway office puts a big red mark by your name and you can kiss your credit rating goodbye. So it seems logical that a country failing to repay the interest on its loans would have that same big mark put against its name. But that just didn't happen in the mid-1970s.

Poisonous petrodollars

The *oil crises* of the early 1970s were felt around the world. Sky-high oil prices affected every corner of our oil-dependent world, and a global recession began. But in every game there are both winners and losers. And the oil crises had a lot of both.

With OPEC (the Organisation of Petroleum Exporting Countries) controlling oil prices, OPEC members — mostly in the Middle East — suddenly found the cash coming in faster than they could spend it. There are only so many silver-plated Ferraris that anyone needs. The remainder of the oil revenue was simply hoarded in the banks.

The banks receiving this oil money were mostly in Europe and the United States. They found themselves in the unique position of being in the middle of a global recession but with huge amounts of cash pouring in. The global recession was pushing interest rates down, so something needed to be done with all those *petrodollars*.

There was one thing that could easily be done with all the money: lend it. And who better to lend it to than developing countries looking to maintain their growth and in need of a helping hand. The problem was that no-one seemed to really care whether the recipients were likely to be able to pay it back.

Everyone got in on the action. Central and South America took on huge loans, as did most of Africa and parts of Asia. But sadly, these loans did precious little good for their recipients.

Burdening thy neighbour

Latin America borrowed big time. Brazil, Argentina and Mexico led the pack. From 1975 to 1983 the continent's debt rose from $75 billion to $315 billion. The Institute of Latin American Studies confirms that amount as about half of the annual economy of Latin America — that's GDP, or gross domestic product to the accountants among you.

As the world economy continued to spiral downward, interest rates rose, and foreign debts became harder and harder to repay. In 1982, Mexico finally declared that it was unable to meet its debt repayments.

It may seem unbelievably stupid, but the response of the International Monetary Fund (IMF) and the federal government of the United States was to offer new loans to help these countries pay off their old ones. What became known as neo-liberal structural adjustments began across the continent. Government spending was cut, foreign investment was encouraged and large infrastructure projects were set in place.

Adding insult to injury: Colonialism's parting gift

The debt spiral of the 1970s was not the first time the poor nations of the world had been weighed down by the yoke of international debt. Many of today's poorest countries can trace the ancestry of their debts partly back to recent colonial times.

Take Indonesia. Upon gaining independence, the former Dutch colony was forced to pick up the debts amassed by its colonial rulers. And how had these loans been spent? Much of the debt had been accumulated by the Dutch while fighting pro-independence rebels. So, lucky Indonesia got to pay for both sides of the fight for its freedom.

Here's another good one. France finally agreed to grant Haiti independence in 1825 in exchange for a 150 million franc payoff to compensate French slave-owners for their loss of property. That 'property' referred to former slaves, now freed Haitians. The 150 million francs is equivalent to US$21 billion today and took the country 120 years to pay off. It's no wonder that Haiti is the poorest country north of the equator.

The justification for these colonial debts is so twisted that it makes the colonial powers look like thugs delivering a final twist of the knife after centuries of slavery and pillaging.

Banking on Mexico

You could be forgiven for thinking that the United States holds all the cards in its dealings with Mexico. After all, the US economy is about 11 times larger than Mexico's. But in 1982 Mexico's economic troubles showed that the relationship was far more complex.

The United States buys 65 per cent of Mexico's exports and sells a similar amount back again. Tourists from the United States bring billions of dollars into the country each year, and Mexicans living north of the border (both legal and illegal) send back billions more in remittances.

So, during the big lending years of the 1970s, who better for Mexico to borrow from than the United States? Mexico enjoyed a few golden years with growth rates of around 7 per cent. But by the early 1980s, the United States recession flowed south across the border. Interest rates and unemployment headed skyward in the United States. With their debt almost exclusively in dollars, the amount owed by Mexico skyrocketed overnight.

Mexicans saw their peso becoming worthless and stashed money overseas in dollars. Some US$50 billion left the country, and with a GDP of US$120 billion in 1981, that became a colossal problem! Mexican goods stopped flowing north and US tourists stopped going south. With no-one buying Mexican goods, cash flying abroad and interest rates at an all-time high, the Mexican economy was squeezed from all sides.

The country's debt had reached US$80 billion by the end of 1982. Rather than turn its back, the United States had no choice but to bail Mexico out. The United States depends on Mexico for cheap labour and cheap processing of its goods. More importantly — to the bankers, anyway — the nine largest banks in the United States had 40 per cent of their capital tied up in Mexico. If Mexico collapsed, these banks would be ruined. Mexico's troubles threatened the entire international credit system.

The irony for Mexico is that the country has never exerted as much influence over Washington as when it was on the brink of collapse.

The *structural adjustment packages* implemented in the 1980s set the economies of South America back dramatically. During the first half of the 1980s, the region experienced negative growth of about 9 per cent a year. If the old debts had been hard to pay, these new ones ensured it was impossible to break even. This period of Latin American economic suffering has become known as *the lost decade*.

Table 20-1 provides a top-five list of who's in the red in Latin America.

Table 20-1	Latin American Nations' Debt Levels
Country	*Debt Level, 2007 (US$)*
Brazil	$230 billion
Mexico	$182 billion
Argentina	$118 billion
Chile	$49 billion
Venezuela	$45 billion

Source: World Factbook 2007.

Following suit

Africa dominates the list of most indebted countries in the world. Of the 32 countries classified by Jubilee USA as severely indebted low-income countries, 25 are in sub-Saharan Africa.

What debt has done for Africa is to permanently fix the flow of capital out of the continent and back to the West. To put this in perspective, the continent of Africa spends four times more on debt repayments than on health. An estimated US$15 billion is needed each year to fight HIV/AIDS on the continent. Coincidently, that's about what Africa pays out annually to 'service' (repay) its debt.

Can't Pay, Won't Pay

Every time the World Trade Organization or the world's richest nations hold a conference, the news focuses on the banners and the protestors shouting 'drop the debt'. In 2005, at the launch of the Commission for Africa report, President Mkapa of Tanzania said, 'It is a scandal that we are forced to choose between basic health and education for our people and repaying historical debt.'

Before he stepped down as US president in 2001, Bill Clinton made noises about debt relief for the millennium. At the G8 meeting in Scotland in 2005, leaders vied fiercely to outdo one another with promises of debt relief. Despite all this, most developing countries' debts haven't been cancelled.

They remain in place. And that's not just because it's costly to relieve debt. Many decision-makers don't believe debt cancellation is the answer. The following section presents some of the arguments at the heart of the debt debate.

Forgiving debt is bad for business

For a bank or a business to write off the debts owed to them is a pretty big ask. It's like asking you to go without your pay packet after you've done a week's work. For obvious reasons, the banks and financial institutions don't think that forgiving debt is a great way to solve extreme poverty. This section examines the arguments they put forward.

Before reading this section, be warned. These arguments are used by international financiers to justify ripping off poor countries. You're not going to make very many friends if you trot them out over dinner — not the right kind of friends, anyway.

The moral hazard

Cancelling debt to poor countries sets a bad example. It encourages other countries to borrow more than they can afford, overspend and default on their loans. It's like writing a blank cheque and encourages irresponsible behaviour.

The fallacy of this argument it that campaigners for debt relief aren't asking for future debts to be written off. They're calling for debt that's mounted up over decades to be cancelled. Lending institutions and governments have to ensure that safeguards are in place for future lending.

The real moral hazard can be traced back to the colonial regimes that passed on their debt to newly independent countries. Or to the moneylenders who threw money around irresponsibly.

Advancing the corrupt

Why cancel debts, anyway? After all, isn't some corrupt official just going to pocket the savings?

This argument offers an easy way out for those reluctant to bite the bullet and drop the debt. But the reality, as described in Chapter 7, is that corruption can be managed. Creditors have to ensure that the impact of debt relief is felt by the poor, and not by the rich. Check out 'Relieving the Burden' later on in this chapter for more on how this can be done.

It's a matter of principle

Debt relief is unfair to those countries that have managed to get by without loans or who have managed their debt effectively.

Fairness isn't about treating people the same; it's about doing what's right for each one as best you can. Being 'fair' would be to cancel excessive debts that force money away from much-needed public services.

Why should we pay?

Why should the strong look after the weak? Let natural selection take its course.

This argument goes against the heart of the matter raised in this book. Extreme poverty is caused by unfair rules. Changing those rules isn't diminishing the strong; it's punishing the greedy. That rule is fundamental to social organisation. If there are no such rules, then crime rules.

Everyone resents tax, whether it's used to contribute to health care and education or goes on bombs and guns. When a natural disaster occurs, or a rash of crime breaks out, though, everyone turns to the nearest authority figure for support. Organising social systems so nobody is desperate is good for the rich, too.

Recognising need is the higher virtue

Several reasons exist for thinking twice before simply writing off developing country debt. The following points raise some very good reasons for doing exactly that.

Lending: The gift that keeps on taking

Interest hikes mean that most countries have already paid off their initial loans — often many times over. The organisation Jubilee USA calculates that Nigeria originally borrowed US$5 billion. So far it has paid back US$16 billion to service that debt, but it still owes another US$32 billion. Go figure!

Across Africa the picture's much the same. Between 1970 and 2002, the poorest countries received $294 billion in loans. They paid back US$298 billion in interest and principal — but still owe more than US$200 billion. Whether you're a maths whiz or not, it should be pretty obvious that these figures lead directly to the impoverishment of the debtor nations!

Being a good Samaritan

Of course, you can't avoid the moral argument. The simple fact is that debt is crippling developing countries and causing huge amounts of human suffering. Relieving the debts of the poorest countries can translate directly into lives saved. That's got to be a good reason to drop the debt.

Angola's US$11 billion debt means that the country puts a third of its revenue into paying the interest. Yet less than 1.5 per cent goes into its health system.

Setting practical limits

For most countries, paying off debt isn't about cutting out luxuries. More than 50 of the world's poorest countries have debts that are quite literally unpayable.

The six million people of Benin in western Africa are faced with an international debt of US$1.6 billion. The debt is so large that it makes up 72 per cent of the entire gross national product (the country's total annual economic activity). The excessive debt contributes to a quarter of all children in the country being malnourished.

Debt bites back

Debt in poor countries causes problems in your life, as well. The *debt boomerang* is the phenomenon that bad debts on the other side of the casino can ruin your night out as well.

Where did the markets go?

If it weren't for the burden of debt, many of today's poor countries would be much better off and would be able to trade with developed countries. Rich countries would benefit from markets for their goods and services. In short, everyone would be better off if extreme poverty didn't exist.

The curse of illegal drugs

Decades of a drug crisis is taking its toll in rich countries. Expanded policing and high-profile campaigns seem unable to halt the demand for illicit substances that tear families apart and ruin lives. If you can't stop the demand, the only course left is to tackle the supply. You can send troops, finance militia, burn fields. But experience shows that the only way to deal with the drug problem is to remove the economic forces that encourage farmers in poor countries to grow the illicit crops.

Baby Doc cripples a nation

Dr Francois 'Papa Doc' Duvalier and his son, Baby Doc, led Haiti for 29 years and racked up nearly half a billion dollars in debt still owed by the Caribbean country.

Papa Doc came to power in 1957 using campaign strategies from assassinations to terror by armed gangs. He sided with the black majority against the *mulatto* elite and won the election. Once elected, Papa Doc murdered up to 30,000 of his opponents.

He appointed himself President for Life after the presidential elections in 1964 — there was not one single Haitian vote against him. The title proved accurate as he held it until his death in 1971. At the age of 19, Jean-Claude Duvalier (Baby Doc) became the world's youngest president. He was content to live the life of a playboy and leave the hard work of governing to his mother. During his 15-year rule, Baby Doc added as much as 40 per cent of Haiti's current $1.2 billion debt to his father's total.

Baby Doc was overthrown in 1986 and fled to exile in France. He publicly boasts that he has $900 million squirrelled away in secret bank accounts. That's close to the entire national debt!

The World Bank and the IMF say that Haiti's debt isn't high enough to warrant cancellation. But the high levels of debt service that the country is expected to pay each year — around $45 million — are one of the major reasons why its people are far and away the poorest in the northern hemisphere. Nearly 80 children die for every 1,000 born; life expectancy is a rather meagre 53 years; and barely half the population is literate.

If there's ever been a classic case of odious debt, this would be it. A vast amount of Haiti's current debt was racked up under the rule of corrupt tyrants, siphoned off into their own accounts and squandered by their cronies.

After years of watching the heroin trade in Afghanistan grow out of control, international peacekeeping forces suggested in March 2008 that a regulated trade in opium be established for legitimate medical purposes. Cultivating poppies appears to be the only realistic means of survival for some impoverished peasants.

You're subsidising the greedy

The old hip pocket nerve. Yes'm. We're going to talk about how this affects you. There's no doubt that the world's poorest countries are going backwards. When a country is going backwards, someone has to pick up the tab.

The irresponsible lending of greedy (or incompetent?) bankers partly created this mess in the first place. But it's not the bankers and their clients that have to pick up the bills. First, it's the poor in developing countries, and when they can't make their repayments, it's Western governments who prop up these irresponsible loans. Your taxes contribute to paying aid to poor countries to repay international banks. Is that why you head off to work every day?

You're in the same boat

Climate change isn't about changes in faraway countries or melting icecaps on the other side of the world. It's about changes in *your* country, in your backyard. Changes that affect you, your future and the future of your children. The economic pressure that debt places on poor countries is leading directly to environmental destruction. The poor are the first to suffer, but sooner or later everyone will feel the effects. It's in your best interest to make sure something is done. And now!

Relieving the Burden

The good news is that momentum calling for debt relief has built up to the point where action is being taken. The even better news is that in those places where it's been applied, it's actually working. (Read about the success of Tanzania's debt relief in Chapter 21.) Those positive results encourage activists to keep pressure on governments to extend debt relief programs. You can participate in a number of exercises to lobby governments and global organisations, such as the World Bank, to get more creative in how they approach the issue.

The legalities of forgiveness

Less than two decades ago, racial oppression under South Africa's apartheid regime was front-page news. While suppressing the black majority, the government led the country into debt. Hey, it's expensive work suppressing 30 million people!

After freeing themselves from apartheid, the new regime was forced to repay the loans incurred under its racist predecessors. Nelson Mandela emerged from 27 years of imprisonment to lead a new country. But unfortunately, he was saddled with his prison bill. South Africans picked up the tab for their own oppression. Sound fair to you?

Many people like to make fun of lawyers for their seemingly hard hearts and their perceived lack of morality. But in cases like this, those legal types have stepped up to the plate and put forward the argument for forgiving debt.

Odious debt

Odious is a great word. It conjures up a despicable smell or an unbearable acquaintance who won't leave. Such a value-laden word seems an unlikely candidate for an objective, legal definition. Because the law has to be exact, ordinary English words are replaced with specific, often archaic, terms. 'Theft' becomes 'larceny', 'planning' becomes 'conspiracy to commit'. Odious is the word of choice for international law when it comes to debts.

Legally, debt is considered to be *odious* if the borrowing government used the money for an individual to profit from or to oppress its own people. It's especially relevant in cases where creditors were — or should have been — aware that the funds wouldn't be used in the interest of the recipients' constituents. Under international law, creditors can't expect repayment of odious debt.

If you want to check into the concept of odious debt in a little more detail, a good place to start is www.odiousdebts.org.

Illegitimate debt

Why should people in poor countries be forced to repay loans that did nothing for them? Up to a fifth of all loans to poor countries have been spent on weapons and to bolster oppressive regimes. And between 1960 and 1987, developing countries spent as much as US$400 billion on arms from rich countries. International law steps in to say such debts should be ruled illegitimate and therefore need not be repaid.

Illegitimate debt is different from odious debt, because it's considered that it wasn't truly borrowed; instead it was foisted on the supposed borrower by the party that is now demanding repayment.

If you look back to the cold war era, communist-phobic Western governments were all too happy to help influence the political climate of foreign lands with a little bit of cash. Well, often quite a lot of cash. The United States in particular threw piles of money at anyone and anything that they believed would resist left-leaning politics.

Nowhere experienced this more clearly than South America. Spurred on by US taxpayers' funds, civil wars broke out in places like Guatemala, El Salvador and Colombia. But although this spending was in keeping with US foreign policy and seen to be in the national interest, many of these payouts weren't gifts. They were loans.

But anyone with a pulse knew that the regimes being propped up by US dollars weren't the friendly peace-lovers who'd bring happiness and prosperity to their citizens. For the most part, these regimes were run by right-wing totalitarian tyrants.

Drops, swaps and repudiation

You've seen what happens when economic policy is imposed on poor countries by rich ones. Structural adjustment packages have brought nothing but misery to millions of people. But new approaches are emerging to help alleviate the suffering brought on the poor by heavy debt.

Taking the first step

Under mounting pressure from international organisations, the International Monetary Fund (IMF) and World Bank teamed up with creditor governments in 1996 to establish the HIPC initiative, which stands for Heavily Indebted Poor Countries. The idea was to reduce the debts of particularly poor and indebted countries to manageable levels.

The IMF reports that under the HIPC scheme, recipient countries are paying around a third less on debt service. Between 1996 and 2005, US$30 billion worth of debt was written off.

But HIPC isn't working as it should. Here are some of the problems that have emerged:

- The relief offered has been too slow, unnecessarily prolonging the effects of poverty in many of the poorest countries.
- Strict eligibility requirements have excluded many countries that any moral judgement would consider deserving of debt relief.
- The conditions put on the countries being relieved are harsh and maintain advantageous trading conditions for wealthy countries.
- Western governments have transferred aid dollars to debt relief, simply moving those aid dollars into the pockets of already wealthy institutions.

Leaping forward: MDRI

Scotland hosted the G8 conference in Gleneagles in 2005. Leaders from the eight countries in attendance recognised that HIPC (see the preceding section) wasn't cutting it. They agreed to write off all debt owed by countries that meet HIPC's requirements (about US$50 billion). What's more, there were no conditions attached to this new scheme.

Called the Multilateral Debt Relief Initiative (MDRI), this represents about one-tenth of all debt currently owed by highly indebted countries. African countries will enjoy the lion's share of the relief. They will have between a half and three-quarters of their debts written off. For Zambia, rates of malnutrition are edging up to around half of all children. But thanks to

MDRI, the country has been able to scrap health-care fees and put money into other much-needed initiatives that makes the world of difference for the country's ten million people.

Around the world, the G8's debt relief initiative allows nearly 300 million people to live debt-free. Eventually, as many as 550 million people may be freed from the bondage of debt.

MDRI is far from perfect. Latin America doesn't fare quite so well, with only about a third of its debt being cancelled. And only about one in ten poor countries will actually benefit from the initiative. Both MDRI and HIPC fall well short of what's actually needed to remove the burden of debt that keeps so many people in poverty. But it's a good start.

Reversing the flow: Debt swaps

HIPC and MDRI are great news but they help very few countries. Not every country that needs debt relief qualifies for these initiatives.

The Philippines, for example, owes more than US$70 billion in external debt, but doesn't qualify for HIPC. In 2005, the Philippines government spent 89 per cent of revenue in interest repayments, leaving just 11 per cent for the nation's military, health and education.

Countries like the Philippines desperately need alternatives to ease the burden of their excessive debt. One proposed solution is debt swaps, or more accurately *debt-for-investment*.

Instead of repaying creditor nations, *debt swaps* allow a debtor country to use the money that would've gone in debt repayments on development activities that target the Millennium Development Goals (MDGs). That means the money goes to reducing poverty instead of making wealthy investors wealthier. This is a reversal of the sleight-of-hand that keeps aid money in rich countries by calling it debt relief.

Debt swaps are still a rather new concept, but the idea is that both the creditor and the debtor work out how the money is to be spent effectively. Then, rather than the sum being transferred to the debtor, it goes towards education or health services, for example, that directly benefit the poor.

Being such a new area, debt swaps are being approached cautiously. It's not yet clear exactly what type of programs benefit from this approach. Despite the justifiable caution, initiatives like this need to be pushed so those countries that don't qualify for debt relief under HIPC or MDRI have some way out of debt.

Saying no: Repudiation

Have you ever wondered why poor countries don't just refuse to pay their debts? After all, it's highly unlikely anyone's going to invade Uganda just because the country stops servicing debts to foreign banks.

The answer's quite simple. Governments in poor countries are afraid that they will never again have access to foreign loans if they repudiate their debts. They know that if they fall on hard times in the future, loans will be a crucial coping mechanism.

Many campaigners suggest odious debts should be repudiated, despite the potential loss of credit rating. One suggested tactic is for many poor countries to band together and repudiate all their debts in the hope that there is no retaliation. So far this hasn't happened. There is a danger, though, that if the debt trap keeps mounting some nations may decide they have no choice but to take this route.

Watching debt relief work

With all the big questions surrounding debt relief, you may despair that it will remain in the too-hard basket for ever. It is working, though. Here are some of the changes that debt cancellation has brought about in Africa:

- In Tanzania debt cancellation led to the elimination of school fees, the training and hiring of more teachers and the building of more schools. Jubilee USA reports that, almost overnight, 1.6 million children returned to school because of debt relief.

- Burkina Faso decided to cut the cost of life-saving drugs and increase access to clean water — things that really made a difference to the poor.

- Uganda's school enrolment rates more than doubled when the country received debt relief. The children now face a brighter future without the burden of their parents' ruler's loan repayments to weigh them down.

Joining the fight for debt relief

The momentum's building. In January 2006, Gordon Brown was the United Kingdom's Chancellor of the Exchequer (the guy responsible for the country's economic and financial decisions); now he is the Prime Minister.

At the time he declared that the 67 poorest countries should receive debt cancellation, and that the United Kingdom would do its part in making that happen. In October 2006, Norway led the way by announcing it was cancelling US$80 million of debt it was owed by Egypt, Ecuador, Peru, Jamaica and Sierra Leone. Now is the time to join the campaign to call for an end to this new slavery. The following sections include some of the ways you can get involved.

Joining Jubilee

Jubilee is the name of a campaign calling for all debt owed by heavily indebted poor countries to be written off. It also says that all unpayable and unfair debt owed by developing countries should be cancelled. It is a coalition of groups and organisations across the world.

Try the following Web addresses to find a Jubilee group in your region:

- ✔ www.jubileeaustralia.org
- ✔ www.jubileeusa.org
- ✔ www.jubileedebtcampaign.org.uk
- ✔ www.s-j-c.net

Making poverty history

One of the ways that the Make Poverty History campaign wants to 'make poverty history' is through debt relief. In part, it was the success of the Make Poverty History campaign around the world that meant the G8 granted so much debt relief in 2005.

Join the campaign at one of the following sites to find out what you can do to get debt relief for poor countries.

- ✔ www.makepovertyhistory.com.au
- ✔ www.milleniumcampaign.org
- ✔ www.makepovertyhistory.org
- ✔ www.one.org

Campaigning your own way

You don't have to join a campaign to make a difference. Why not become an anti-debt advocate? First up, find out what your government's doing about debt. Speak out about debt at your local community groups, churches or schools and at work. Organise a letter-writing day to support debt relief.

How about a workplace morning tea? Invite your colleagues, share a cup of tea, talk about debt and get them to sign a petition.

Flexing your muscles at the ballot box

What does your elected representative think about debt relief? What is the position of the politician's party? Why not find out? Write a letter and ask the politician to state his or her position. While you're at it, see what the opposition has to say about it as well. Then, next time you vote, don't just vote for yourself and your family, vote for the millions of people who suffer from a debt burden that's not their own.

Part VI
The Part of Tens

Glenn Lumsden

*'I'd love to help, but I've got a lot
on my plate right now.'*

In this part . . .

Our traditional Part of Tens, a feature in all *For Dummies* books, looks to the future, and the good news is that it's not all doom and gloom. Massive social change benefiting millions has happened before and can happen again. So first up, get inspired by our ten stories of change, albeit followed by our hazards on the horizon that the world needs to include on its to-do list. Also, we include a list of movies you can see to help you get a better understanding of poverty — and how every day people can and *do* make a difference. Finally, we get practical and list ten things you can do right now to help end poverty. Together, everyone can change the world.

Chapter 21

Ten Most Exciting Stories of Change

*O*ver two billion people struggle to survive because they have the spending power equivalent to an American citizen trying to live on US$2 a day — grinding poverty in anyone's book. Addressing problems on this scale can be difficult and disheartening — a little like that fairground game where you have to whack a gopher with a mallet. Every time you score one victory, another challenge pops up somewhere else. Despite the challenges, efforts to address the underlying problems go on, working to create the framework for positive change — all the more reason to celebrate when breakthroughs do occur.

In this chapter, we list ten of the most stunning victories in the fight to restore human dignity. Turn to this chapter every time you begin to wonder if you really can make a difference — yes, you can, and here's the proof, in black and white.

Millennium Development Goals

The best news of all is that the world has a plan, the know-how and the money to end world poverty. The plan is known as the Millennium Development Goals (MDGs), and it aims to halve extreme poverty by 2015.

The goals include things like providing health services to pregnant women, ensuring environmental sustainability and sending children to school. You can find out more about the goals in Chapter 18.

If you want to see how countries are tracking to achieve the goals, go to www.un.org/millenniumgoals. The 2007 report marks the halfway point. Many countries have succeeded well in some areas. For example, the number of underweight children in the developing world has dropped from 33 per cent to 27 per cent!

The Abolition of Slavery

The transatlantic slave trade, which led to the forced removal of up to 12 million African people over 300 years, is one of the ugliest periods in human history. By the end of the eighteenth century, three out of four people on earth lived under some kind of slavery. The slave trade changed Africa, the Caribbean, Europe, and North and South America economically, demographically and culturally. The trade in human cargo also created a global market and stimulated major economic growth and the transfer of vast amounts of wealth into the hands of European and American companies. But, through a mass movement that brought together enslaved Africans, anti-slavery campaigners and ordinary members of the public, the slave trade came to an end during the mid-nineteenth century. The abolition of the transatlantic slave trade is one of the modern world's greatest moral triumphs. This makes the re-emergence of modern slavery described in Chapter 11 all the more shocking.

Small-scale Banking

The Grameen Bank, founded in 1976, provides a chance for millions of the world's poorest people to work their way out of poverty. It's a small-scale banking system based on mutual trust, accountability, participation and creativity.

The bank provides credit to the poorest of the poor in rural Bangladesh who don't have access to traditional banks, and its clients are mostly women. As of May 2007, the bank had 7.16 million borrowers and 2,422 branches, covering more than 93 per cent of the villages in Bangladesh. Micro-credit programs have proven their value in reducing poverty: Estimates put the average household income of Grameen Bank members at about 50 per cent higher than those in villages who aren't involved with the bank.

Grameen Bank's founder, Muhammad Yunus, won the Nobel Peace Prize for his life-changing work in 2006.

Fair Trade Movement

If poor countries could get access to just 1 per cent more of the value of world trade, millions of people would be lifted out of poverty. Trade creates jobs, provides incomes for producers, encourages investment and economic growth, and generates more revenue for governments to provide essential services. The fair trade movement ensures that producers get a fair price for their goods and the security they need to grow and expand their businesses. Also, fair trade gives consumers the power to make the choice to support some of the world's poorest people. The important distinction between fair trade and free trade is discussed in Chapter 19.

The Economic Miracle in East Asia

The economic development of East Asia gathered steam during the second half of the twentieth century, proving that it's possible for countries to create wealth and transform themselves into globally competitive economies. Between 1965 and 1990, Hong Kong, Japan, Malaysia, the Republic of Korea, Singapore and Taiwan grew faster than nations in any other region in the world. Not only was the growth remarkably fast, it was also fairly equitable. Many reasons contributed to their success, but basically all these countries got the fundamentals down pat:

✔ Their governments developed the financial systems and structures to ensure stable economies.

✔ They invested in infrastructure and innovation, and they traded with richer countries.

✔ Their citizens enjoy property rights, good health-care and education.

✔ Their standard of living has increased remarkably and their populations are wealthier, healthier and living longer.

Eradication of Smallpox

Smallpox has been around for at least 3,000 years and is one of the worst diseases known to humanity. It's also the first disease to be officially eradicated from the planet. Throughout history, epidemics of smallpox swept across continents and as many as 30 per cent of people who contracted smallpox died from the disease. Those who survived were likely to be scarred and blinded. It's not surprising that, in 1798, the first vaccination ever developed was for smallpox.

In 1967, the World Health Organization launched a campaign to eradicate smallpox for good. The goal was to vaccinate populations en masse. It was a massive endeavour and a huge success. The last natural case of smallpox occurred in 1977. The World Health Organization declared the planet free from this ancient scourge in 1979.

South Africa's Political Reform

For decades, South Africans lived under *apartheid,* a discriminatory political and legal system that allowed the ruling white minority to segregate, exploit and terrorise the vast non-white majority. Apartheid was racism made law. It dictated how and where non-white citizens of South Africa could live, work and die. Despite its long history and institutional character, apartheid was brought to an end by global pressure and the tireless work of activists within South Africa. In the 1990s, South Africa peacefully transformed into a democratic society and South Africans enacted a process of forgiveness, justice and reconciliation. The end of apartheid is one of the biggest human rights success stories of the twentieth century.

Debt Relief and Education in Tanzania

Tanzania is a very poor country in southern Africa that's been struggling to develop for decades — even before independence was granted from Britain in the early 1960s. Many of its children didn't get the chance to go to school. That all changed in 2001, when Tanzania received a partial debt write-off that reduced its debt burden by 54 per cent, or over US$2 billion.

With the money it saved from not repaying debt, the Tanzanian government abolished school fees for primary education. Enrolment increased by 50 per cent between 2000 and 2003, an extra 1,000 primary schools were built and hundreds of extra teachers were trained. Amazingly, approximately 1.6 million children were then able to go to school for the first time.

Girls in School in Bangladesh

Bangladesh is in the midst of one of the most profound social changes in its history: Bangladeshi girls are now being educated as part of a campaign to ensure equality between men and women. Bangladesh has about 19 million children of primary school age and almost half are girls. In the 1990s, huge investments were made in schools, materials, teachers and administration. An intensive program educated families about the benefits of educating girls and provided incentives for poor families to send their daughters to school. The program brought about a significant change in family attitudes towards the value of girls. Now, the rates of children enrolling in primary school are equal for boys and girls. This will have a lasting positive impact on the whole society.

Stopping the Spread of HIV in Uganda

When HIV and AIDS first began to spread through southern Africa at the close of the twentieth century, Uganda was one of the worst affected countries. But the Ugandan government took decisive action and set up an AIDS Control Program in the Ministry of Health. The country was one of the first to work with the World Health Organization to create a national HIV and AIDS control plan.

The results have been impressive. Today, the overall infection rate has dropped to a low of about 7 per cent of the adult population. This shows that even very poor countries can reduce the spread of HIV and AIDS, given the resources and the political will.

Chapter 22

Ten Plus Hazards on the Horizon

Addressing the structural imbalances in the world economy is an enormous challenge. It requires agreement between wealthy and poor nations to work together to give a hand to the world's poor. That help almost certainly will come at the expense of some advantages that rich nations take for granted.

In addition to the basic fundamental challenge, there are a number of emerging hazards that will test the world's dedication to eradicating extreme poverty. This chapter gives you the 11 biggest hazards on the road ahead.

Food Shortages

Theoretically, the planet can grow enough food to feed about ten billion people. Chapters 6 and 19 detail how economic pressures prevent the fair and equitable distribution of this food. Shortages of energy, water and the impact of an increasingly chaotic climate are also placing pressure on world food supplies. The increasing scarcity of oil has a twofold impact. As well as making it more expensive to grow food, it encourages some farmers to turn their food crops into ethanol for fuel.

In early 2008, all these pressures came together, driving up the price of staple grains (such as rice, wheat and corn). The price of rice trebled in two months. Protests over food prices erupted in 35 countries. These price pressures had been building over three years. The sudden increase, though, caused governments to stockpile food, and introduce new tariffs and trade barriers. The impact on the world's poor if this situation continues will be devastating.

Climate Change

Climate change is the big one. The world is getting warmer and all the plans to cut carbon emissions will only slow down climate chaos, not stop it. International efforts to implement a united climate plan are bogged down in arguments over who should make what sacrifices.

In the meantime, more hurricanes and cyclones will wreak havoc. Farming will become impossible in more regions because of prolonged droughts, leading to food shortages. Some plants and animals won't survive. Weather-dependent diseases like malaria and dengue fever are likely to spread to new areas.

As the earth warms, oceans will rise, affecting coastal regions like the heavily populated delta on which Bangladesh is built. Whole regions will disappear and so too will many low-lying islands in the Pacific, for example, wiping out whole countries. Millions of environmental refugees may flee their homelands, creating a massive humanitarian crisis.

Market Crash

For the last 20 years, the world economy has been strong. You're living in boom times. But that's what people thought on 23 October 1929. By lunchtime the next day the Roaring Twenties had ended with a crash, bringing on the Great Depression. The share market in early 2008 showed all the signs of an end to those 20 years of uninterrupted growth.

The oil shocks during the 1970s, the Wall Street collapse in 1987 and the Asian market crisis of 1997 are all reminders that endless growth and prosperity is never certain. Today, the spectacular economic growth of China and India has lifted literally hundreds of millions of people out of poverty. Yet these economies aren't immune from the cycle of boom and bust. Neither is your country's economy.

War in the Middle East

Nothing wrecks an economy or a society like war. Natural disasters, droughts, floods and storms have caused much less famine and misery in modern history than wars. Since the cold war ended in the early 1990s, the number of armed conflicts in the world has declined. Wars between countries are fewer, but civil wars and protracted local conflict are becoming more common. The scale of local conflicts has also increased, causing more people to be killed, injured or displaced. Many conflicts have started along ethnic and religious lines, leading to more deliberate targeting of civilians and acts of 'ethnic cleansing' and genocide.

Some wars have implications for the entire world. The escalation of the ongoing conflict in the Middle East has destabilised the entire region. The concentration of the world's known oil reserves, religious divisions and its geographic importance between Europe, Asia and Africa make it a hot spot for trouble, waiting to erupt.

Excessive Artillery

The threat of nuclear war didn't end with the cold war. The United States and Russia claim to be reducing their arsenals at the same time as the slow but steady proliferation of nuclear arms goes on. Israel, India, Pakistan and North Korea all have nukes, and Iran may be on the way. About a dozen other countries have had a nuclear research program at some time or other. With this amount of nuclear hardware lying about, terrorists, as well as governments, can acquire nuclear bombs.

Nukes terrify people because of the physical damage they cause, and the fact that the radiation kills for a long time after the bomb goes off. Biological and chemical weapons, though, could also cause mass casualties. Again, the United States and Russia have led the way, creating these deadly weapons and, inevitably, the prospect of global proliferation.

Despite the alarming nature of these high-tech weapons, the real weapons of mass destruction in the world today are small arms — cheap, readily available and killing 500,000 people each year. Small arms are fuelling conflicts in all parts of the world; and once they're in communities, they stay there even after conflict is over. The death toll from landmines, for example, remains steady for decades after a war.

Dirty Governments

A corrupt government can wreck a country's economy and ruin millions of lives. So can a violent and repressive government, or a government controlled by the military or by small self-interested cliques. Even a well-intentioned but inefficient government can undo past progress. But the worst results flow from corruption and repression, which often go hand in hand. Leaders who systematically loot their countries become ever more unpopular. As their popularity sinks, they resort to bribes and handouts to shore up their support, and to violence and threats to shut down their opposition. Corruption and violence discourage investment, and the most skilled workers often leave the country.

The situation in Zimbabwe is a perfect example of what happens to a country when it's run by a corrupt despot and his cronies. Food production has decreased dramatically because farms have been taken away from people who've been working the land for generations. The price of food has skyrocketed. Inflation is out of control. The life expectancy in Zimbabwe has dropped by more than 20 years and HIV has spread throughout the country. More and more people are fleeing over the border to South Africa, where as refugees they slide into greater poverty.

Failed States

Some governments are so bad, and their country's problems so intractable, that the whole system of government collapses. Nature hates a vacuum, so, violent mobs or organised criminals can take over. Sometimes, the country splinters into fragments, each controlled by local warlords. Most often, the end result is a neighbouring state invading or 'offering support', either because they fear the chaos will spill over into their own territory, or just because they can see an opportunity to grab resources.

For decades life in Somalia has been desperate for many of the ordinary people who live there. The ongoing violence and brutality of the civil war makes the country unsafe for any kind of activity that doesn't involve fighting. There's very little food produced; education and health services have broken down; and there are whole cities of refugees on the borders of the neighbouring countries. It destabilises the whole region. If there's a bad year, and there's a drought, the people have nothing to fall back on and many die.

Bird Flu

A large-scale outbreak of avian flu could kill millions and seriously disrupt the world economy. Some short-term strategies may help stop a pandemic — such as selectively killing poultry in areas of concern, vaccinating poultry workers and isolating areas where the virus is found. But wild and migratory birds are impossible to control, and they don't care about borders! In any case, a virus might adapt well enough to humans that it could infect millions in a very short time.

In rich countries the damage may be reduced by using antiviral drugs and other treatments. But poorer communities, especially ones where people live in crowded conditions, or where people are in daily contact with chickens and ducks, are likely to suffer most.

The Further Spread of HIV and AIDS

If bird flu is the massive pandemic on the horizon, AIDS is the one that's already here and could get much worse. The United Nations estimates about 40 million people now live with HIV — 25 million of them in Africa. Globally, in 2006, 4.3 million new cases were reported, while 2.9 million people died. Up to 90 million Africans could become infected by 2025. Such a high rate would be devastating — especially because AIDS, unlike most diseases, hits hardest in the most economically productive age groups. This is because people are generally sexually and economically active at the same time.

The Emerging Fossil Fuel Crisis

You live in world that runs on fossil fuel. All transportation uses it, and industry sucks it up. Anything that's made of plastic started its life as oil. Oil is so important to industrial economies that they're willing to go to war for it. But there's only a finite amount of oil around the world and experts think that more than half of it has probably been used. There have certainly been no major new discoveries of oil in the last 30 years. The worst part is that demand for it is growing faster than ever.

So far, the world doesn't have any alternatives that will produce as much energy as needed. The current proposals amount to burning food or forests for transport fuel, which can only accelerate the problems of extreme poverty. The world may literally be heading into a new dark age.

Bzzz — Disappearing Bees

The earth is losing animal and plant species at a catastrophic rate. It's hard to imagine how the death of a frog species in a far-off rainforest affects you, but biodiversity is fundamental to the health of the planet. Each species plays a role in keeping the earth's ecosystems working smoothly.

Some species are more directly important to your wellbeing than others. One of the most important is the common honey-bee. Bees pollinate the vast majority of flowering plants, including most fruit and vegetables, and seed plants like canola. If they become extinct, much modern agriculture will be under serious threat.

In the last couple of years, across the northern hemisphere, bee farmers are waking up to find that their bee colonies have disappeared. Millions of bees are dying and no-one knows why. However, mobile phone towers, genetically modified foods, parasites, overworking of bees in agriculture and their undernourishment from monocultures are possible explanations. Only one thing is certain — life on this planet is going to be much worse off without them.

Chapter 23

Ten Informative and Inspiring Movies

What better way to find out about poverty than to sit back and immerse yourself in a couple of hours of high-quality silver screen entertainment? In this chapter, we give you our top ten informative and inspiring movies about poverty, starting with the most recently released and working our way backwards from there. The films deal with a cross-section of the subjects covered in this book: Economic inequity, human greed and the environment.

Because of the nature of the topic, these films are hardly light entertainment, and many of them are far too gruesome to share with your children.

Blood Diamond (2006)

Blood Diamond is a piece of issue-tainment that stars Leonardo DiCaprio as a mercenary from Zimbabwe. He's on a hunt for a diamond across war-torn Sierra Leone. The film touches on the issues of the arms trade, child soldiers, civil war, slavery and, of course, the resource curse. It's a gruelling story, but this is a Hollywood blockbuster with a conscience, and well worth a couple of hours of your life.

An Inconvenient Truth (2006)

An Inconvenient Truth is an Academy award-winning documentary about climate change starring former vice-president of the United States, Al Gore. The film has had a stunning impact around the world and completely changed the global debate on climate change. It's now broadly recognised that climate change is real, potentially catastrophic and caused by human activity.

The film itself intersperses an informative and entertaining presentation about climate change that Gore has delivered more than a thousand times around the world, with his own story. The movie presents a wide range of science to prove that climate change is actually happening, while refuting common arguments against climate change. This flick ends on a positive note and shows how everyone can do something to slow global warming.

Al Gore won the Nobel Peace Prize in 2007 for the far-reaching work he has done to raise awareness about climate change and putting action against it on the agendas of all world leaders.

The Girl in the Café (2005)

Occasionally the charming tale of *The Girl in the Café* degenerates into a bit of a lecture about poverty — unlike the stimulating reading contained within these pages — but it's still a fantastic film that will inspire you to ask the hard questions about global justice and poverty.

The Girl in the Café could be called a political drama, but don't let that put you off. It's actually a love story (but don't let that put you off either). It pairs an unlikely couple — Bill Nighy, a political adviser to the British government, and Kelly Macdonald, a young girl full of questions about the world. Romance blossoms while you find out more about the Millennium Development Goals (also covered in Chapter 18), international politics and the impotence of Western governments. Grab some popcorn, kick back and enjoy the ride.

Born into Brothels (2005)

Winner of an Oscar for best documentary in 2005, *Born into Brothels* gives an unsentimental insight into the lives of several children who live in the red-light district of Calcutta where their mothers work as prostitutes.

The film chronicles a year that the filmmaker, US photographer Zana Briski, spends with the children. She follows their transformation when she gives them photography lessons and cameras so they can photograph their lives. The heartfelt and sometimes funny film provides a glimpse into what it means to live in extreme poverty — not just lack of money, food and clean water, but also the stigma and discrimination that the children live with daily.

Lord of War (2005)

The title is reminiscent of a typical Hollywood action film, but *Lord of War* is actually an intelligent movie that takes you into the underworld of international arms dealing. Nicholas Cage plays the protagonist, a young man who gets a head start in life by selling guns to mobsters, before moving on to the big leagues where he sells illegal weapons to war-torn regions across the globe.

The Constant Gardener (2005)

Many people come out of the movie *The Constant Gardener* saying, 'Sure, it was good, but it's not really like that . . . is it?' Well yes, sadly it is.

Based on a book of the same name by John Le Carré, this film stars Ralph Fiennes and Rachel Weisz. It takes you deep into the sinister underbelly of Big Pharma — the global pharmaceutical industry that's worth US$500 billion a year. Fiennes plays a British diplomat who investigates drug testing being carried out by a fictitious pharmaceutical company on unsuspecting Kenyans. It's exciting from start to finish and will leave you with a bitter taste in your mouth, a bit like medicine.

Hotel Rwanda (2004)

Hotel Rwanda recounts the dreadful events of 1994 that led to the murder of 800,000 Tutsi at the hands of their Hutu brothers and sisters. Don Cheadle plays the real character of Paul Rusesabagina who helped save hundreds of fellow Tutsis from certain death while frustrated United Nations peacekeepers stood by helplessly. The sensitive way in which this film deals with the political issues and violence makes it compulsive viewing.

For a film that deals with one of the worst genocides in modern history, *Hotel Rwanda* is pretty close to being family-friendly. Don't get us wrong, you'll still bawl your eyes out by the end of this triple Oscar-nominated movie. Based on real events, it's ultimately optimistic and restores belief in the human spirit.

Cidade de Deus [City of God] (2002)

Whether you're into subtitles or not, *Cidade de Deus* [*City of God*] is a Brazilian film well worth the watching. It's easily the most graphic from our selection, but it's unrivalled in its ability to take the audience deep into the lives of the poorest of the poor in the slums of Rio de Janeiro.

City of God tells the tale of several characters in the 1960s who live in a slum in Rio — a housing estate with the ironic name of 'City of God'. The narrator is a poor teenager living in the slum with the odds stacked firmly against him. He grows up with a love for photography, but despite his artistic disposition, he keeps getting swept up in the violence and madness around him.

You may not find this an easy couple of hours, but *City of God* will stay with you long after the credits roll. If you've got the stomach for it, put this film at the top of your list.

Not One Less (1999)

Directed by Zhang Yimou, this movie tells the story of Ming, a 13-year-old girl living in a poor village in the Chinese countryside.

When the regular school teacher goes away for a month, Ming is left in charge of the class – with strict instructions that when teacher returns, all 28 students must be there. When the class troublemaker runs away — heading for the city to make some money to pay off his parents' debt — she follows in hot pursuit.

As well as being a great piece of entertainment, *Not One Less* is a reminder that while China might be the new economic superpower, life for hundreds of millions of Chinese remains harsh and grinding. The movie throws light on how the lives of individuals are distorted by the pressures of poverty. But it also shows how people find the resources and inner strength to take control of their situation.

City of Joy (1992)

No, we're not hung up on films with 'city' in the title, it just happens that some of the great films have the word 'city' in them. *City of Joy* is a little easier to stomach that *Cidade de Deus* (see the earlier section) but is also a little less realistic because of its slight Hollywood flavour. It's loosely based on the French novel of the same name, and follows a young American doctor, played by Patrick Swayze, who flees his crumbling life in the United States to redeem himself in the slums of Calcutta.

Swayze's character meets a range of slum dwellers in another one of those ironically named slums, the 'City of Joy'. You get an idea for why people are forced to flee to the cities, you find out about sexual prejudice, the caste system, the cycle of poverty and a host of other challenges faced by India's poorest. *City of Joy* presents the poor as inspirational and strong characters, rather than helpless victims to be pitied. In the end, this little tale will also leave you with a sense of hope and optimism.

Chapter 24

Ten Actions You Can Take

*I*f you're feeling overwhelmed by the scope of the challenge extreme poverty presents, this chapter's for you. Hard to believe that one person can actually change the world? Just look back in history to all the individuals who've made a difference — for the better and for the worse. Maybe you won't be a world leader — who knows? The point is that most heroes didn't set out seeking adventure, they just stood up to a bully when the time came.

The sections in this chapter help you take the first steps towards tackling poverty.

Discovering Your Options

You've started the process of discovery by reading this book — good job! Now follow some of the suggestions below for discovering more information:

✔ Check out the website www.globalissues.org.

✔ Research more about the Millennium Development Goals.

✔ Read books.

✔ Browse the Internet.

✔ Talk to people.

Find out about poverty and stay informed about how the world works. After you start on this journey, you'll find yourself tracking down information that you didn't know existed. One way to make the journey more exciting is to share what you've learned by spreading the word. But that's a different step.

Joining the Club

No movement has ever been successful without the support of people. One of the greatest advantages of working with other people is that you're more effective as a team. You get feedback on your thoughts, and the extra energy created by the discussions you have makes the group more effective than if you each acted on your own.

As well as potentially increasing the impact you make, you may enjoy the process more. Everyone has something to offer. Whatever your skills, you can play a part in ending poverty. Here are some suggestions:

✔ Join a social movement such as Make Poverty History.

✔ Join a political campaign to ask your politicians to get on board and do their part to end global poverty.

✔ Sign up for newsletters that keep you informed of what's going on and how to get involved.

Wielding the Pen

The pen is mightier than the sword. It's an old cliché that gets reused because it's true. Share the information that you've uncovered. Share your experience and the stories about battling extreme poverty that touch you. Write letters to the paper and letters to your friends. Submit comments to websites that report on global poverty.

Write to your local politicians. Tell them what motivates you. Tell them about justice and poverty. Ask them to do their part in the fight to eradicate global poverty. Be assertive: Politicians are your chosen representatives who've been elected to act on *your* behalf.

When you deal with officials, follow these pointers:

- **Don't waffle.** Be brief and to the point. Yours won't be the only mail they open today.

- **Be respectful.** Don't be rude or aggressive. You get a much better response if you're polite and respectful.

- **Use your own words.** Personalising your letter has a much bigger impact than using a form letter. That way, they know you mean it.

- **Request a response.** Ask your politicians to get back to you. Make them think more carefully about the issues, but listen to what they have to say. They may even agree with you.

- **Give your information.** Include your full name and address in the letter you write.

As well as your local politician, give the editor of a local newspaper a try. Write to them about something that's current — something that's making headlines today. Most of the same rules in the bulleted list in this section apply though — keep it short and sweet. One or two points are enough, and try to keep it under 200 words. They also like it if you've got a quirky angle.

Using Your Voice

Use your voice to shout for justice. Use it to call for an end to poverty. Talk to your friends and family. Tell them what's going on, tell them why it's important that they care, and tell them what they can do. Word of mouth is one of the most effective ways to change community attitudes. It helps you sharpen your arguments along the way.

You can talk to your local politician, if you can get hold of them. Sometimes it's more powerful to get your message across face-to-face. Be respectful, make an appointment in advance, keep to the message, and listen to what they have to say. Don't just tell them the problems; suggest what *they* can do about it — maybe start with what others have done successfully.

Call a talkback radio show to get your opinion heard by a wider group. Do your research — find out what sorts of issues the show will be interested in. And when you're on the air, don't panic (now, that's easier said than done), don't waffle and keep to the point.

The easiest way to do that is to write down what you're planning to say and tick off each point as you say it.

Oh, and a top tip that radio DJs will thank you for: Turn off the radio before you make the phone call. They play the radio station in your ear while you're waiting.

Organising Events

Are you good at pulling people together? Then why not put your social skills to good use and organise an event. You don't have to pull off a multi-national rock concert to get the message out there; start simple. You could run a dinner party with your friends, host a morning tea at your workplace or even organise a benefit night at your local pub. Your event will get people thinking and talking about the issues. That's when real change can happen.

There are a couple of tricks to running a good event. Keep it manageable. Check what time and resources you have, including what help you're likely to get, and shape your event around that. If there's an organisation already working on the issue, give them a call to see if they've got any materials you can use. Get their support to promote the event outside your immediate circle.

Be clear about what you want to achieve and what action you want people to take, and let them know what difference it will make. Promote your event. You could use flyers, email lists or friends, or send out a media release. If it's a public event, invite your local MP and get in touch with your local newspaper. They might cover it in the next edition!

Working in the Field

Some people want to spend their lives working on issues like global justice and poverty. If you're one of them, suggestions on how you can break into this world can be found in Chapter 4. But it's not for everyone, and there are plenty of opportunities in both your home and your workplace or school to make a difference.

Many people decide to volunteer at a charity. Volunteering often suits part-time workers or people who've retired or who have more time than income for some other reason. Whatever skills you have, chances are someone would love to make use of them.

You can offer to work on a specific project. That's when volunteers are most needed and it gives you a clear timeline for when your contribution is complete. You can sometimes be well rewarded; getting access to a special event or a great meal you would normally not be able to afford, for example.

If you plan to make a career change, volunteering can be a great way to get experience in an area that is new to you. The world benefits as a result of your efforts and so do you.

Praying for Others

If you're part of a faith community, pray for change. Pray for an end to global injustice and chronic poverty. If you're a church-goer, ask your faith leader to include a prayer for the poor in the service.

Get involved in activities with your faith. Participate in discussion groups, charities that can have an impact on world poverty and activities that spread the good word. Many faith communities have active international organisations that go out into the world and work hard to eradicate world poverty. Support them.

Donating What You Can

Of course, everyone's always happy to take your hard-earned cash. So, be discerning. Don't just throw money away in the hope that you'll sleep better. Look into what agency you think can make the most of it. Do research, investigate different charities and organisations to find out which is the most suitable for you.

Most agencies offer a range of ways to give. You have to choose what's right for you. Depending on the agency and the nature of the work they do, you may be able to:

- Sponsor a child
- Purchase products that directly benefit people who struggle
- Contribute to a specific project — say, a new well or school
- Donate your time and money by going to the location and working on a project
- Simply give money to the organisation

Shopping for Effect

You don't need to feel guilty about spending your cash. After all, you earned it — well, most of you, we hope. Spend it thoughtfully. Don't blow it on a new pair of shoes that were manufactured in a sweatshop in a developing country. Do your research: Find out where products were made and who made them. Try writing to the company. Let them know that you care about where the stuff you buy comes from.

Choose fair trade if it's on offer. Make sure that your office or school offers fair trade coffee or tea — if they offer any at all — so you can be sure the growers are getting a fair price. If you're a caffeine addict — as we are — you'll thank us when you sample the delights that fair trade coffee has to offer.

Look out for locally grown and manufactured products. That way you're supporting your local economy, and you're reducing the impact of the global economy on countries that are being ripped off by it.

Investing Your Money Wisely

If you have money in the bank or in a pension fund, do you know where that money's being invested? Is it propping up corrupt regimes? Is it supporting child labour? Is it helping fuel global warming? Check out the companies that receive your cash and make sure they report on the triple bottom line — that's people, planet and profits.

Investigate ethical investment organisations and check out what they can do with your dollars. Your superannuation or pension fund might be the best tool you have to make the world a fairer place.

If you're an active investor and are directly involved in your investment decisions, you can have an even greater impact.

Index

•I•

•J•

FOR DUMMIES®

Business

Small Business For Dummies
1-74031-109-4
$39.95

Share Investing For Dummies
1-74031-146-9
$39.95

Investing in Real Estate For Dummies
0-73140-724-5
$39.95

Charting For Dummies
1-74031-124-8
$39.95

Buying & Selling Your Home For Dummies
1-74031-166-3
$39.95

MYOB Software For Dummies
1-7314-0541-2
$39.95

Sorting Out Your Finances For Dummies
0-7314-0746-6
$29.95

Superannuation For Dummies
0-73140-715-6
$39.95

Reference

Work / Life Balance For Dummies
0-73140-723-7
$34.95

Sustainable Living For Dummies
1-74031-157-4
$39.95

Wedding Planning For Dummies
0-73140-721-0
$34.95

Australia's Dangerous Creatures For Dummies
0-73140-722-9
$29.95